F. Meyer-Krahmer   J. Müller   B. Preißl   (Eds.)

Information Technology: Impacts, Policies and Future Perspectives

Promotion of Mutual Understanding Between Europe and Japan

With 7 Figures and 11 Tables

Springer-Verlag Berlin Heidelberg New York
London Paris Tokyo Hong Kong

Dr. Frieder Meyer-Krahmer
Dr. Jürgen Müller
Dr. Brigitte Preißl

DIW-Deutsches Institut für Wirtschaftsforschung
Königin-Luise-Straße 5, D-1000 Berlin 33, FRG

ISBN 3-540-52396-0 Springer-Verlag Berlin Heidelberg New York
ISBN 0-387-52396-0 Springer-Verlag New York Berlin Heidelberg

Library of Congress Cataloging-in-Publication Data.
Information technology: impacts, policies, and future perspectives: promotion of mutual understanding between Europe and Japan/F. Meyer-Krahmer, J. Müller, B. Preissl (eds.).   p.   cm.
ISBN 0-387-52396-0 (U.S.)
1. Information technology – European Economic Community countries. 2. Information technology – Japan. 3. European Economic Community countries – Foreign economic relations – Japan. 4. Japan – Foreign economic relations – European Economic Community countries. I. Meyer-Krahmer, Frieder. II. Müller, Jürgen, 1943 –   . III. Preissl, Brigitte, 1953-   .
HC240.9.I55I56   1990   303.48'33'094–dc20   90-9562

This work is subject to copyright. All rights are reserved, whether the whole or part of the material is concerned, specifically the rights of translation, reprinting, reuse of illustrations, recitation, broadcasting, reproduction on microfilms or in other ways, and storage in data banks. Duplication of this publication or parts thereof is only permitted under the provisions of the German Copyright Law of September 9, 1965, in its current version, and a copyright fee must always be paid. Violations fall under the prosecution act of the German Copyright Law.

© Springer-Verlag Berlin Heidelberg 1990
Printed in Germany

2142/3140(3011)-5 4 3 2 1 0 – Printed on acid-free paper

Table of Contents

I. INTRODUCTION, SUMMARY AND RECOMMENDATIONS 1

WELCOME FOR TIDE 2000
Hans Günter Danielmeyer 3

JAPANESE-EUROPEAN DIALOGUE
Opening Speech
Hiroshi Inose 6

SUMMARY OF THE CONFERENCE SESSIONS
Frieder Meyer-Krahmer, Jürgen Müller, Brigitte Preißl 9

CHAIRMAN'S CLOSING STATEMENT
Hiroshi Inose 21
1. Major Observations 21
2. Recommendations 23

II. THE IMPACT OF INFORMATION TECHNOLOGY WITHIN THE EUROPEAN-JAPANESE RELATIONSHIP 25

THE SOCIAL AND CULTURAL IMPACTS OF INFORMATION TECHNOLOGY
Youichi Ito 27
1. Introduction 27
2. Impacts in the Domestic Area 28
3. Impacts in the International Area 34
4. Summary and Conclusion 37
References 38

III. POLICY MAKING IN THE AREA OF INFORMATION TECHNOLOGY . 41

NEW DIMENSIONS OF TELECOMMUNICATIONS COMPETITION
Charles Jonscher 43
1. Introduction 43
2. Case Study: The UK Cellular Mobile Communication Industry 45
3. Further Details Regarding Competitive Structure in the UK 48
4. Implications for Future Marketing of Telecommunications Services .. 49

COMMENTS ON NEW DIMENSIONS OF
TELECOMMUNICATIONS COMPETITION
Laurent Virol 53

PRODUCTION ORIENTED INFORMATION TECHNOLOGY POLICY
IN JAPAN AND EUROPE
Graham Vickery 60
1. Introduction 60
2. The Patterns of Use of Advanced Manufacturing Technology 61
3. The Role and Function of Policies to Improve Industrial
   Performance 70
4. Recent Government Initiatives 71
5. Key Features of Programmes 84
6. Summary 86
References 87

COMMENTS ON PRODUCTION ORIENTED INFORMATION
TECHNOLOGY POLICY IN JAPAN AND EUROPE
Mamoru Mitsugi 88

IV. EUROPEAN-JAPANESE COLLABORATION 97

EURO-JAPANESE COOPERATION IN INFORMATION TECHNOLOGY
Hellmut Schütte 99
1. Background and Framework 99
1.1 Agreement and Objective 99
1.2 Definitions and Methodology 99
2. International Cooperation 100
2.1 Changes in International Business: The Stage 100
2.2 Developments in Information Technology: The Game 102
2.3 Europe, Japan and the USA: The Players 104
3. Cooperative Agreements between Japanese and European Firms 107
3.1 Characteristics of the Agreements 107
3.2 Categories 109
3.3 Quantitative Analysis 115
4. Strategic Alliances: Experiences and Perceptions 119
4.1 International Agreements: A Comparison 119
4.2 Asymmetries in Partnerships 123

EXPERIENCES OF A JOINT VENTURE
(ENDRESS + HAUSER / SAKURA)
Klaus Riemenschneider 131

SCENARIOS OF 1992 AND CONSEQUENCES FOR
EURO-JAPANESE RELATIONSHIP
Jürgen Müller 151
1. Introduction 151
2. The Goals of a Single European Market in Telecommunications
   Equipment and Services 152
2.1 The Evaluation of the Single Market Concept 152
2.2 The Myth of 1992 152
2.3 The Major Policy Aspects of the Green Paper 153
2.4 The Likely Effects of the Green Paper's Policies in the
    Telecommunications Equipment Market 154
2.5 Reasons for a Lack of Market Integration 158

	3.	Completing the International Market for Telecommunication Services 160
	3.1	Expected Effects 160
	3.2	Better Network Utilization 161
	4.	Japanese Policies Concerning Telecommunications Equipment and Services 164
	4.1	Policy Focus 164
	4.2	Opening up the Equipment Market 164
	4.3	Opening up the Service Market 165
	5.	Areas of Conflict 166
	5.1	Japanese Trade Surplus and Administrative Reactions 166
	5.2	Export Restraints and Antidumping Threats 167
	5.3	Controlling Standards 168
	5.4	Excessive Specialization and Dependence or International R&D Races 168
	6.	Gains of Joint Problem Resolution 170
	References 171

V. THE FUTURE WORLD MARKETS FOR INFORMATION TECHNOLOGY 173

FUTURE WORLD MARKETS FOR INFORMATION TECHNOLOGY
William H. Melody 175
1. Introduction 175
2. Major Trends 175
3. Key Factors Influencing Market Growth 178

THESES ON THE CONDITIONS OF FUTURE WORLD MARKETS FOR INFORMATION TECHNOLOGY PRODUCTS
Brigitte Preißl 181

COMMENTS ON FUTURE WORLD MARKET FOR INFORMATION TECHNOLOGY PRODUCTS
Seisuke Komatsuzaki 194

INFORMATION AND RELATED TECHNOLOGIES AND THEIR IMPACT ON EAST-WEST RELATIONS
Peter Havlik 197
1. Introduction 197
2. The Gap in Information Technologies Between East and West 198
3. Eastern Policies Aiming at Reducing the Technology Gap 207
4. Implications for the West and East-West Relations 212
References 214

THE UNBALANCED TRIAD
Francois Bar and John Zysman 216
1. Introduction 216
2. The Trade Context 217
3. Telecommunications and American Policy 219
4. Reregulation and Deregulation in Japan and Europe 221
5. The Crucial Fact Left Out 224
6. New Issues for American Policy 228
7. A Changing Structure of Telecommunications Policy 229

I. INTRODUCTION, SUMMARY AND RECOMMENDATIONS

WELCOME FOR TIDE 2000

Hans Günter Danielmeyer
Vicepresident of the Japanese-German-Centre Berlin
and Member of the Board at Siemens AG, Munich

Your Excellency, Ladies and Gentlemen:

It is an honour for me to welcome you as distinguished participants of this meeting to the Japanese German Center Berlin. Thank you for coming, and thanks to the organizers, hosts and sponsors: The Governments of Japan and Germany, and the German Institute for Economic Research.

We start with the Impact of Information Technology on the Relationship between Japan and Europe. The chairman of this session, Mr. Garfinkel, reminded me of my time 1966 through 71 as a postdoc in AT&T's Bell Telephone Laboratories. Already then, optical communications and the picturephone were at the center of interest. How long it takes for ideas to develop into markets! We also see that corporate and market structures are quite stable: Telecommunications was and still is to a large extent a national affair while data processing was and remains, of course, a highly competitive private market. The integration of these closely related business activities proceeds not as smoothly as R&D people thought in the sixties - be it within the market or within a corporate culture.

Our second topic will be Policy Making, chaired by Mr. Martin-Löf. In a visit to MITI in 1988 I was informed about Japan's commitment to the "informatization of society". For investments in industry and job security the perspectives given by such long term public authority commitments are certainly much more effective than direct R&D funding by government. The former provide the basis for effective competition within a common market and this in turn is the basis for competitiveness in the world market.

That would be a model for a European policy as well. Developing from a fragmented into a larger market, however, we have some specific problems which Japan and the US do not have. E.g., there are at least five domestic companies in Europe competing for the public networks. In the US there are AT&T and Northern Telecom, in Japan there is practically only NTT. Knowing that just the software package of the next ISDN system contains 10 to 20 million lines of code, the order of magnitude known from manned space flight, we see that we have but the alternative for mergers or exits in European industry.

Presently we formulate our general R&D-Framework-Programme with the European Community. Besides, we have to address such problems as economies of scale, European vs. national authority and regulation, and standardization. We know perfectly well that peace and fair trade are the most precious goods in our world. As every state of nature with a high degree of order they require just for maintenance intensive work and attention, not to speak of achieving a new and higher order, which is our present task: We need the best people and the best ideas for 1992 and beyond.

Our third topic is the European-Japanese Collaboration, chaired by Mr. Perucca. This gives me the chance to introduce you to the Japanese German Center Berlin, hosting this meeting.

In 1927 the world's first Japan Institute was founded here in Berlin. That Berlin is the last site of a Wall between East and West does not fit into tomorrow's world. This building here was erected as the Japanese Embassy 1938 through 42 and destroyed during the war.

In the spirit of tomorrow's world and the trilateral solidarity between Japan, Europe and North America, Mr. Nakasone and Mr. Kohl decided at the Williamsburg Summit in 1983 to found the Japanese-German Center Berlin and to use this site for scientific and technical conferences concerned with the future of our world, strengthening the Japanese-European leg of the triad. The Atlantic and Pacific legs had developed more strongly after the war. The funds for the foundation and the building came so far from the Senate of Berlin, from both governments and from KEIDANREN, the Japanese Business Society.

In saying that, we are already at our last topic of this meeting, the Future World Market, chaired by Mr. Nambu. There is a need for economic balance in order to achieve and maintain peace in our world. Fair trade is essential in order to achieve this economic balance. With respect to Information Technology the future looks very bright: It is a truly global technology; its components such as chips and its systems such as networks have leading growth rates; its impact on society will be larger than that of nearly all the other technologies; and it is itself a generating technology for achieving fair trade and economic balances. On the consumer level we are equally confident: trust that we will see the world communication plug before we will have the privilege to use our razors without a collection of main adaptors.

At any level, I wish you for the meeting of TIDE 2000 a lot of success.

JAPANESE-EUROPEAN DIALOGUE

Opening Speech

Hiroshi Inose
Director General, National Center for Science Information System, Tokyo

Distinguished Guests:

It is with pleasure that I note the opening of the Japanese-European Dialogue in Berlin, the meeting place of Eastern and Western Europe. I am highly honored to serve as the chairman of this follow-up project to TIDE 2000. I think that many of you are familiar with TIDE 2000; that stands for Telecommunication, Information and Interdependence of Economies in the year 2000. But by way of brief introduction, let me say a few words in the beginning. This project, initiated by the Ministry of Foreign Affairs of Japan to mark the 20th anniversary of Japan's joining to OECD, has been concluded with the third symposium held in February 1987.

The first symposium took place in Tokyo in November 1985 with the theme of "Information and Communications Technology in North-South Relationship". The second symposium, held at the East-West Center in Hawaii in May 1986, took the theme of "IT's Role in Enhancing the Interdependence of OECD Economies". Each occasion was characterized by the lively exchange of opinions. The third symposium was convened at INSEAD near Paris to conclude the two previous symposia, where a number of significant policy proposals were adopted.

One of these was the need to promote IT cooperation through continous dialogue and exchange in all fields and at all levels. Based on this, The Pacific Cooperation and Information Technology Conference (PACIT 88) was held in Vancouver Canada, last September, as a TIDE 2000 follow-up project, where the current state of cooperation in the Pacific Basin relative to IT was examined. The present Japanese-European Dialogue represents the second TIDE 2000 follow-up project. The purpose of this meeting is to consider specific measures to promote mutual understanding between Japan and Europe and to encourage cooperation in the fields of information and communications technology and services. These goals are to be realized by the bilateral exchange of views between representatives of industry, government and academia. For those reasons I look forward to the active contribution of all the distinguished delegates who are participating in this meeting.

Now, ladies and gentlemen, we are all aware that the international situation revolves around the three poles, Europe, Japan and the United States, a tendency that is expected to gain momentum in the future. To ensure the stable development of international politics, economies and society, the harmonization of policies among Europe, Japan and the United States will increase in importance. In particular, Europe's initiative is quickening as it moves towards a single market. The continent can be expected to exert greater influence over international politics and economies following the year 1992.

A quick survey of recent relations between Japan and Europe reveals that bilateral exchanges over the last few years have progressed to an extent unknown in the past. In the political arena, Prime Minister Takeshita's successive visit to Europe, and more recently visits of the Heads of states, prime ministers and other dignitaries of Europe to Tokyo on the occasion of the funeral ceremony of the late Emperor, were accompanied by the frank exchange of views. In the field of economics, the volume of bilateral trade has rapidly increased and Japanese investments in the EC have expanded. Such exchanges, however, are still insufficient when compared with Japan-U.S. and Europe-U.S. relations. I believe that the expansion of Japan-Europe cooperation should be a major priority within the framework of trilateral harmonization among Europe, Japan and the United States.

Ladies and gentlemen, let me now touch upon a few ideas of mine concerning measures that will increase cooperation between Japan and Europe. First, there is a need to create a forum for continuing bilateral dialogue and information exchange to deepen international harmonization and cooperation from a global perspective. It goes without saying that the foremost task in furthering mutual understanding is to accurately perceive the other party's situation. Next, thinking about what can be done to promote this kind of dialogue by means of IT, clearly the first thing that comes to mind is the accerleration of liberalization. It may be best to distinguish communications services into appropriate component functions and promote liberalization function by function. Further, I think that the nations that have introduced communications liberalization, such as Japan, Great Britain and the United States, should assess and publicize their policies and outcomes in full detail. Also, the expansion and strengthening of communications networks can be mentioned as another priority. In particular, I believe it is necessary to promote the development of Japan-Europe information and communications network including those, such as ISDNs and international VANs, and to ensure their effective utilization. Where data bases and their services are concerned, the United States presently holds an overwhelming market share. To be comparable to and complimentary for this efforts of the United States, Japan and the countries of Europe should cooperate in their endeavors to promote the construction of data bases and to encourage informations vendors. The furtherance of Japanese-European joint, research and development projects is, I feel, also a subject for serious consideration. In addition to explore possibilities of establishing joint Japanese-European research and development arrangements and of participating in existing government-sponsored projects, I also consider it of utmost importance to promote cooperative ventures between European and Japanese companies.

Furthermore, it would be extremely valueable if Japan and Europe were to draw up guidelines for solving such international problems as standards, protection of intellectual property rights, security measures, computer crime etc. We should also work together to develop IT policies that will promote technological innovation as well as to explore the role IT can play in promoting cultural exchanges.

Ladies and gentlemen, at the close of the fifteenth century, European navigators embarked on their great ocean voyages, and thereby successively expanded the range of the known world. This enabled the people of the world to become acquainted with each other. Unfortunately a long period of colonialism followed but these colonies have now gained independence and are acquiring self sufficiency, with generous economic support of the industrialized nations and their own determined endogenous efforts. At the close of the twentieth century, we stand at the beginning of a new age, a new Age of Great Navigation. I believe that the industrial countries should fully open their doors to deploy their activities world over and, hand-in-hand with the developing countries, strive for the sustained economic growth, the eradication of proverty, hunger and environmental disruption, and the enhancement of the quality of life of the whole world. I look to the countries of Europe, who initiated the first Age of Great Navigation, to serve as the advance guard in realizing another Age of Great Navigation by disseminating the enormous vitality they will gain from the integrated market in the year 1992. In closing, I should be happy if these remarks might serve to initiate free and frank exchange of opinions and to help conduct ensuing discussions.

I thank you very much for your kind attention.

SUMMARY OF THE CONFERENCE SESSIONS

Frieder Meyer-Krahmer, Jürgen Müller, Brigitte Preißl
German Institute für Economic Research (DIW), Berlin

The conference theme "Information Technology - Impacts, policies and future perspectives" covers a broad variety of issues. Furthermore, one of the priorities of the meeting was to promote "Mutual understanding between Europe and Japan". The design of the conference programme and the choice of papers presented in two-and-a-half days reflect the complexity of facts, trends and problems in the field. Economic and political as well as cultural and social questions were addressed, always keeping in mind the European and the Japanese side and their interactions. The structure of the conference was the following:

- The impact of information technology within the European-Japanese relationship
- Policy making in the area of information technology
- European-Japanese collaboration
- The future world markets for information technology.

Information Technology (IT) is quite a new field for investigation and discussion. Research as well as disputes therefore normally start with definitions of problems and issues. Thus considerable time and effort was dedicated to this task in the first conference session. Most of the papers will be published in a special journal, edited by Prof. Ito, "Keio Communication Review, No. 12". To avoid duplication only the contribution of Prof. Ito is included in this volume.

The impact of IT on the macro-economy, the firm and on society and culture meets considerable public interest, because IT is seen as a key technology with huge potentials for change in the economy and society. It can be expected that its adoption produces similar as well as completely different problems in Europe and in Japan.

The session started with a paper on the conditions and patterns of IT diffusion in a European country (Italy). The discussion showed that Europe includes countries with a whole variety of economic and social backgrounds. So generalizations of the Italian example seem to be as problematic as talking about "Europe" as a unity. Italy can be considered as a special case because of its pronounced dualism which is also reflected in Antonelli's paper on the adoption of fax machines in various Italian regions.

Nevertheless, it has been shown that IT-diffusion follows the traditional ways of the spreading of new technologies: they are first used in advanced, economically prosperous areas, poorer regions are following much later, if at all.

Antonelli's arguments are convincing: The adoption of IT results in an increasing demand for fixed capital and for skilled labour, whereas it reduces the use of unskilled labour. Therefore, IT is used earlier and more intensely in geographical areas where capital and trained manpower are relatively abundant and where unskilled labour is scarce and expensive.

However, in a sense, this empirical result is surprising, becuase the very nature of telecommunication technology seems to favour decentralization and deconcentration. Its diffusion therefore raised hope for improving economic chances for remote areas. But Antonelli's study as well as empirical research for the Federal Republic of Germany point out that IT has rather centralizing than decentralizing effects. In macro-economic terms: IT will not diminisch regional imbalances, it might even accentuate them.

One of the central issues in the analysis of macro-economic impacts of IT is its contribution to economic growth. The question is rather complex, because IT acts as a key factor in the production of goods, and services and thus its effects often show only indirectly. Impulses and stimuli are given by IT that influence intermediary variables which in turn produce changes in the overall economic performance. This makes it difficult to attribute a change in macro-economic figures directly to the use of IT. Research in this field is further complicated by synergetic effects characteristic for IT networks.

In the paper of Oniki and Kuriyama the contribution of IT to economic growth in the Japanese economy was estimated using input-output-analysis and data on factor productivity.

The many aspects of IT innovations - changes in IT production, innumerable forms of IT adoption including the creation of new products and markets - however, demonstrate the need for further research in this field to confirm existing results and investigate more profundly the complex effects of IT on the economy.

Macro-economic developments reflect changes on the micro level, especially in the firm. Traditionally, the first point to look at in technology assessment is productivity. Therefore the introduction of IT raises questions about the returns to large investments. Generally, no significant cost reductions or productivity increases were observed. The clue to this obvious contradiction lies in the fact that in the adoption of IT improved quality of products and services as well as the opening up of new markets are more important effects than direct productivity gains which no doubt occur but remain far behind euphoric expectations.

Successful strategic IT management requires a whole range of factors to be taken into account. Among these are: qualification requirements, the network character of IT, organizational adjustments, standardization and the redefinition of inside and outside logistics. Research on these topics presents an extremely differentiated picture. The adoption of various IT products and services and its effects on the firm vary according to the size, the location and the organizational structures of firms. A distinction has to be made between production plants, enterprise units and holding societies.

Production processes and products contain different "amounts" of information. Thus different industries/services branches show varying effects of the adoption of IT. Industries which produce, process or transmit information goods or even information itself will be more deeply affected than those which only use these products and services.

Finally, diffusion rates and patterns of organizational adjustment within the firms differ from one branch to another due to varying competitive pressure.

Because of the very complex set of possible effects each piece of empirical or theoretical research on the impact of IT in the firm can only cover a very limited part of the subjects mentioned above. New research methods have to be developed for the specific phenomena of IT adoption, e.g., the identification of causal relationships in synergetic processes.

Pogorel's paper concentrated on the influence of IT on the structure of firms. His distinction between trend effects (in activities with a low information content), in-depth effects (in activities which consist to a large extent of information processing) and thorough structural change (in firms which are engaged in the production, processing and transmission of information itself) and his analysis of the impact of IT on structural change within the firm were broadly accepted. However, more research is needed to find out if his results hold for enterprises in other countries, too.

Communication technology causes revolutions in mass media. Social scientists are very much concerned about the impact of these developments on socio-cultural factors and, more specifically, on national identities.

Cultural identity of a nation could be threatened in two respects:
1. The creation of many small local radio and tv-stations gives minorities (resp. ethnic groups) possibilities to undermine the cultural unity of the nation as a whole. (This aspect was discussed intensely in Prof. Colas' paper).
2. Unwelcome cultural influences are poored over the country via radio and tv programmes, causing the domination of international cultural scenes by one leading entertainment producing country.

The enormous expansion of broadcasting possibilities, however, also gives a chance for the cultural diversity of a country to stay alive and prosper. Colas' concern about a nation's cultural identity which is expressed by <u>one</u> language and <u>one</u> cultural herity seems to reflect a problem which might be of greater interest in countries like France or Spain than in others. The extent to which a country has cultural unity or cultural diversity affects the attitude and difficulties to be encountered in regulation of mass media. Safeguards are required - and they seem to be legitimate - to prevent the cultural domination of one society over others. It might be difficult, however, to balance out this concern with the overall accepted free flow of information.

Another problem of new mass media scenarios is their effect on human communication. The rather naive idea that communication technology brings people together has to be replaced by more differentiated analyses of different forms of communication and of the perception of information. The electronic transfer of information which has tremendously increased over the last decade also showed some aspects fo deprivation in human interaction. Only a very limited part of the complicated process of communication can be transmitted electronically. While the limited possibilities of non-interactive communication like tv-watching are quite obvious, it is not entirely clear what makes the difference between e.g. video conferences and personal meetings. Undoubtedly, more research on sensual perception in communicative situations is needed.

The growth of TV provides potential for multi-lateral presentations of society. But everything depends on the content of information which is transmitted through mass media. It is a question of media policy and a country's communication and information culture, if the potential will be fully used. In order to be attractive, TV has to convey complex concepts in a simple fashion. (A similar tendency shows in the growth of comic books and magazines to explain complicated material). Especially in Germany, there is some concern about a loss of differentiation and of critical aspects in arguments which are presented in a show-like manner.

Prof. Ito's paper expressed optimism in some of these issues. By comparing visual messages made possible with new IT with printed information, he emphazises the more holistic perception of the world in modern media. It has to be asked, however, if the comparison should perhaps be extended to visual messages and actual "live" experience. Personal experience - not regarding selective perception - is "holistic".

TV programmes may contribute to perceiving information more completely than, for example books, by adding the visual component. On the other hand they filter the real world and leave important sensual aspects apart. Prof. Ito hopes that TV will reduce manipulation and give a more objective picture of reality. But television does not seem to be the "cool medium" which he has in mind. TV programmes in dictatorial regimes prove that pictures can very well be used selectively and thus influence people more effectively than by using only print or accustic media.

The following conclusions might be drawn from the first conference session: IT translates into societal change and presents several political and volatile factors. To defuse extreme reaction the beneficial aspects must not be hidden but identified and become a part of planning. Progress has been made in deployment of IT. It has been recognized by major firms and countries that information, as a basis of timely and more informed decision making, can create strategic advantage in a competitive environment.

The second session on "Policy making in the area of IT" was divided into two parts, one on telecommunications and one on information technology.

Whereas policy making for telecommunications is mainly concerned with competition and deregulation, in the field of information technology it deals primarily with the support of IT adoption, with R&D subsidies and with international competitiveness of national firms. The need to abolish state monopolies in the telecommunications sector seems to be broadly accepted. Discussions now focus on the necessary degree of deregulation and various forms of market organization which may follow from it.

Three modes of competition were discussed by Ch. Jonscher:

a) Parallel basic network infrastructure has been introduced only in US, Great Britain and Japan. The total impact is not yet significant and this type of reform seems improbable in many other countries. It has been criticized as a wasteful duplication of resources and potentially threatening the viability of ISDN introduction.
b) The second mode is competiton in the provision of value added services (in the technical sense). This is under way, even if problems of defining the boundary between basic and value added service will prevail. The value added market is so far only a few per cent of total and less than 5% even in GB.
c) The third mode is competition in the provision of value added services in a business sense (or outplacement). As examples Minitel in FR and cellular telephony in GB were given. The latter has grown very fast by international comparison.

A slightly modified version of form b) is adopted after the deregulation of the German telecommunications sector. Here the monopoly sphere includes the network infrastructure and the simple telephone service. All other services and user equipment are supplied under competitive conditions.

The large variety of regulatory patterns in different countries shows that no single economic answer for the "right" organizational frame of telecommunication markets exists. Policy making must take into consideration specific national structures and historical backgrounds, and it must take a broader view of implications beyond the economic ones. Existing supply and demand constellations, aspects of industrial and entrepreneurial culture, industrial relations and traditional regulatory instruments and institutions have to be considered.

A central question in the deregulation debate is what happens after the establishment of new regulatory patterns. The introduction of competition stimulated the supply of basic telecommunication and value added services in the US, Great Britain and Japan. It led to a restructure of tariffs with a tendency towards lower prices for most of the new services. New forms of "package services" are offered in Great Britain: Network capacity retailers are subsidizing the terminal dealers in return for subscription contracts, so that customers only pay a fraction of the real price for terminals. Customers have had benefits from this, but the national industry has lost the terminal market to foreign competitors. Competiton in Japan increased after the introduction of type I and type II operators in 1985. Long distance telephone, mobile communications and international services are offered in competitive markets, and 1989 is expected to be a year of strong rivalry. International tariffs are being reduced. Transborder value added services will soon gain in importance.

The new systems still require a considerable amount of regulation in order to prevent "unfair" marketing or price-setting behaviour and to assure the technical functioning of the network.

In the discussion it was emphasized that due consideration must be given to all actors in the global market place and that the increased pace in developments puts stronger demands on speed and efforts on standards. L. Virol emphasized that also the specific national and economic contexts should be considered.

Regular consultations about all these issues are being held between Japan and the EC. IT policy in Europe focuses on the diffusion of advanced manufacturing technologies. Emphasis is put on the support of small and medium sized companies. Increased productivity and efficiency are important for industries which are labour intensive and subject to competition from low-wage countries. Data from a few OECD countries show that the diffusion of IT is rather uneven. The impediments of a more wide-spread adoption point towards the major fields of IT policy, as H.-P. Gassmann explained:

- A lack of qualified personnel requires the expansion of training facilities in the firm and in private and public institutions outside the firm. School and university programmes have to reflect qualification needs for new IT;
- software and system operation have to become more user-friendly. IT policy should support the respective R&D programmes;
- especially small and medium sized firms mention the high cost and lack of finance as an obstacle against more intensive use of IT. Interest subsidies or government guarantees could ease the situation;
- firms often need support from outside to acquire know-how for the necessary organizational and technical changes which are a precondition for productive adoption of IT. In Germany good results were achieved with technology transfer centers;
- cooperation between firms seems to become increasingly important. Efforts to link existing elements and to develop more efficient standards should be encouraged.

National support programmes have already taken up these issues. It seems that the Japanese efforts are more long range oriented.

In the third session of the conference, aspects of European-Japanese collaboration were discussed.

Not long ago cooperation between firms was a rather ambiguous field. Companies feared their comparative advantages might disappear if they shared knowledge and stragtegies with competitors. But then cooperation turned out to be a necessary instrument to survive in highly competitve markets. Rapid technological change in IT, decreasing life cycles of related products, an enormous rise of R&D costs and a quickly proceeding partition of world markets require cooperation even between direct competitors. The most important advantages of cooperation are: a more favourable level of production in terms of economies of scale, mutual stimulation and enhancement of technological competences, avoiding or diminishing barriers to entry in a foreign market. The paper of H. Schütte contributes to the better understanding of the actual dynamics of European-Japanese cooperation in IT and its constraints. Especially he emphasizes on strategic alliances; this group of agreements represents the care of broad-based accords which are truly cooperative and long-term in nature and approach.

Despite these apparently positive aspects there are very few examples for European-Japanese cooperation so far. Usually Europeans feel that the Japanese partner gains more from joint ventures. So an imbalance of strategic objectives as well as a lack of accordance about the "rules of the game" leave potential partners with rather reluctant feelings about possible cooperations. Nevertheless, the case study presented in this third conference session showed that these diffuculties can be overcome if some conditions are met.

The experience of the joint venture mentioned above shows some main features of difficulties to be faced by European firms in Japan. Very often collaboration is used to enter the Japanese market. This approach has proved to be useful because it is not easy for a new-comer to understand business rules in Japan. Foreign firms generally encounter a lot of traps that could be avoided. Many problems which are due to misunderstanding the Japanese way of doing business are misinterpreted as barriers to entry. In the light of these difficulties K. Riemenschneider's paper is very useful. It gives a comprehensive list of typical problems of European firms which intend to enter the

Japanese market and can serve as a guideline to understand the complicated mechanisms of an undisclosed economy.

The discussion concentrated mainly on two points: First, why are there so little examples of cooperation? Second, are the difficulties to be faced in Japan similar for big, medium-sized and small companies?

Firms still seem to be rather suspicious about the possible benefits of cooperation. Furthermore, it turned out to be difficult to find arrangements which served the strategic aims of both partners. Cooperation is certainly not restricted to small companies, though the ways into the Japanese market may differ considerably for companies that are bigger than the one presented in the case study.

The second part of the third session was dedicated to the problems arising from the Single European Market for the Japanese-European relationship. It was argued that cooperation between firms might become even more important in the view of 1992. But a coordinated approach to trade policy is required, to prevent an increase of unproductive political pressure due to fears of protectionism.

In the market for telecommunications equipment, the major economic restructuring in the process of forming a Single Market is already taking place. Changes and adjustments have still to be expected, however, in the services sector, where Japan has moved much faster, in line with the US and Great Britain. Policy decisions in the telecommunication sector are undoubtedly one of the critical policy areas, because they involve not only technical and market aspects but also regulatory and standardization issues. Concerns were expressed that while concentrating on the effectiveness of implementing the Green Paper, the efforts towards international cooperation may fall behind.

Research cooperation of European and Japanese firms presents some difficulties for these activities that fall outside the rules of European research programmes. It is obviously difficult for Japanese firms to get access to European research funds and circles, which are now being opened ot US firms. To overcome this disadvantage, some firms from Japan intend to establish R&D centers in Europe. They thereby hope to eventually gain a position equal to that of large American companies with respect to participation in European research programmes.

To sum up, European-Japanese collaboration in the IT sector presents a great challenge, but it can also be a mutually rewarding experience, if the gains of cooperation in international specialization can be fully realized.

Future world markets for IT, the issue of the fourth conference session, offer a broad variety of topics to be discussed. The aggregate volume of future IT markets is as difficult to assess as its structure in terms of various goods and services and in terms of the geographical location of supply and demand. IT might change the actual partition of world markets bringing about new dominating firms or countries. Changes in the distribution of economic power and in the relative status of countries will affect the relationship of Japan, Europe and the US. All these problems could only be shortly commented on in the session. Some important conclusions can be drawn, however.

W. Melody's paper concentrates on the structural changes occuring in the global economy, and examines how these changes are likely to influence the size and structure of future world markets for IT. There is a reciprocal relationship between IT and the performance of economies: Trends in the global economic performance will influence the size and structure of IT world markets. On the other hand, IT has got a key role for the dynamics of overall economic development. Hence a sensitive simultaneous process is going on with promising and solid but not overwhelming results so far.
Problems of IT production and adoption seem to be quite similar on the national and on the international level. IT was supposed to bring nations together, but again, increasing volumes of transmitted information do not necessarily mean better communication or mutual understanding, especially if processes of diffusion and access to IT products and services are unbalanced.

Nevertheless, IT seems to have special characteristics which help to overcome institutional and spatial barriers. So there is some justification in calling it an "international commodity", as Prof. Komatsuzaki did in his contribution. To fully realize this internationalization, the crucial problem of how underdeveloped and developing countries can be integrated in the world markets for IT has to be faced. Today it is far away from being resolved. Third world countries may be confronted with a vicious cycle: They need IT to be able to participate in major processes of technical progress. But they can absorb IT productively only, if a relatively high level of economic and technological development is reached. A way out of this circular problem can be found, if IT products and services are offered which adjust to the specific needs of countries in different stages of development. Furthermore, IT offers niches for countries with particular comparative advantages, for example, low wages for manpower with good basic qualifications in data processing and programming. However, quick technical progress in dominant parts of the world market includes the danger to further widening the gap between advanced and underdeveloped countries. It can therefore not be said today, if IT tends to increase or decrease the stability of the international economic system.

A group of countries which have been mostly excluded from the world market of IT products are socialist countries, i.e., Eastern Europe and China.

P. Havlik pointed out the difficulties to promote the production, processing, transmission and diffusion of information in countries where information is supposed to be under strict governmental control. Thus current reforms in the Soviet Union might not only bring about more democratic rights and more economic efficiency but they might also produce a big push in the development of IT markets. The same holds for China, though here expectations cannot be very optimistic after the recent attempts to stop and reverse liberalization. Y. Mine pointed out with respect to China that security aspects in data processing and transmission should be given more attention.

The actual situation in most Comecon countries usually requires that the delivery of IT products is accompanied by services like training, repair centers or organizational know-how. Thus some western firms have been engaged in joint ventures with eastern European states.

A lack of technical equipment and infrastructures does not mean, however, that there is also a lack in all skills and qualifications connected with IT. The contrary might be the case. Recent developments, e.g. in Hungary, showed that the country has got good chances in international markets for programming services, mostly for routine purposes, for which it has got comparative advantages due to solid basic qualifications and low labour costs.

It is particularly interesting to analyze the new role which the US might play as one of the world powers besides Japan and Europe (and not necessarily the leading one). Of course, the US are very much concerned about opening of the Japanese markets and keeping the European ones more or less open. F. Bar and J. Zysman point out that US influence in telecommunications on Europe and Japan has come through three different channels: Deregulation, opening the American market and an unbalanced trade bill. Since one traditional advantage of the US economy, the technological superiority which partly stemmed from spill-over effects from the military to the civilian sector has lost its importance, access to foreign markets requires other instruments, such as negotiations and dialogue.

This statement leads back to the overall theme of the conference - mutual understanding. It was generally agreed upon that communication and cooperation were the most important factors to forward the realization of considerable potentials which IT offers both in Japanese and in European markets.

CHAIRMAN'S CLOSING STATEMENT

Hiroshi Inose
Director General National Center for Science Information System, Tokyo

The conference was organized by the **German Institute for Economic Research (DIW)** and the Japanese-German-Center Berlin with the participation of academic, government and private sector experts from 12 countries in Europe and Japan and head- and or representatives of three relevant international organizations. The Conference was convened as a result of the recommendations put forward in the past meetings of TIDE 2000 project, which was initiated in 1985 by the Ministry of Foreign Affairs of Japan.

It has been widely recognized that the development of IT has greatly influenced the economic and social development of countries and that it is of utmost importance to examine measures for realizing the maximum benefit from the development of IT.

Taking into account of the widely held vies that the European-Japanese relations are not as extensive as those of Japan-US and Europe-US relations, it has been felt necessary for Europe and Japan to promote dialogue and exchange to promote international cooperation between the two regions. From this point of view, it is very important for Japan and Europe to exert their efforts to promote exchange and dialogue by making maximum use of IT.

More specifically; the following major observations have been made during the three-days discussions at the Conference.

1. Major Observations

a) Continuing promotion of telecommunications liberalization

Liberalization should be promoted in the field of basic service as well as value added services taking into account of future technological progress and at the same time, taking into full account of institutional and social environment of respective countries.
Japan, Great Britain, and the United States will be urged to provide their own experience of liberalization to other countries. And at the same time, it is expected that the proposals included in the EC Green Paper on Telecommunications will be implemented and further developed.

b) Enhancement and strengthening of networks

It is important to enhance and strengthen information networks between Europe and Japan, in particular to make full use of newly developed ISDN facilities and interantional VAN services. Emphasis also should be placed on the promotion of human networks between Europe and Japan.

c) IT for enhancing industrial competitiveness

IT related policies must be incorporated into economic policy on a long term perspective. Specific attention should be directed to more effective diffusion policy, manpower training and promotion of small and medium sized enterprises.

d) Promotion of European-Japanese joint projects

Considerable support was expressed for the establishment of joint research and development projects. Cooperation between enterprises need to be improved and expanded.

e) Promotion of social and cultural exchange

The importance of the function of IT for facilitating social and cultural exchange between Europe and Japan was recognized, in the context that cultural understanding plays an important role for the promotion of the cooperation between European and Japanese firms.

f) Coping with IT related problems

It was widely recognized that it is highly appropriate for Europe and Japan to attempt to solve such international issues as standardization and interoperability of systems and services.

g) Relations between free market and centrally planned economies

It is important to encourage technology transfer between these different economies for facilitating the development of science and technology, while paying particular attention to national security problems. Dialogue among Western industrialized democracies is needed in this regard.

2. Recommendations

a) The Conference recommends that continued and further intensified dialogue on IT impacts on the economies, society and culture of Europe and Japan should be maintained. In this regard, it would be appropriate to hold a similar conference on IT related cooperation by an European initiative at an appropriate time and place.

b) Considering the fact that great attention has been focused to commercial relations between European and Japanese firms, the Conference recommends that these relations should be strengthened by industry, government and academic organizations, to promote direct investment, joint ventures, technology transfer, research and training.

c) The Conference also recommends that considerations are given to the examination of these IT developments and cooperation on a more global basis and with other economic regions, that include newly industrializing economies and centrally planned economies.

II. THE IMPACT OF INFORMATION TECHNOLOGY WITHIN THE EUROPEAN-JAPANESE RELATIONSHIP

"Impact on society and culture"

THE SOCIAL AND CULTURAL IMPACTS OF INFORMATION TECHNOLOGY[1]

Youichi Ito
Institute for Communications Research
Keio University, Tokyo

1. Introduction

Many social critics, jounalists and scholars have speculated about the impacts of information technologies. Speculation, however, is not a science. Many of the descriptions regarding the impacts of information technologies are nothing but wishful predictions without convincing grounds. What will become possible technologically and what will happen actually are often different. A distinction must be clearly made between arguments about technological feasibilies and scientific predictions about the future.

A scientific prediction about the future must be based on a social theory supported by facts or current or recent factual trends. It is not easy to identify scientific predictions among numerous irreponsible predictions regarding information societies and the impacts of information technologies (see Masuda 1980, Slack 1984, English 1985, Miles and Gershuny 1987, Miles, Bessant, Guy and Rush 1987 for various predictions on the impacts of information technology).

Information technology is similar to transportation technology in the sense that they both bring different individuals and societies closer. Therefore, in a sense, the impact of information technologies resembles the impact of transportation technologies. Transportation technologies made it impossible for non-Western countries in the 18th and 19th centuries to seclude themselves from the Western world. They were forced to join international competition. Today, information technologies are making it impossible for many socialist countries to seclude themselves from the capitalist bloc. The impacts of information technologies have domestic and international aspects.

---

[1] The writer would like to thank James W. Dearing of the Annenberg School of Communications, University of Southern California for helpful comments on an earlier draft.

2. Impacts in the Domestic Area

Decline of mass media influence?

McLuhan (1964, p. 36) divided communication media into two categories, a "hot medium" and a "cool medium".

> "A hot medium is one that extends one single sense in 'high definition'. High definition is the state of being well filled with data. A photograph is, visually, 'high definition'. A cartoon is 'low definition', simply because very little visual information is provided. Telephone is a cool medium, or one of low definition, because the ear is given a meager amount of information. And speech is a cool medium of low definition, because so little is given and so much has to be filled in by the listener. On the other hand, hot media do not leave so much to be filled in or completed by the audience. Hot media are, therefore, low in participation, and cool media are high in participation or completion by the audience. Naturally, therefore, a hot medium like radio has very different effects on the user from a cool medium like the telephone."

McLuhan suggests that "hot media" such as radio and movies are superior as propaganda media to "cool media" such as television. Not only that, he suggests that "cool media" that are "high in participation" have an effect to "cool off" the audience.

> "It was no accident that Senator McCarthy lasted such a very short time when he switched to TV .... TV is a cool medium. It rejects hot figures and hot issues and people from the hot press media .... Had TV occured on a large scale during Hitler's reign he would have vanished quickly. Had TV come first there would have been no Hitler at all." (McLuhan 1964: p. 261).

McLuhan's definition of being "hot" and "cool" is not very clear. In order to clarify his definition, major media described as "hot" or "cool" in McLuhan's book are shown in Table 1.

Table 1
Hot media and cool media

Hot media	*Cool media*
paper	stone
alphabet	hieroglyphic and ideogram
printed matter	face to face communication
photograph	cartoon
radio	telephone
movie	television
lecture	seminar

(characteristics)	
high definition	low definition
one way	two-way or interactive
uni-channel	multi-channel
less participation	more participation
highly specialized	general or holistic

Which kind of media is likely to become more dominant in the coming information age? While "hotter" television such as high definition television (HDTV) is expected to be commercialized in the near future, more two-way, interactive media such as videotex, personal computer networks, facsimile, two-way cable television are expected to flourish. In other words, "cool media" are likely to become more dominant in the near future. What do "cool media" do to individuals and society?

According to McLuhan, while "hot media" make people passive, individualistic, specialist, and their thought patterns linear and logical, "cool media" make people active, participatory, group-oriented or others-oriented and their thought patterns more holistic and intuitive. According to McLuhan (1964):

> "The printed word with its specialist intensity burst the bonds of medieval corporate guilds and monsteries, creating extreme individualist patterns of enterprise and monopoly. But the typical reversal occurred when extremes of monopoly brought back the corporation, with its impersonal empire over many lives" (p. 36).

The medium of money or wheel or writing, or any other form of specialist speed-up or exchange and information, will serve to fragment a tribal structure. Similarly, a very much greater speed-up, such as occurs with electricity, may serve to restore a tribal pattern of intense involvement ...
Specialist technologies detribalize. The non-specialist electric technology retribalizes" (p. 38).

Whether McLuhan is dicussing superficial short-time effects (media effects) or deep long-term effects (basic change of thought patterns, ways of perception or personality) is not clear. It is possible to argue that the thought pattern of a person who is always exposed to "hot media" will become logical, linear, specialist, analytical, individualistic and susceptible to propaganda. On the other hand, the thought pattern of a person who is always exposed to "cool media" may become holistic, intuitive, general, balanced, and group-, interaction- or harmony-oriented. It is also possible to argue that personal thought patterns or personality never change. What is affected is short-term media effects. A "hot medium" will make the audience think linear and logical at least while they are exposed to that medium. If they are exposed to a "cool medium" after a while, their way of perception may change to become more holistic. It seems to the writer that it is not realistic to think that a basic thought pattern or personality is changed by the media to which one is repeatedly exposed. Most people are usually exposed to both "hot" and "cool" media in their daily lives.

The effects of propaganda or mass media campaigns are basically determined by two factors, i.e., the degree of control of the media environment (for example, by the government) and the kind of media used. As discussed later in the section entitled "intensification of international competition", the control of media environment is becoming more and more difficult in the coming "information age". At the same time, "cool media" are becoming more dominant. Under these circumstances, it is very probable that the effects of propaganda including campaigns through mass media decline.

Social organizations

How will information technologies affect social organizations including family and local communities? Printing technology, increased literacy rates and an enhanced educational level of the masses enabled rapid development and diffusion of science and technology and brought the industrial revolution. As a result of the industrial revolution, modern economic organizations and political systems were created undermining traditional roles born by families and local communities. The family size has become smaller and smaller and people have lost many traditional functions. Many local villages in remote areas have collapsed and many new urban communities have become nothing but a collection of anonymous, atomized individuals.

Under such circumstances, it was expected that new communication media such as interactive two-way cable television and videotex might contribute to the halt of these trends. These new media were expected to save atomized lonely people in large cities through increased interactions within the community. This wishful prediction, however, has not been supported by facts so far. According to several surveys conducted in the communities that experimentally introduced highly sophisticated interactive two-way cable television or videotex, people did not use these media as frequently as expected to communicate with other community members. Moreover, it was found that these media were used more in rural communities where there were interactions anyway than in urban communities where a number of isolated lonely people live (see Ito and Oishi 1987 for survey data and further discussions).

It was also expected that new communication media would contribute to the development of underdeveloped areas within the country and the decentralization of the Tokyo-Yokohama-Nagoya-Osaka-Kobe corridor in Japan. The reason given was that new communication systems such as teleconferencing and video telephones would eliminate or diminish the disadvantage of building factories or offices in remote areas. For example, Pool (1977, p. 5) once wrote that "the telephone contributed considerably to urban sprawl and the mass migration to suburbia ... and the location of offices and factories." In old times people had to see each other to discuss business. According to Pool, however, automobiles and the telephone changed that. As a result, "the city grew from a walking city to a vehicled one" and then to a telephone network city enabling the city to expand to the suburbs.

In advanced information societies, facsimile, teleconferencing, ISDN networks, video telephone, and two-way cable television are expectd to join the existing communication networks. In Japan, which suffers from over-centralization, there was a strong expectation that as "informationization" proceeded, more offices, factories and companies would be built outside Tokyo where rent, labour, and all other costs are less high than in Tokyo.

Actually, however, what is happening is the opposite, more centralization. Now experts give different explanations. The land productivity of information industries is extremely high. Think of a software house, for example. Work stations placed in small offices are generating a large amount of profit. For these industries, high rent is not a problem. Quality of labour is more important than the average cost of labour. Creative and original ideas are crucial in information industries. These ideas are born in dynamic and energetic megalopolises full of intellectual stimulation. Ideas grow through the communication of ideas and information with colleagues and competitors and by attending conferences and symposiums. Whatever the reason, the concentration of population, capital, information, and everything else in Tokyo is still increasing under "informationization" (see Oishi 1986, 1988a, 1988b).

On the other hand, a new kind of communities which did not exist before informationization are emerging. They are called "network communities". People who have never met each other and do not even know each other's real names are regularly communicating through personal computer networks. According to a newspaper report, for several days after Emperor Hirohito's death on January 7, 1989, heated electronic discussions took place in the world of personal computer networks regarding Emperor Hirohito's responsibility for the Pacific War (Nihon Keizai Shimbun, 1989). Nobody knows yet, however, what kind of social and political functions these PC network communities have.

Productivity and efficiency

Technological innovations make possible what was previously impossible. Business corporations are severely competing with each other to provide higher quality commodities at a lower cost. Computers, telecommunication networks, and other information technologies contribute a great deal to increases in productivity and efficiency and to competitive success. This is a major reason why information technologies have rapidly been incorporated into business corporations, changing the structure of their organizations, offices and factories. The number of manufacturing factories completely controlled by computers and industrial robots is increasing. In some factories robots are producing robots. Computers and robots are not only efficient and productive but also seldom make mistakes, unlike humans. Therefore, the quality of products produced by robots is usually higher than of those produced by human workers. The quality of products in information societies tends to be superior to those produced in pre-information societies. Government agencies are also under pressure for different reasons to increase efficiency and productivity. They are also introducing new communication and information processing facilities to increase efficiency.

Eisenstein (1983) wrote that printing technology drastically increased the amount of literature available for reference by scientists, making it possible for them to acquire far more knowledge than before the printing revolution. This contributed a great deal to the acceleration of the "science revolution" in Europe. The same situation is emerging in information societies by the diffusion of xerox machines, personal computers, word processors and fax machines. Moreover, scientists can use large-scale data bases for finding scientific information and literature. Twenty years ago I used to write articles using a pencil and manual typewriter (when I wrote in English). Now at home I have two personal computers, an electronic typewriter, a Japanese word processor, a xerox machine and a fax machine. My personal computer at home can be connected to large data bases in Japan or outside Japan through telephone lines. The number of articles I can write per year has drastically increased. The same change must have occured, or must be occuring, to other researchers and scholars in the world. As a result, the accumulation of knowledge and the development of sciences are being accelerated. During the past several centuries, the number of scientific journals has increased exponentially. At present, the increase is better described as an "explosion" (Anderla 1973, p. 15).

Convenience and the increase of productivity, however, do not necessarily give people more free time. It seems that people in information societies are busier than those in pre-information societies. The reason is the same as when considering the change to industrial societies, when people in industrial societies seemed busier than those in agricultural societies. It seems that people's sense of pace or speed increases as productivity and efficiency of the whole society increase. The society takes the increased speed and efficiency for granted. Younger generations speak faster and walk faster than older generations. Twenty years ago, I could tell the publisher that my manuscript is in the mail even if I was still working on it. Nowadays, however, the publisher asks me to send my manuscript by fax and I cannot respond that it is in the mail.

3. Impacts in the International Area
Cultural identity

There is no culture on this earth which has never learned anything from another. Learning from other cultures is a natural phenomenon and there is nothing wrong with it. However, when foreign influence is overwhelming, beyond the control of the receiving country, or when influence is unidirectional for a long period of time, psychologically delicate problems emerge.

A friend of mine, an economist, once said to me that even if a country imports information products and exports raw materials and agricultural products, it should not be a problem as long as an even balance of trade is maintained. He even said that trying to retain a country's cultural identity is like believing in superstition and is irrational. His view is certainly "rational", especially from an economist's viewpoint. He ignores, however, (irrational?) human psychology that people need a "balance of influence" apart from a "balance of payment".

All people in the world want to be equal, not only in principle, but also in practice. If Nation A always influences Nation B and Nation B never influences Nation A for an extended period of time, people in Nation B will begin to feel that their culture is inferior; their cultural identity may be endangered. Under such circumstances, people in Nation B may suffer from an inferiority complex and begin to resent Nation A. In the extreme case, Nation B looses cultural integrity, imagination, creativity and energy and is eventually led to a complete cultural and social collapse. Unfortunately, a few examples of this extreme case exist.

On the other hand, if Nation A and Nation B influence each other and learn from each other, the cultures of the two nations will be enriched and the welfare of both nations will be enhanced. In the past, new leaps in human cultures and civilizations have often been brought about by the blending and synthesising of different cultural elements. Such cultural leaps benefit the people of the world and there exist many examples of this kind of progress.

The extremely rapid development of modern information technologies has accelerated the speed of transmitting culture between nations. If the present world situation follows the second scenario, that is, an increase of mutual cultural influence between countries, there is no need for concern. However, many experts, particularly those in Third World countries, are afraid that the world might be following the first scenario, that is, cultural domination on one hand, and cultural subordination and collapse on the other. (For further discussion, see Ito 1988).

Between culturally dissimilar areas such as West and East Asia, cultural differences work as an effective barrier against excessive importation of foreign cultural products. If cultural industries develop to a certain level, domestically produced cultural products become more competitive than imported products and eventually replace them. This occurred in Japan in the late 1960s, Asian newly industrialized economies (NIES) in the late 1970s, and it is now occuring in many less developed Asian countries. Therefore, between culturally dissimilar countries, there is not much to worry about.

Between culturally similar countries, however, such as between the United States and Canada, the United States and Western Europe, large European countries and small European countries, and Japan and Korea, this problem can be more serious. Direct broadcast satellites (DBS), for example, will increase the influence of more populated and economically powerful countries on less populated and economically weaker countries within the same region. There are two ways to avoid this: (1) Restrict the flows of information from more populated and economically powerful countries to other countries within the same region, or (2) *expand* the object of cultural identity from a country to an international region. For example, French, German, Italian and British people might give up their traditional identities and adopt the identity of Western Europeans (see Schlesinger 1987 regarding this issue). Similarly, Japanese, Chinese and Korean people might give up their traditional identities and adopt identities as Northeast Asians; Indian, Pakistani and Sri Lankan people might adopt identities as South Asians; and American and Canadian people might adopt identities as North Americans.

Although the latter solution may sound difficult due to historical reasons, it may be more suited to the information age. Two hundred years ago, the identities of Japanese people were limited to the feudal territory to which they belonged. Transportation technologies in the late 19th century, however, expanded their object of identity from the feudal territory to Japan as a whole. Modern information technologies may encourage people to further expand their object of cultural identity from a nation to a larger international region.

Intensification of international competition

It was the military and economic strength of the West and their modern transportation technologies that made it impossible for Japan and other East Asian countries to seclude themselves from the Western Word. In the mid 19th century, Japanese leaders realized that unless they joined international military and economic competition, their countries would be colonized and exploited by the Western powers. Without the superior transportation technologies of the West at that time, Japanese leaders would not have felt such a strong threat.

It was only after two disastrous world wars in the 20th century that people all over the world agreed for the first time in history that every nation in the world had a right to exist and be independent regardless of its degree of military strength. Military aggression based on ethnocentric motives was clearly denounced. Thus, military and economic competition continue to flourish in today's world.

Another feature of the world after World War II was that demands from the general masses for a higher quality of life became increasingly stronger. The diffusion of movies and television sets and other information technologies as well as the increase of overseas travel have enabled the general masses to compare their quality of life by seeing that in other countries. Economic indicators such as per capita income are used in ordinary mass media reports and stimulate people's competitiveness.

The Soviet Union and other socialist countries have long objected to the idea of a "free flow of information" across national borders and have instead insisted on the idea of "information sovereignty". "Information sovereignty" means that each government has the right to control the flow of information coming into and going out of the country just like it controls the flow of individuals and commodities across national borders. This idea, however, is rapidly becoming obsolete due to the development of information technologies.

Back in the days when journalists and other individuals sent their messages across national borders by letters, cables, and sound or video tapes, governments could control the flow of information. Nowadays, however, messages are sent by direct dial telephone, telex, fax, or via communication satellites. It is becoming more and more difficult for national governments to intervene in the flow of international information. The principle of a "free flow of information" across national borders desired by the Western block is now being realized on a global scale chiefly due to the rapid development of information technologies.

If information flows freely between socialist and capitalist countries, people in socialist countries can easily compare their standard of living and their freedom and welfare with those in capitalist countries. As a result, the governments of socialist countries are obliged to give highest priority to raising the standard of living and the welfare of the general public. If information from foreign countries flows in freely, it becomes more difficult for central governments to hide facts or information from the masses. Recent policy changes in China and the Soviet Union towards more openness, more competition, and more freedom were caused by this new reality. Consider a recent joke in the Soviet Union: "Socialism is an agonizing intermediate stage that some nations experience when they shift from capitalism to capitalism". Information technologies are probably having stronger impacts on socialist countries than on capitalist countries.

4. Summary and Conclusion

Many predictions made so far regarding the impacts of information technologies were not scientific. Many of them only foretell what will become technologically possible. Some of them were nothing but wishful predictions. Scientific predictions must be based on social theories, facts or recent trends.

In this paper the domestic and international impacts of information technologies were discussed. Domestically, information technologies are likely to undermine mass media influence, change social organizations, and increase productivity and efficiency. Internationally, information technologies are likely to influence personal cultural identity and intensify international competition.

Some of the predicted influences are socially desirable, but some are not. Policy makers must be prepared for the predicted impacts and wisely cope with them.

References

Anderla, Georges (1973): Information in 1985: A Forecasting Study of Information Needs and Ressources. Paris: Organization for Economic Cooperation and Development (OECD).

Asahi Shimbun (1989a): "Keizai Komikku Doitsugoba mo (A Comic Book on Economics Translated into German)", February 8, p. 2.
Asahi Shimbun (1989b): "Tetsuwan Atomu no Messeiji (Message from the Iron-Handed Atom)", February 10, p. 5.

Eisenstein, Elizabeth L. (1983): The Printing Revolution in Early Modern Europe. Cambridge, MA, Cambridge University Press.

English, Maurice (1985a): "The Four Stages of Impact: The Primitive, Widespread, Cultural, and Full Impact of Information Technologies", in Altenpohl, D.G: Informatization: The Growth of Limits. Düsseldorf, FRG: Aluminium-Verlag.

English, Maurice (1985b): "Research and Development in Advanced Communications Technologies for Europe". Unpublished report available at the Information Technologies and Telecommunications Task Force, the Commission of the European Communities.

Finnegan, Ruth, Salaman, Graeme and Thompson, Kenneth (1987): "Information Technology: Social Issues". Sevenoaks, Kent, U.K., Holder and Stoughton.

Freeman, Christopher (1987): "The Case for Technological Determinism", pp. 5-18 in Finnegan, Salaman and Thompson (1987).

Freeman, Christopher (1988): "The Factory of the Future: The Productivity Paradox, Japanese Just-in-Time and Information Technology", Policy Research Papers, London: Economic and Social Research Council (ESRC).

Innis, Harold A. (1951): "The Bias of Communication". Toronto, Canada, University of Toronto Press.

Ito, Youichi (1981): "The 'Johoka Shakai' Approch to the Study of Communication in Japan", pp. 671-698 in Wilhoit, G.C. & de Bock, H. (eds.), Mass Communication Review Yearbook, Vol. 2, Beverly Hills, CA, Sage.

Ito, Youichi (1985): "Telecommunications and Industrial Policies in Japan: Recent Developments", pp. 201-230 in Snow, M.S. (ed.), Marketplace for Telecommunications: Regulation & Deregulation in Industrialized Democracies. New York and London, Longman.

Ito, Youichi (1987): "Mass Communication Research in Japan: History and Present State", pp. 49-85 in McLaughlin, M.L. (ed.), Communication Yearbook 10. Beverly Hills, CA, Sage.

Ito, Youichi (1988): "International Competition and Domestic Harmony as Driving Forces of Social and Cultural Change in Japan", unpublished paper delivered at the symposium entitled "Japan and Europe: Looking Towards the 21st Century" held at the Université Libre de Bruxelles in Brussels, Belgium, March 25-26, 1988.

Ito, Youichi and Oishi, Yutaka (1987): "Social Impacts of the New Utopias", pp. 201-220 in Dutton, W.H., Blumler, J.G. and Kraemer, K.L. (eds.), Wired Cities: Shaping the Future of Commuications. Boston, MA, C.K. Hall.

Masuda, Yoneji (1980): "The Information Society". Tokyo, Institute for the Information Society.

McLuhan, Marshall (1964): "Understanding Media: The Extensions of Man". New York, McGraw-Hill.

McLuhan, Marshall and Fiore, Quentin (1967): "The Medium is the Massage: An Inventory of Effects". New York, Bantam.

Miles, Ian (1988): "Information Technology and Information Society: Options for the Future", Policy Research Papers. London, Economic and Social Council.

Miles, Ian and Gershuny Jonathan (1987): "The Social Economics of Information Technology", pp. 209-224 in Finnegan, Salaman and Thompson (1987).

Miles, Ian, Bessant, John, Guy, Ken and Rush, Howard (1987): "IT Futures in Households and Communities", pp. 225-242 in Finnegan, Salaman and Thompson (1987).

Nihon Keizai Shimbun (1989): "'Tokumei Shakai' no Dengonban (A Message Board in an 'Anonymous Society')", January 17 (evening edition).

Oishi, Yutaka (1986): "Johoka deha Tokyo Shuuchuu wo Fusegenai (Informationization Cannot Halt the Tokyo Centralization of Japan)", in Ekonomisuto 64(50), pp. 46-50.

Oishi, Yutaka (1988a): "Impact of Informationization on Regional Development: Implications for Japan", in Keio Communication Review 9, pp. 23-31.

Oishi, Yutaka (1988b): "Japan's Informationization Policy and the Urban-Rural Gap: A Critical View". Unpublished paper delivered at the international colloquium sponsored by "Media, Culture & Society", held in London, October 21-24, 1988.

Oishi, Yutaka (1988c): "'Joho Kaihatsu' no Hikari to Kage (Light and Shadow of 'Information Development'", in Telemedia 1.

Pool, Ithiel de Sola (ed.) (1977): "The Social Impact of the Telephone". Cambridge, MA, The MIT Press.

Rahim, Syed A. (1989): "The Information Society Concept and Research: A View from Another Window", in Keio Communication Review 10.

Rogers, Everett M. (1986): "Communication Technology: The New Media in Society". New York, The Free Press.

Schlesinger, Philip (1987): "On National Identity: Some Conceptions and Misconceptions Criticized", in Social Science Information 26(2), pp. 219-264.

Slack, Jennifer D. (1984): "Surveying the Impacts of Communication Technologies", pp. 73-109 in Dellin, B. and Voigt M.J. (eds.), Progress in Communication Sciences, Vol. V, Norwood, NJ, Ablex.

III. POLICY MAKING IN THE AREA OF INFORMATION TECHNOLOGY

"Telecommunications policy in Japan and Europe"

"Production oriented information technology policy in Japan and Europe"

NEW DIMENSIONS OF TELECOMMUNICATIONS COMPETITION

Charles Jonscher
Booz Allen & Hamilton International Ltd., London

1. Introduction

During the 1980's Japan and the countries of Europe have all taken steps to reduce the extent of domination of the telecommunications service sector by the former monopoly provider. Many reasons can be put forward for this trend: a general swing in the political climate in favour of more decentralised management of the economy; technological developments which have made the range of services which can be provided by telecommunications systems wider; and the convergence of telecommunications with two other activities, namely computing and broadcasting, which have made it necessary to rethink certain regulatory boundaries. Trends such as these have caused practically all the countries of the industrialised world to reappraise the appropriate scope of the monopoly of the PTT within the telecommunications sector.

I suggest that a useful measure of the extent of this regulatory reform or liberalisation is the percentage of the total revenues which used to fall within the domain of exclusivity of the PTT, which has been yielded to competition. This previously exclusive domain is being yielded to competitors along two dimensions.

The first dimension is sharing the market for basic network facilities. In Japan and the United Kingdom (amongst other countries), additional carriers have been licensed to construct networks which parallel those of the major carrier, either using terrestrial technology or carrying signals by satellite. The extent of reduction of the former PTT's market share is still tiny in both cases. In the UK, Mercury has little more than 1% of the country's network revenues, and the newly licensed specialised satellite services carriers are expected to have smaller shares still. In Japan, the new networks are also carrying a very small proportion of total traffic at present. These percentages will grow through time, but it is not expected that the dominant carrier's share will fall to a level associated with normally competitive industrial markets (say, 50%) for a very long time into the future - perhaps decades.

The second dimension is the introduction of competition into parts of the value added chain, the term value added being used in the technical sense. The provision of telecommunications services involves on the one hand the provision of a basic infrastructure of circuits and circuit switches enabling electronic signals to be routed between distant points, and on the other hand the provision of equipment which is attached to nodes in that network, enabling or assisting the customer to make use of it. If this equipment is located on the customer's premises, it is called terminal or customer premise equipment; if it is operated by a third party vendor of processing facilities, its provision is regarded as a value added service activity. The dismantling of the former monopolies in these two areas (terminal equipment provision and value added service provision) is much more widespread than the introduction of parallel networks as discussed above; all countries of Western Europe and Japan have introduced competition to a greater or lesser extent in these fields. The introduction of new enterprises along these two dimensions of telecommunications service provision can be regarded as a response to an underlying problem faced by all industrialised countries. This is the fact that the growth of information technology as a tool of business and personal life has made the complexity and sheer size of the telecommunications industry reach a point where it is becoming inconceivable that it should be so monopolised or dominated by one institution. The operation of an advanced country's telecommunications facilities already consumes approximately 3% of the GDP. Given that this figure is rising by some 6% per year in real terms, in a typical European country, against real economic growth in the vicinity of 2 - 3%, we can look forward in the near future to a situation in which telecommunications activity represents 5% of the total economic activity of the nation. The desire to reduce the role of a single private or government institution in such circumstances becomes clear.

However both approaches to reducing this extent of domination in the sector have their problems. The construction of parallel networks arguably represents wasteful duplication of infrastructure facilities, given the enormous economies of scale in point to point communication through fibre optic technology. The construction of multiple parallel networks may also, it is feared, inhibit the deployment of the next generation of integrated digital services, be they of the narrowband or broadband type. For this reason the licensing of parallel networks has not gone ahead in any country of Europe other than the United Kingdom.

The introduction of competitors in the value added services area does not suffer from this problem but gives rise to considerable difficulties in the delineation of a boundary between basic and value added business activity. Attempts to draw this boundary have generated enormous controversies in the United States surrounding the Second and

Third Computer Inquiries in 1980 and 1985 respectively, and to similar difficulties in certain European countries. Furthermore, the extent to which competitive provision of value added services achieves results by the measure proposed at the beginning of this paper, is at present extremely small; in the United Kingdom, which probably has the largest value added sector among European countries, total revenues amount to less than 5% of telecommunications network revenues overall.

In the last few years there has emerged a third dimension of competitive entry into the former domain of PTT provision. This is the outplacing to competitive companies of downstream activities in the value added chain, the term value added being used in the business rather than physical sense. Specifically, we refer to the outplacement of the marketing, sales, customer service and account administration (billing and collection) functions. The relationship of these functions to those of network operation is illustrated in Exhibit 1.

In the remainder of this paper we consider the potential of this third dimension of competitive entry for stimulating growth in the telecommunications industry. We take as a case study, the provision of cellular mobile telecommunications services.

2. Case Study: The UK Cellular Mobile Communication Industry

The cellular telephone service industry presents a most illuminating case study of the effect on industry growth of the different dimensions of competition discussed above.

Developed countries have adopted a series of models for the competitive structure of that industry, yielding a rich variety of alternative industry structures for the delivery of essentially identical technology to their respective national markets. We therefore have available as close an approximation to a controlled experiment in the dynamic behavior of different industry structures as is likely to present itself in the telecommunications sector (or indeed in many other sectors of business activity).

The different competitive arrangements are:

1. Monopoly

A complete monopoly of network infrastructure provision, of the marketing and distribution of service (ie value added functions in the business sense), and of the marketing and distribution of terminals (ie value added functions in the technical sense). This situation obtained from example, during the early years of cellular development in Japan.

2. Free entry into the terminal provision market

As above, but with competitive marketing and distribution of terminals. This has been the case in the Scandinavian market.

3. Duopoly network infrastructure provision

Licensing of two or more carriers to provide and operate the network infrastructure; terminal provision is then usually also open to competitive market entry. This is the position, for example, in the United States, two carriers being licensed to provide service in each major metropolitan area.

4. Free entry into.the market for service marketing and distribution (ie value added functions in the business sense).

This regulatory structure was introduced in the UK. Two competing network infrastructure operators, Cellnet and Racal, are required to delegate the marketing and distribution of their network services to third party operators. The result of the UK arrangements has been to produce an unusually complex competitive industry structure, in which there is free entry not only into the terminal provision market, but also into the market for cellular service provision. Specifically, the network provision business is split into two layers; a layer which is occupied by the two primary carriers and which is concerned with the consortium operation of the cellular infrastructures, and another layer consisting of dozens of competing "airtime retailers" which perform no technical or engineering functions but are concerned with marketing the service, signing-up customers, billing and collecting customer payments and dealing with service inquiries. Each of the two network operators in the primary layer does have a subsidiary active in this second layer; however the subsidiary must operate on an "arms-length" basis, on equal terms with the independent competing providers. In both Cellnet and Racal's cases this subsidiary has a non-dominant market share (of some 20-30%) of customers on their respective networks; the remaining 70-80% of the market is served by independent service providers.

The best measure of the development of the industry under these different competitive structures is the rate of penetration of cellular telephone per 1000 members of the population, beginning with the date of cellular service infrastructure introduction. The relevant data for the major markets of the world (those with more than 50,000 cellular service customers) is given in Exhibit 2. We can see from this exhibit that markets fall into essentially three groups.

a) The slowest industry growth was exhibited by those countries which had, at least in the early years, a monopolistic industry structure (eg. Japan; note that the German terminal market, while not monopolised, is subject to special PTT-set specifications which have had a comparable influence on prices).

b) A much faster rate of growth was experienced in those countries which adopted the competitive infrastructure provision model (USA) or the competitive sale of terminals (Scandinavia). It is interesting to note that the competitive provision of infrastructure itself (which is also associated in practice with competitive terminal provision), does not appear to add greatly to the rate of uptake. We would not be able to draw this conclusion with any confidence based on the very limited data set presented; however, this conclusion is supported by anecdotal evidence to be presented for the case of the UK.

c) The third case is that of the UK, which has shown market growth substantially faster than that which would have been expected bearing in mind the experience of other countries having similar or indeed higher standards of income and wealth. This, we will argue, is attributable to the extremely vigorous marketing activity which evolved under the competitive arrangements imposed in that country.

3. Further Details Regarding Competitive Structure in the UK

Inspection of the UK market for cellular telephone service reveals two features which distinguish it from other markets;

- unusually low prices for equipment
- an exceptionally high level of advertising and selling effort

Prices for a standard car cellular telephone, which costs the customer in excess of £2,000 ($3,500) in markets such as those of France and Germany, were as little as £1,000 ($1,750) from the early days of provision of cellular service in the UK. Intense competitive pressure in the industry has forced the price steadily lower ever since. By 1987 many car telephones of this kind were being sold for as little as £500 ($875). During that year and also 1988, prices continued to fall steadily, reaching £200 ($350) by the end of 1988. At the time of writing (March 1989) the price advertised by most low-price suppliers had dropped to £150 ($260). This price includes delivery of a working connected telephone to the customer within 24 hours of his telephone enquiry regarding the requirement for service.

The level of advertising and selling effort is more difficult to quantify than the price trends, but all evidence shows that it is exceptionally intense. National newspapers carry in each daily issue several advertisements for identical telephones from competing suppliers. Weekly magazines carry an even larger volume of advertising, often spreading to dozens of advertisements covering many pages of an individual issue. This advertising exposure is backed up by very vigorous selling by individual sales agents, selling on a door-to-door basis in various establishments such as car dealers (to encourage sales to new car purchasers) small and large business establishments (to encourage purchase among employees), and individual potential buyers such as estate agents, doctors and stockbrokers. The industry structure which produces this very competitive pricing and marketing behaviour is illustrated in Exhibit 4. The two competing network operators offer network time to service providers at a "wholesale" rate which allows the service providers a margin of 15%-20% when reselling the service at retail prices. These two network operators, therefore, have no direct dealings with the consumer and do not themselves engage in any significant advertising or competitive discounting. Consequently relatively little conventional evidence of competitive behaviour is perceived at this layer of the industry structure; prices have been remarkably stable, at £25 per month service rental charge and 25-33 pence per minute usage charge during the day throughout the period of development of this industry.

Instead, intense competition occurs at the next level, that of service provision. Service providers offer terminal distributors a cash incentive, typically in the range £300 - £500, for each customer signed up for service. This amounts to more than an entire first year of service rental charge. Despite these payments, the service provider industry is clearly thriving, with suppliers spending intensively (as we have noted) on advertising and other means of market development.

The cash payments offered to dealers have risen to the point where, in some cases, they exceed the cost of telephones to the distributor. It is therefore possible that car telephones will be distributed free to users, in return for a contract to take the service for at least one year. Indeed, examination of price trends in the past two years, showing falls from £1000-£150 for an item delivered from the factory for £450, shows that a forecast of a zero price within a year or two from now is not unreasonable.

4. Implications for Future Marketing of Telecommunications Services

The UK cellular telephone market experience is illuminating because it shows how much can be achieved, by way of stimulation of industry growth, by setting up arrangements which encourage vigorous sales promotion activity and deep discounting of the entry price faced by consumers. This example is particularly important because it has achieved such dramatic results in a product area which is so standardised or undifferentiated that it could easily be said that little could be gained by having many alternative distribution channels. The cellular telephone service quality and coverage offered by the two competing network providers is practically identical, so the competitive service providers which compete to sell these services are selling an item which comes very close to having perfect commodity characteristics. The case for having many competing selling channels would have been more obvious if the service being sold was, for example, a complex set of information sources available on a Videotex system.

The implication is, clearly, that reselling arrangements of this type could be very effective in other parts of the telecommunications service industry in which the service being sold is also of essentially a commodity nature. The most important instance would be that of the basic telephone service itself. It is fair to say that, in essentially all countries of the world, basic telephone service to the broad mass of residential subscribers has never been subject to marketing or selling effort of the kind considered normal in most consumer goods industries. At best, a modest level of national advertising is used to encourage, in a general sense, subscriptions to and use of the telephone.

Following from the cellular radio experience, let us consider what might happen if say, telephone companies or PTTs offered local selling and marketing agencies a commission of perhaps 10% of sales revenues in order to encourage use of the basic telephone service. Salesmen would no doubt be visiting households on a door-to-door basis, making every effort to encourage awareness of the benefits which telephone service can bring (in the case of existing non-subscribers), and encouraging the installation of extra extensions, push button telephones, answering machines and other usage-enhancing items (in the case of existing subscribers). As in the case of the UK cellular industry, terminal subsidies would no doubt become a standard feature of the industry.

In many European households, for example, the only telephone in the house is located in a position where members of the household are rarely present, often the entrance hallway of the house. In these circumstances, the placing of an extension in the living room, supplied free of charge, would almost certainly generate revenues justifying the subsidy of the terminal within a very small number of months. Provision of other, more advanced terminal devices, such as cordless telephones, which encourage telephone use by making it more convenient, would have a similar effect. These items are available to consumers who choose to order them from the PTTs, or in some countries, purchase them from a shop. But they are not marketed or promoted in the manner which they would be if private sector agencies could obtain some of the benefits of the additional telecommunications use which they encourage.

There is of course no reason, in theory, why a PTT or telephone company should not itself introduce the kinds of incentives and sales efforts that we have described in this paper. In practice this is generally not possible given the nature of large institutions. The two competing national telephone companies in the UK (British Telecom and Mercury), can and do employ their own sales forces, but they could never achieve the variety of approaches to different customer groups which is actually effected by the many competing cellular service providers. Differentially trained, managed and motivated sales forces are not sent out to tackle, locality by locality, the special needs of different kinds of local business people, different professional groups, and different residential sectors. Terminal prices could be discounted to a modest extent, but a PTT would face great political difficulties if it risked almost giving away items which have a cost (in the case of cellular telephones) of several hundred dollars each. Advertising can and is purchased by telephone companies in national media; but what advertising agency would recommend to such an organization that it takes out several pages of advertisements competing against one another, and competing under different brand names, for the sale of the same product or service. Yet it was precisely this kind of competitive, if slightly confusing, media exposure which has encouraged British consumers in the cellular telephone market.

It would not be realistic to expect PTTs to adopt such a policy (of outplacing marketing and customer account handling with separate agencies) in the case of their main infrastructure services. The loss of revenue on those customers for whom use of the services has (after many decades) reached a level which would not be further enhanced by marketing efforts, would be too high.

However a proposal along these lines may well be appropriate in the case of new infrastructure services to be offered by PTTs and telephone companies, for example the Integrated Services Digital Network (ISDN). While there is no doubt of the technical improvements which the introduction of ISDN facilities will bring, the telecommunications industry is frankly uncertain as to the extent to which the majority of potential users will find they can usefully exploit this extra capability. This is precisely the situation in which, instead of attempting to create service and marketing packages within the existing telecommunications organisations (in the hope of identifying one or more which may appeal to a broad mass of customers) the correct solution may be to encourage private third party participation in the creation and marketing of service. As was the case with the UK cellular telephone experience, a large number of competing "retailers", adopting a variety of approaches to attract various different customer segments in which they each specialize, may stimulate the market more than a large institution acting on its own.

Whether relinquishing these value added functions - marketing, sales, billing and account administration - results in a net loss or gain to the revenues and profitability of the main network operator depends on the extent to which demand is stimulated through the presence of such a competitive industry structure. There is little doubt that in the case of the UK cellular telephone industry the two network operators have achieved greater revenues and profitability than they would have done had they been granted monopolies of marketing and distribution of their respective services. Thus, ironically, the mandatory delegation of these functions to third party competitors, while initially regarded as disadvantageous, has worked very much to their benefit. Last year's revenues for each of the two network operators exceeded by a large margin any forecasts which these corporations (or the industry generally) was making of the sales volume which they would achieve in the 4th year of operation. Indeed, the actual result has exceeded most forecasts of the entire industry's revenue in the 4th year, showing that by having only one half of the network revenues and only some 80% of the value chain, the British Telecom - led consortium, Cellnet, is doing better than it would if it had a complete monopoly of both network operation and of all functions in the business value chain. PTTs, in their role as future providers of ISDN services, could find that the relinquishing of certain functions in that business chain yields a net gain in their overall returns for the same reasons.

The idea that revenues and profits are stimulated by active marketing of a service, as opposed to passively allowing a customer to subscribe or purchase, is so familiar to most industries that it seems unnecessary to state. Yet it is a relatively new concept in the telecommunications industry. Clearly, considerable strides have been made in the past decade or so, in the direction of marketing of telephony and other services, notably through the use of advertising campaigns and the setting up of retail outlets. However the industry should recognise that it has an enormously long way to go before it attaches as much importance as it could to the elements of the business value chain downstream of infrastructure provision, and that creative solutions to the provision of such functions could yield large benefits in the long run.

COMMENTS ON
NEW DIMENSIONS OF TELECOMMUNICATIONS COMPETITION

Laurent Virol
Ministry of Posts and Telecommunications, Paris

This text that describes the regulatory situation for the telecommunications in France, was intended to be delivered at the March meeting in Berlin, during the session dedicated to regulatory matters. In fact, the paper presented by Charles Jonscher to open the session and to be discussed focused on the analysis of the competitive situation in the cellular phone market in the UK and tended to show that free entry into service provision as well as terminal markets helped to sustain dramatic growth through subsidization of the terminals from the traffic revenues.

In addition, the time schedule of the session did not allowed a full presentation of the text. The result has been a short synthesis of the french situation and a comment of the Jonscher's paper: quite enligthening about the possibility to achieve a quick and effective take-off in communications services through competitive means, but rather limited about non purely economic motivations (sovereignty, universal access, ...) of regulatory activities in the telecommunications sector.

Whatever the similarities of situations and trends that may be noticed in different countries, these are often embedded in specific national and economic contexts and appear to be confusing and unclear from an external point of view.

My name is Laurent Virol, I am Deputy Head at the "Mission à la réglementation", in the french Ministry of Posts, Telecommunications and Space. The creation of the Mission, two years ago, witnessed the recognition that the telecommunications environment was changing and that essential questions pertaining to it were to be adressed in a new way.

This creation was also a significant step to have the regulatory and the operational activities progressively separated:
- the "Mission à la réglementation" on the regulatory hand,
- the public telecommunications operator - France Télécom -, its subsidiaries, as well as other operators and services providers, on the other hand.

One may notice that this move anticipated, several months in advance, the corresponding proposition of the European Commission's "Green paper" that invites the European Community's Member States to separate their telecommunications regulatory activities from the operational ones.

At the same time, an independant administrative body has been created --under the CNCL acronym -- essentially dedicated to broadcasting and media regulation, and the advice of which was also required by the government where new operators should be authorized.

So far, regarding the "Birth of a Mission" ... how may I now describe the french regulatory situation that we have found at that time ?

The pivotal point is to recognize that telecommunications in France have never been covered by a legal monopoly but come under an authorization scheme which goes way back in our history. The relevant authorizing powers have been placed into the hands of the Minister who is in charge of telecommunications, about one and a half century ago.

The resulting situation, two years ago, showed specific characteristics, depending on which aspect of telecommunications you were talking about:
- you had a "de facto" monopoly for the public network infrastructure and for the provision of the essential switched services: this was not surprising and quite similar to what you could find almost everywhere;
- second aspect: you had not this vertical organic integration between equipment manufacturing and network operations activities that may exist elsewhere, particularly in North America.
- third aspect, quite specific to France at that time: the terminals market had already been liberalized for several decades. That means that all kinds of terminals, including telephone sets, modems, PABXs, and other CPE equipment, could be directly bought by the end user and be installed and maintained by private installers - for there is no privilege for the Administration in the field. One or two figures: we have four hundred private telephone installers and eight hundred radio installers in a country the demographic and economic size of which is about one fifth of the US size.

- the fourth and last aspect that we found two years ago, is linked to what you call "value added network services" (VANS), that we have christened "réseaux et services télématiques". We had here a double sided situation:
  o on one side, a quite exciting dynamism in the private provision of a multitude of such services, boosted by an open network philosophy put into practice by the public operator, as far as the switched network could allow it. This situation, that includes the videotex-Minitel phenomenom but goes far beyond, derives from a partnership where the public operator and the telematic services providers tacitly restrain themselves to impinge on the activities of the other party. This dynamism is partly supported thanks to a large packet-switched data network (Transpac), the existence of which diminishes the need to rely on leased lines that prevails in some other countries.
  o on the other side, an interrogation and a potential confrontation: how to tackle the question of the leased lines usage in order to provide telematic services similar to those already offered through the switched network ? Such an evolution was considered to be necessary but fears were expressed, relative to the potential financial unbalance that could affect the public operator, due to its public service duties, to the cross-subsidization practices that resulted from them, and to the correlative risks if leased lines were to be used for a pure resale of traffic, without value added to it ...

To sum it up: (1) a classical situation for the infrastructure and for "basic" services; (2) one of the most liberalized situation for the CPE and terminals market; (3) a burgeoning world of telematic services; (4) but a question mark about the usage of the leased lines.

Along these two years, the activities of this new entity, "la Mission", have been three-fold:

- "la Mission" has undertaken several studies, met with a large spectrum of persons and organizations, in France and abroad, and set up a communication programme in order to have interested people aware of to-day's and to-morrow's issues.
- second activity: "la Mission" has been given the responsability to manage the radio frequencies necessary for the telecommunications networks that provide services to third parties and it advised the Minister in his decision to allow new competitors to the public operator, for paging and for mobile telephony. The new mobile telephony company "Société Française de Radio-téléphone" (SFR) will be operating in the first

quarter of eighty-nine. For paging as well as for mobile telephony, foreign companies such as Bell South participate in the new authorized consortia.
- the third activity that I shall describe in a little more detailed fashion, adresses the new opportunities for the telematic services providers to use leased lines for their purposes.

Where do we come from?

Two years ago, a company could rent leased lines uniquely for its own needs; special agreements were required for this company to connect one line to another in its own premises, or to the public network; connection to third parties were generally not allowed.

After a phase of concertation where France Telecom was involved as well as the telecommunications and computer industry, the services providers, and the users... the Minister signed a decree:

1. That allows a far more flexible use of all kinds of leased lines: provided that they do not convey traffic between third parties, they may be connected in the premises of the company in order to constitute a network, and be connected to the public network; in addition, a leased line may interconnect two different companies.

2. The restriction against the interconnection of third parties does not hold for telematic services, provided that these services incorporate a sufficient share of added value. The authorization scheme placed in the hands of the Minister is then replaced by a simple notification form that is sent to the "Mission". Once this form has been completed and signed, the telematic services provider may begin to operate its business and sell the services to its customers under its own responsability. The authorization scheme becomes valid again if the size of the network is too important: the present level has presently been fixed to be equivalent to about two thousands simultaneous two-point-four kilobits per second user access ports to the network. There is only one service-provider to have reached this threshold for the moment.

3. Thus, a user may now build a telematic network, not only for its own usage as before, but also to be shared with its suppliers, dealers or traditional customers. He may

also become a telematic services provider to third parties on a commercial basis thanks to its own computers and devices, and to leased lines connected or not connected to the public network.

4. This regulatory device is a quite pragmatic one: parameters have been devised to adapt the situation to an evolutionary context: if necessary, the Minister may set the threshold (under which a simple notification procedure is sufficient) to an higher level; he also may decrease the required percentage of added value to be incorporated in the telematic services. Thus, larger opportunities may be progressively available to the potential services providers.

5. A Consultative Commision composed primarily of telecommunications and computer industry representatives and users - only five of its seventeen members come from the Ministry - has been created to appreciate the conditions and impact of the decree; it reports directly to the Minister. This Commission is assisted by a Group of twenty-five technical advisors that includes representatives from all economic players, that oversees and propose to the Minister those of the international standards to be prescribed for the network accesses. This prescription is intended to promote more open telematic networks and services and may be proposed to the customers concurrently with proprietary procedures. This on-going contact between the regulatory authorities and the business and professional communities provides an official vehicle for expression of both users concerns and technical considerations.

6. This regulation has been elaborated on a quite non-discriminatory basis: it is evenly applied to french and to foreign competitors and does not contain any restriction related to this criterion. One may also notice that large world-wide computers manufacturers - IBM, Digital Equipment, and Unisys - are represented in the group of technical advisors.

To sum up, la "Mission" newly created as an office of regulation has recognized that the public network infrastructure should be preserved, that France enjoyed a relatively liberalized situation for the terminals market, and that something had to be pragmatically done to transfer towards telematic networks supported by leased lines, the dynamism of the telematic services market based on the public switched network. Thus, the main efforts have been oriented in that direction.

At the same time the separation of the regulatory and operational activities comes within the context of the European policy on telecommunications as expressed in the Green Paper, that forms a basis for reflexion and a reference point whereby the changes that have taken place in each country may be assessed:

- maintaining an infrastructure of homogeneous public network throughout Europe;
- preserving the public service and a small number of "basic" services;
- ensure the free provision of the other services in compliance with european-wide rules to open the infrastructure network to these services;
- liberalizing the terminals market;
- promoting standards in order to create a better inter-connectivity.

Along these lines that have been approved, in June 1989, by the Ministers in charge of telecommunications in their respective countries, our Minister has decided that the "Mission" would be upgraded to a full Directorate. This development will further the evolution of separate regulatory and operational telecommunications activities in France.

According to the EEC's Green Paper, the regulatory activities to be separated from the operational ones cover, in particular:

- the licensing of the operators,
- the control of the interfaces specification procedures,
- the control of the corresponding approval procedures,
- the allocation of the spectrum frequencies,
- the overall supervision of the network usage conditions.

The Minister has announced that the Directorate (the enlarged regulatory entity) should be set up soon - that means in the first semester of eighty-nine.

Well - I wanted to bring to your knowledge some essential facts and milestones about the telecommunications regulatory policy in my country:

- for more than one century, the pivotal practice has been the authorization scheme that I have already described;
- the results of which have been:
    o a quite modern and digitized network,
    o a terminal market considered for years to be amongst the most liberalized,

- o a remarkable dynamism in the market of private information and value-added services using the public switched network;
- we are quite conscious however:
  - o that we are in a world of changes, technically, economically, internationally,
  - o that new needs arise,
  - o that new issues must be adressed;
- we also know that some of these issues are not always easy to tackle: the process and the debate that has been experienced for years, in the US for instance, could support that affirmation;
- since its creation, la "Mission" participated to a similar and fruitful debate and process by:
  - o helping to increase the awareness of interested parties on these issues;
  - o experiencing new competitive situations through the authorization of other networks operators;
  - o developing the opportunities for a more diverse and dynamic market of telematic services;
- other steps will follow, where the propositions of the Green Paper, supported by all the EEC Ministers in charge of telecommunications, is playing a sizeable catalytic effect. The next step is the creation of the Directorate that has recently been announced by the Minister, and that will further the separation of separate regulatory and operational activities.

PRODUCTION ORIENTED INFORMATION TECHNOLOGY POLICY IN JAPAN AND EUROPE[1]

Graham Vickery
Principal Administrator, OECD, Paris

1. Introduction

A key feature of international economic and industrial development over the last ten to fifteen years has been the rapid rise of Japan, some European countries, and a few rapidly industrializing developing countries such as Korea, Singapore and Taiwan, to be highly competitive in a widening range of products. This has been particularly marked in a number of high-technology and consumer goods industries where high quality, new and innovative products have captured an increasing share of world markets. These products have been based on rapid industrial innovation and introduction of new goods which consumers will buy, and on efficient, high quality manufacturing techniques.

Following these successes many governments have become increasingly interested in promoting the use of advanced manufacturing technologies which can produce a range of high quality products under different conditions and respond rapidly to changing markets. At the same time countries which have taken the lead - Japan, the rapidly industrializing countries and European countries such as Sweden and Germany which maintain a strong tradition in producing industrial products - and good firms in all countries have redoubled their efforts to introduce new products and to use the most efficient manufacturing techniques to respond to rapidly changing markets and to develop new markets.

In this paper we discuss the recent evolution of government policy in Europe and Japan aimed at improving the competitiveness of industrial firms by enhancing their ability to use advanced manufacturing technology intelligently and efficiently.

---

[1] This paper was written by Graham Vickery, Principal Administrator, Industry Division, Directorate for Science, Technology and Industry, OECD, Paris. It was delivered at the Conference by Hans-Peter Gassmann, Head, Information, Computer and Communications Policy Division, Directorate for Science, Technology and Industry, OECD, Paris.

Definitions

Advanced manufacturing technology (AMT) includes computer controlled or micro-electronically controlled equipment, such as computer numerical control (CNC) machine tools, robots, flexible manufacturing systems (FMS) and computer aided design (CAD) and resource planning, and just in time manufacturing, and the use of associated management methods and organizational techniques. Advanced equipment can be used as individual stand-alone pieces or it can be linked into increasingly complex computer-integrated manufacturing systems. The efficient introduction and use of such equipment and systems is a key determinant of firms' competitiveness and its importance is increasingly recognized by governments.

2. The Patterns of Use of Advanced Manufacturing Technology

Complex equipment and highly-integrated equipment is still not widely used. It is concentrated in a few firms, in a few industries and in a few countries. For example, computer aided design or robots have only recently begun to be used extensively and there are wide differences between countries in the use of these technologies. The leading countries use approximately five times as much advanced technology per 10,000 workers in the using industries as other major industrial countries (see Table 1). The same pattern of wide differences between leading and lagging countries is shown for integrated flexible manufacturing systems, where different kinds of equipment are linked together into complex networks capable of rapidly switching between a range of different products and functions. But a well-established technology such as numerical control machine tools is widely diffused through manufacturing industry. There is relatively little difference between countries such as Japan and Sweden with the highest levels of use of established technology, and those with lower levels of use.

Table 1

The Density of Flexible Automation in Selected Countries: 1984

Units per 10,000 employees in metals and machinery industries, ISIC 38

	NCMTs	Robots	CAD	FMS
Germany	135	19	32	0.07
Japan	245	95	15	0.21
Sweden	162	47	51	0.41
United Kingdom	149	12	41	0.05
United States	128	16	74	0.07

Source: Adapted from Edquist, C. and Jacobsson, S., Flexible Automation, Basil Blackwell, Oxford, 1988, Table 7.2. Employment from OECD/ISIS

Some of the differences between countries in their use of AMT reflect their industrial structures. A few industries have taken the lead in the use of advanced manufacturing technologies. And countries which have a strong presence in these industries are leading in AMT applications. For example, the highest use of robots is to be found in the automobile and mechanical engineering industries, the electronic and electrical engineering industries, and for very specialized activities such as injection moulding in plastics. In other industries the use of robots is much lower (see Table 2). There are some variations in these patterns however. Local area networks which tie together pieces of monitoring and controlling equipment tend to be concentrated in process industries, such as pulp and paper making, printing and publishing, metal refining and in chemicals. But by and large, advanced manufacturing technology is concentrated in the metals and machinery industries, even though some equipment may be widely used in other industries.

There is, however, scope for much wider use of information technology-based equipment in almost all industries for tasks such as stock management and monitoring of inventory, storage and handling, testing and quality control. Most industries have not yet realized anything like their full potential use of advanced, computer-controlled equipment.

Table 2

Type of Manufacturing Equipment used: UK Process Users by Industry: 1987
Percentages of sample establishments

	CAD work stations	Machine tools	Programmable logic controllers	Pick and place machines	Robots
Food/drink	17	2	68	10	6
Chems. metals	31	15	72	9	4
Mech. eng.	41	63	24	9	16
Elec. eng.	52	41	41	23	9
Vehicles	58	62	41	23	28
Metal goods	17	38	49	21	7
Textiles	22	3	41	3	2
Clothing	20	11	32	1	1
Paper/print	19	5	46	4	2
Other	19	20	43	13	4
Total 1987	31	28	46	12	8
Expected 1989	46	32	50	21	15

Source: Northcott, J. and Walling, A., The Impact of Microelectronics: Diffusion, Benefits and Problems in British Industry, Policy Studies Institute, London, 1988.

Large establishments and firms also have far higher levels of adoption of AMT than small ones. This pattern of use is determined by the greater technological, management and financial resources available to larger establishments and firms compared with those available to smaller ones. To take one example, almost all large firms in Germany in the mechanical engineering and electrical and electronic engineering industries use computer aided design (CAD) systems, to help design and specify new products and improve existing ones (see Table 3). Yet in these same industries the level of use in smaller firms is very low. The same high levels of use in large plants in Germany is seen for computerized production planning and control systems, where 70 per cent of firms with more than 1,000 employees in the capital goods industries were using these systems in 1986/87 whereas less than 10 per cent of firms with 50 to 99 employees, and only a very small share of firms with less than 20 employees did so.

As equipment and systems become more complex, small firms are even less likely to use them. There is great potential however for expanded use of AMT by small firms and for reaping flexibility, quality and productivity gains from efficient applications in the small firm sector.

Table 3

Distribution of CAD Systems by Firm Size in Germany: 1986
Percentage of all firms

	Turnover in DM million			
	< 50	50-100	100-250	> 250
Mechanical engineering	5	70	85	95
Electrical/electronic	4	73	80	95
Construction	0	12		37
Chemicals/pharmaceuticals	0	12	15	45
Other	0	1	7	26

Source: Diebold quoted in Bessant, J., "Computer-aided design in the Federal Republic of Germany", Brighton Polytechnic, August 1987.

Benefits

Firms investing in advanced manufacturing technology usually seek to:

- Improve quality and flexibility of production;
- Improve productivity and the use of labour, machinery and equipment;
- Reduce overheads and stocks.

Many of these improvements are difficult to attain and they may also be difficult to measure. Nevertheless, analysis carried out at the OECD shows that growth in labour productivity and total factor productivity across industries is positively associated with the use of advanced manufacturing technology as measured by the level of robot investment in Japan. And in Japan labour productivity growth over time is positively associated with the growth of robot investment in total investment - particularly in the electrical machinery and automobile industries. The level of capital productivity is also positively associated with the level of investment in robots.

Labour productivity in the metals and machinery industry group across all OECD countries is also positively associated with the use of robots. And there is a strong positive correlation across OECD countries between the use of advanced manufacturing technology and good trade performance. There are larger export surpluses and strong comparative advantages for the metals and machinery industries in countries where there are more robots per 10,000 employees.

Improvements in trade and output are important reasons why industrialists and governments try to spread the use of computer controlled and micro-electronically controlled technology more widely. Because of the concentrated patterns of use of AMT, governments have focussed their attention on attempting to help lagging sectors and small firms, particularly in those countries which are also lagging. Before examining government industrial technology policies, however, it is useful to discuss some of the constraints on wider applications of AMT.

Constraints on Wider Use

Despite the potential improvements in competitiveness, flexibility and productivity which flow from the wider use of advanced manufacturing technology, there are a number of constraints on its use. These constraints are seen in all countries although they are even more acute in countries which do not have a well-developed technological infra-structure, where there are no strong national firms in advanced sectors of engineering and electronics, and where most firms are small.

Surveys in many European countries and in Japan have shown that there is a continuing set of impediments hindering applications of new technologies. In order of importance these are:

- Lack of people with the necessary expertize with advanced manufacturing technology.
- Problems with software, and in some cases, general problems linking systems together and making them operate.
- A set of inter-related economic difficulties such as high costs of development of new systems, lack of finance for new applications, and uneven demand and a macro-economic outlook which has not been consistently good in some countries.

Since the start of the 1980s these problems have been persistently cited as the major ones limiting applications in countries as diverse as Austria, Denmark, Finland, France, Germany, Italy, Sweden, and the United Kingdom and in Japan. The problem always listed as the most important is the lack of people with the necessary expertise to introduce the new systems and to make them work properly. If anything, mismatches and shortages of skills and problems with software and organizational problems have become more acute recently (see Figure 1).

Figure 1

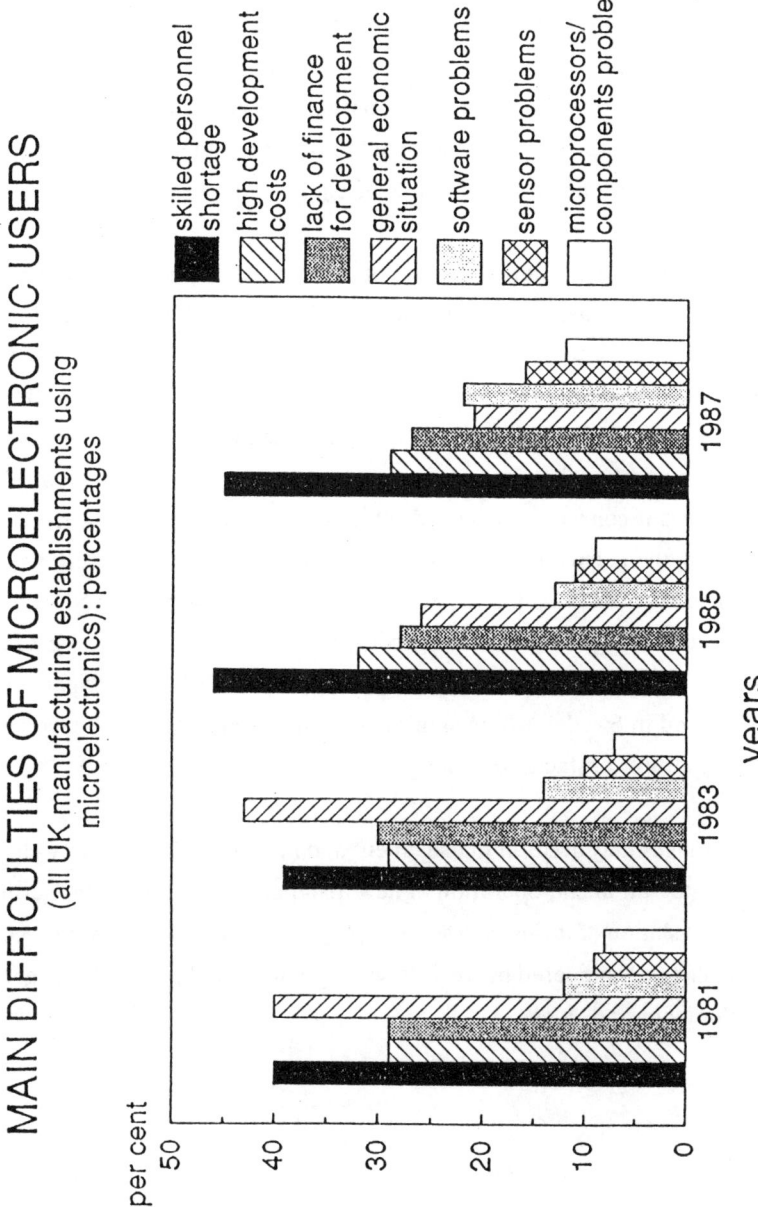

Changing Skill Requirements and Skill Shortages

Surveys show that the principal barriers to the introduction of new technologies into the workplace are changing skill requirements and skill shortages. The major obstacles are, in some cases, shortages of technological skills such as design capabilities and skilled machine operators, in other cases they are problems with skills related to production organization and software. These problems are most serious in industries using advanced equipment, but they are acute for all kinds of equipment.

Even in Japan and Sweden where there has been a long-standing accent on training and skill development, there are continuing shortages of skills and a widespread awareness of the necessity to redouble training efforts. In Japan in the early 1980s when the first round of AMT investment was being implemented, a survey reported that almost two-thirds of Japanese industrial workers affected by the introduction of new automation technologies saw vocational training and improved training and acquisition of skills as their most important concerns. Two-thirds of managers with problems introducing new technologies saw the acquisition of new technical skills as their most serious one, and shortages of necessary skills as the most serious impediment to the introduction of new manufacturing technology in the future. Projected shortfalls in technical areas related to software and engineering are seen as a continuing constraint in Japan. A similar picture is observed in Sweden where shortages of competent personnel have been seen as the most important obstacle to wider use of AMT.

These skill shortages may occur in management and market exploration as well as in the development, integration and operation of new manufacturing systems. In Germany, for example, the translation of technically successful new products into market successes has often been significantly hindered by weaknesses in planning and production organization, market development and sales.

Organizational Constraints

Organizational problems are among the most important impediments to widespread applications within firms. Successful introduction of new processes and products usually requires reorganization of work practices, redeployment of new and different skills, physical reorganization of production and in many cases a complete revamping of the enterprise structure and operations.

The importance of reorganizing work and organizational structures to take better advantage of the potential of advanced manufacturing technology is increasingly being recognized. The introduction of AMT applications involves effective integration into an existing enterprise of long term planning on a continuous basis, increasing attention to inventory and suppliers and increased attention to deliveries and sales. The aim of reorganization in most cases is to improve the flow of information within the enterprise and between the enterprise and its suppliers and customers so that the operations of the enterprise become a smooth flow system.

Reorganization of the relationship between the central firm and its suppliers and sub-contractors is also receiving greater attention. In many cases smaller supply firms are taking much more responsibility for design and development of sub-components and parts. They are adopting or being responsible for higher levels of quality control and for ensuring that deliveries meet the broader schedules of the central coordinating enterprise.

Firm Strategies For the Use of AMT

There are considerable differences between firms from different countries in their strategic use of new technologies. Japanese firms have long focussed on quality and the control of stocks. This has enabled them to reach high quality standards and ensure that they do not have unused material and components waiting to be processed and undelivered completed products. Japanese firms are now focussing even more on day-to-day efficiency and flexibility to underpin their commitment to new technologies and new markets. They have realized that to compete on a global scale it is important to be highly efficient and flexible and to continually search for new product and process technologies so that they can develop new markets.

In Europe and in the United States firms have generally been slower to realize how important the effective use of new technologies is in their day-to-day operations. For example, because US firms have much greater pressure to produce short-term profits, they tend to see technology as a way of meeting those short-term profit deadlines. They are using their manufacturing technology to improve stock control and to improve quality, but tend to concentrate on established markets and established products, and are less interested in more risky commitments to develop new markets and new technologies.

In Europe the focus has been on cost cutting and rationalisation when investing in AMT because of the rapid changes taking place in national markets and the potential for expansion within a broadened European market. This has been spurred by the recent wave of pan-European acquisitions and mergers and alliances between firms, many of which are aimed at reaping the benefits from the enlarged single European market.

3. The Role and Function of Policies to Improve Industrial Performance

The kinds of policies and programmes introduced to improve the functioning and efficiency of industry are often determined by the relative competitive performance of industry. But even more important are the institutional structures and political traditions which shape the kinds of government actions which are called for, and which governments can successfully implement. Japan, for example, has had a long tradition of helping small and medium enterprises to improve their management and technological skills. This has largely been carried out through the comprehensive prefecturally-based guidance system. On the other hand, many policies introduced to assist small and medium firms in other OECD countries have concentrated on financial assistance: for example, in France, through government regulation of the banking system, or more directly in Germany through the activities of the banks themselves. This is in contrast with the situation in the United Kingdom where a different pattern of government involvement has often focussed in the past on regional industrial restructuring.

The common aim of these policies has been to create an appropriate climate in which firms can grow and flourish. But to be successful all government policies and programmes must be based on a consensus on goals and methods between those designing policies, those implementing them, and those that policies are aimed at reaching.

The establishment of consensus is the basis of successful policy delivery. The consensus between government and industry in Japan has ensured that government policy is perceived as being highly successful over the long term. This consensus also explains the continuity and incremental nature of Japanese industrial policy. New initiatives build on previous or continuing ones, and programmes are changed and re-oriented to adapt to changing circumstances. There is an incremental learning, exploring and improving character to government policy.

In Europe policy often has had much more of a stop-go nature, often reflecting changes in the political viewpoint of policy makers with changes in government. There may also be a less stable consensus between industry policy makers and their labour and management partners. But the building of this consensus and clear exploration of what governments are called upon to do and of what they can do will determine the success or failure of government programmes - particularly in such complex areas as increasing the use of information technology to improve competitiveness and flexibility in manufacturing industry.

Government production-oriented technology policy has generally aimed to improve the environment for more efficient applications, to raise the level of awareness of the scope for applications and, in some cases, to increase the level and structure of investment in AMT.

4. Recent Government Initiatives

Japan

Japanese policy has followed two main directions:
1) A series of large scale, co-operative projects involving large firms in applied research. AMT projects include advanced robotics, opto-electronics, automated garment sewing systems and laser based production in engineering.

2) A range of measures to help up-grade small and medium-sized firms and provide support with research and development, the application of new technologies, awareness and information, and advice on management and training, often through the established prefectural "guidance" system.

Both strands of Japanese industrial policy follow a long series of similar measures.

Large Scale Projects

The first Large Scale Projects (co-operative research and development programmes generally involving a group of large firms) were introduced in 1966. Since then there has been a series of co-operative research ventures covering a wide range of carefully defined development areas. Projects were initially in applied technologies, but since 1980 they have been increasingly aimed at basic research. By 1988, sixteen large scale projects have been completed and eight projects are ongoing. All of these projects are government initiatives in the private sector, financed on a 100% contract basis by the central government. The results of the projects are generally owned by the Agency of Industrial Science and Technology (AIST). The results are diffused through the Japan Industrial Technology Association which has exclusive rights to license all industrial property and know-how.

There are also a series of other projects on new energy sources begun in 1974 known as the Sunshine Project, a series of energy conservation projects begun in 1978 known as the Moonlight Project, and other special programmes on basic technologies for future industries. Incentives for applied research in the private sector also operate through the tax system.

The best way of illustrating how the large-scale projects work is to describe one of them - the Optical Measurement and Control Large-Scale Project. This was initiated in 1979 and ran until 1985. The development of the project followed a pattern common to most of them.
First, an under-developed area with high commercial potential was delineated by MITI following extensive formal and informal discussions with interested private companies. Then appropriate research projects, a timeframe and an approximate R&D budget were worked out. Once the budget was approved a formal Research Association was set up

to begin R&D under contract with the Agency of Industrial Science and Technology. The Research Association consisted of fourteen large companies mainly in electronics, and included a group of firms combined into an industry association. A joint research laboratory, the Opto-electronics Joint Research Laboratory, with close government/private industry co-operation was established to develop basic technology in collaboration with individual firms responsible for specific areas of the project. The Agency of Industrial Science and Technology's Electro-technical Laboratory carried out some of the basic high risk research for the project.

The research project had clearly defined aims and a final demonstration project to test the technology developed. The aims were to monitor and control large amounts of information under adverse conditions. The final demonstration project lasted two years, and consisted of putting all of the accumulated development and research into a working system: an opto-electronic process control system in a functioning oil refinery. Research covered: a total system; sub-systems which can handle high-speed and high-quality image, process and control information; and optical element technologies such as laser diodes, optical fibres, opto-electronic integrated circuits and gallium arsenide technology.

This particular project was a considerable success in increasing the rate of diffusion of opto-electronic technologies for communications and control. The project focussed attention on a particular area where there was great commercial potential but where there was little co-ordinated work being carried out, and by grouping and combining research efforts of a large number of firms in generic research it enabled considerable advances to take place. However, total expenditures on the project of US$ 65 million were low compared with private sector expenditures on electronic research. Annual expenditures were less than 0.5% of annual R&D expenditures by electronic companies.

A similar large scale project has developed flexible manufacturing systems equipped with laser technology. This particular project ran through to 1984 and was aimed at developing new automatic integrated production systems that are flexible and provide quick through put in the manufacture of small batches of machine components. A number of new machining cells and systems were installed and used as demonstration systems in a pilot plant. The major result of this work has been the development of welding, cutting and surface processing technology and there have subsequently been rapid increases of applications of laser technology in these areas. The success of this project relied on focussing the attention of a considerable number of firms simultaneously on one particular area which would subsequently have considerable potential for widespread applications. Total expenditure was again rather low, around US$ 56 million, equivalent to approximately 0.2% of business R&D expenditures in mechanical engineering per year.

Other projects are currently developing automated sewing systems and advanced robot technology. In the case of automated sewing systems the companies involved are medium size machinery and textile firms rather than the large ones which are usual for large-scale projects. Because the textile industry spends rather little of its turnover on R&D the amount of government expenditure involved (total US$ 67 million) is relatively larger than for other projects, but it is still only approximately 1-1.5% of business R&D expenditures in the textile industry. Again the volume of funds is not as important as the aim of developing very precisely targeted technologies and ensuring that results are diffused rapidly into participating firms and throughout Japanese industry.

The project on advanced robot technology is following the usual pattern. A joint research association involving a large number of companies and organizations has been set up with participation by all leading robot and electronics companies. Research is carried out in member companies but with basic research in national research laboratories. There are very precisely defined prototype production and demonstration projects. The aim is to develop robots to work in extreme or hazardous conditions such as in nuclear power plants, ocean oil exploration, fire fighting and other disaster prevention areas. Funds involved are equivalent to approximately 0.2% of business R&D in mechanical engineering or electrical machinery.

Programmes for Small and Medium Sized Firms

Government policies for small and medium-sized firms (SMEs) are part of a long term effort to improve performance through guidance and advisory services, training, and a series of investment and R&D-related incentives. Here again total central government funding is rather low compared with firms' own expenditures. Tax expenditures (government revenue forgone due to special tax concessions) are now the most significant form of assistance to SMEs, but in fiscal year 1986 special research and development tax credits for SMEs were equivalent to only about 7% of their own R&D expenditures. The investment tax incentive for advanced manufacturing technology was equivalent to less than 3% of SMEs' own investments in machinery and equipment. And government tax expenditures for SMEs have been worth more over the last few years than loan subsidies and credit insurance which were the previous major instruments of central government financial support for SMEs. This focus on tax incentives rather than credit rationing and allocation shows an important shift in Japan's central government support mechanisms.

Direct support mechanisms are still used however, and if they are structured to include technical and management assistance they have positive effects on industrial investment and development. For example, the Japan Robot Leasing Company (JAROL) was set up in 1980 by a group of robot manufacturers and private sector insurers with funds borrowed from the government-backed Development Bank of Japan to buy robots and flexible manufacturing systems from member manufacturers and to lease them to SMEs. The advantage to SMEs in this scheme comes not so much from the subsidy element involved in government-backed loans, but rather from the quality of technical advice and services available from this group of manufacturers and insurers. It is estimated that some 10% of robots in SMEs have been leased through JAROL thereby increasing their diffusion.

The established infra-structure to assist small firms is highly developed in Japan. There is a comprehensive system of central government and prefectural up-grading assistance and "on-the-spot guidance". These are integral parts of the rationalisation and management measures contained in the Small and Medium Enterprise Basic Law enacted in 1963. This law stipulates that the government must take measures to modernise and upgrade small firms, overcome disadvantages in business activities and take whatever finance, investment, tax and small business measures that are appropriate to achieve modernisation and upgrading. These measures are designed to help small firms raise their technological level, improve product quality and production methods and raise overall performance through extensive investment in firm-based training, improved management practices and organization adaptation.

But in many areas, including those which have always received highest priority in Japan such as firm-based training and skill formation, there is relatively little direct central government intervention despite the comprehensive approach outlined in the Basic Law. Firm-based and short-term industrial training activities supported by the central government are limited and selective. Training courses generally concentrate on improving the level of technological skills of local guidance and extension officers.

The Institute of the Japan Small Business Corporation plays the most important role in training prefectural guidance officers and technicians and managers from smaller firms. It gives training in factory automation, industrial design, mechatronics, telecommunications and management. Courses last from a few days to one year and there are about 6,000 trainees per year.

The Institute provides an initiating role rather than attempting to directly cover the approximately 425,000 small manufacturing enterprises, or the close to 2 million technically skilled production workers. It spends less than 0.05% of the training expenditure of Japanese small firms. But by concentrating on improving overall quality of training, coupled with increasing the level of training in small enterprises and operating through the established guidance system, its impact is probably greater than the amount of money involved. Guidance personnel from the prefectures and small enterprise business organizations spread the results of new, best-practice techniques to where most training takes place - within Japanese firms.

Overall, the Japanese approach to production oriented information technology policy does not involve comprehensive schemes spending large amounts of money compared with firms' own efforts. The focus has been on precisely targeted areas of applied research and development, mainly involving collaboration between large firms, government laboratories and cooperative groups, combined with efficient mechanisms of demonstrating project results and diffusing these results widely through Japanese manufacturing industry. The support given to small and medium enterprises is incremental and continuing in its approach; on-going policies are reoriented to take into account the needs of Japanese small and medium sized businesses, to improve their technological level and increase their use of advanced manufacturing technologies.

Selected European Policies

Rather than listing all of the approaches which have been tried in Europe, only a few are outlined to illustrate government efforts to improve the technological and competitive performance of manufacturing industry. Programmes covering Denmark,

France, Germany, Sweden and the United Kingdom, and some European Community programmes are briefly described.

Denmark: The Technological Development Programme

The Danish Technological Development Programme was introduced in the Summer of 1984 with a total budget of DKr 1.5 billion (approximately US$ 150 million) to run over five years. The programme was aimed at overcoming the problems posed by the small scale of Danish industry by diffusing microelectronics and information technology throughout the small firm sector. There are relatively few large firms in Denmark operating in high technology sectors such as aerospace and advanced electronics, and in 1984 there were only a total of 88 industrial firms in Denmark with more than 500 employees. Denmark has had both a deteriorating trade performance in traditional exports and a weak performance in advanced products. The programme focusses approximately 35% of total industrial support on a broad approach to apply advanced manufacturing technology and increase applications of micro-electronics in products. The programme has largely operated through reorienting and extending existing programmes and reorganizing the inputs of existing institutions into manufacturing industry.

Over 50% of total funds go to joint and co-operative activities and projects involving groups of companies, industry associations and the network of technological service institutes. These group projects cover such diverse areas as the development of robots for meat cutting and for the food processing industry, computer aided design and manufacture in textiles, and computerized manufacturing in the metal fabricating industry. Another one-third of programme funds has gone to individual companies in the form of development grants, loans and contracts to support development of new applications in production processes, products and improved software.

A considerable effort is going into education, particularly in-service, in-firm and part-time training courses, into awareness campaigns, into the acquisition of know-how, for example foreign studies and visits by foreign consultants, and into demonstration projects from joint development programmes.

The Network of Technological Institutes

Denmark has a well developed network of private, self-owned, non-profit, technological service institutes, which play an important role in promoting applications of new technologies. There are two major technological institutes covering a wide range of technological areas, a group of specialized technical institutes concentrating on particular subject areas and technologies, and a decentralized network of information centres.

The Institutes obtain roughly 70% of their total revenue from industrial clients by providing consulting services, training, technology development, quality and standard setting and similar services. The other 30% of funds comes from the government Technology Council to support independent research and upgrade the Institutes' technological facilities and capabilities. As an example of the services provided, the Copenhagen Institute provides short training from a few days to a few weeks or a month or so, to over 15,000 engineers, technicians and skilled workers every year. It also carries out several hundred co-operative and individual research projects and provides about 10,000 consultations and testing services every year as well as conducting extensive awareness activities.

Results of the Programme

The number of small firms reached by this programme has been very impressive. Around one-sixth of all industrial firms with more than ten employees were involved in demonstration, development and joint projects. Total programme expenditures are equal to about 3% of total industrial investment on fixed assets and they have largely gone to intangible forms of investment in research, training and software, information and know-how. Government expenditures have helped to reinforce the re-orientation of firms' investment activities towards higher levels of intangible investment in the development of new processes, new products and new markets and ways of servicing new markets.

France

France has introduced a wide range of programmes designed to increase the use of micro-electronics in industry, to improve the performance of the electronics industry and to improve the functioning of manufacturing industry in general. Because of the wide range of these programmes and the many changes which they have undergone, only the activities of one long-standing agency are described here. This is L'Agence Nationale pour le Développement de la Productique Appliquée à l'Industrie (ADEPA).

The Agency was established in 1969 by the Ministry of Industry and by the leading industrial federations and it operates as a private undertaking. Funding is approximately half government contracts to develop technologies in particular areas, and half contracts with firms, and the operating budget has been about FF 100 million per year. ADEPA provides a pool of technical expertise for industrial companies wishing to modernize their production facilities and upgrade their staff skills. It provides consultancy, technical assistance, training and information. Most assistance goes to the metal processing and machinery industry, followed by plastics and textiles.

Because small and medium firms generally lack the technical, human and financial resources to adopt complex equipment, ADEPA has focussed its attention on assisting them to adopt new, computer-integrated manufacturing methods and equipment. The Agency also aims at bridging the gap between the supply of specialist engineering consultancy skills and the demand for these skills in industry.

ADEPA also administers the MECA scheme (Machines et Equipements de Conception Avancée) designed to improve or increase investment in advanced design machinery and equipment. Grants are given to firms to help them purchase machinery of a new kind. The grants also partly cover the costs a firm incurs in reorganization, training and all of the other necessary software and management expenditures which are required for the successful introduction of new technology. Although the amount of money involved in the MECA scheme is currently being reduced, it has been FF 125 million per year and 4,000 firms have been assisted, most with less than 100 employees. The amount of money involved in this scheme is not high; expenditures under the MECA scheme in 1985 were approximately 0.3% of the total investment in fixed assets of the electronic and machinery sectors.

The MECA scheme and schemes like it usually do not create new investment. What they usually do is advance investment so that it takes place earlier than it would otherwise have occurred. Possibly more importantly, they also encourage firms to invest in more advanced equipment than they otherwise would have done. However, as is the case with all investment schemes, there are the usual obstacles such as shortages of skills, organizational problems and technical problems which cannot simply be solved by the application of investment incentives.

It is in the areas of skill enhancement and organizational change that bodies like ADEPA can be effective. They give high quality technical assistance, and they enjoy a certain flexibility and comparative advantage because of their role as quasi-public agencies. They are not entirely profit driven and they do not suffer from problems of inflexibility and slowness to react that totally public agencies often suffer from. By having a mixed governing organizational structure involving employers, trade unions, trade associations, and government representatives, and by providing consultancy services for which they are paid they can occupy a unique technical service-providing niche. Such bodies have an important role in boosting intangible investment in training, software and marketing; areas where small firms have traditionally been weak.

Germany

The German Ministry for Research and Technology (BMFT) has introduced a series of programmes to widen the use of micro-electronics in processes and products. For example, over the period 1982-1985 there was a major project to expand the use of micro-electronics in products. This was followed by a programme to increase the use of sensors and micro-peripherals particularly in small and medium sized firms. These programmes have for the most part financed approximately 40% of the cost of applications, and they have involved government expenditures of DM 100-150 million a year.

The programme which is of more interest here is that on industrial automation running through 1984-1988. The total funding envelope for the entire programme on industrial automation is DM 610 million spread over CAD/CAM, robots and university-industry co-operation. For the manufacturing technology part of this programme funding has been DM 450 million. The scheme supports 40% of the cost of development and application of CAD/CAM and production planning and control systems hardware and software. Robots, intelligent peripherals, materials and component costs can be financed up to DM 800,000 per firm. The main beneficiaries are small and medium-sized enterprises.

The programme works in two steps. Firms must initially prepare a thorough feasibility study over at least a six month period before direct investment support for CAD/CAM is made available in the second stage. There are also a number of demonstration and information services which have spread information on CAD/CAM and production planning system applications, and seminars and information services have been provided in conjunction with industry associations. The effect of such a thorough spread of information has meant that about 30% of intermediate capital goods producers targeted in the scheme have been able to take some advantage of it.

This has been a highly successful programme with approximately 1,500 applications approved in the first three years of its operation through to the end of 1986. Firms with less than 500 employees accounted for almost 75% of applications. A crucial feature of these schemes is their efficient methods of ensuring rapid diffusion of new production methods by operating through established networks of industry and professional associations, technology transfer agents and information services.

Sweden

Sweden's approach to introducing advanced manufacturing technology has had two sides, as has Japan's, focussing on research with potential for wide applications and on efficient diffusion of best-practice techniques. Sweden currently has a broad National Information Technology Programme comprising support for systems engineering and information technology applications and micro-electronics and component production. The Programme began in Autumn 1987 concentrating on computer, control and communications systems applications, largely in engineering and process industries and it continues previous production-oriented IT support. An earlier National Micro-electronics Programme focussed on design and production of integrated circuits which could be broadly applied in products in Sweden.

The National Information Technology Programme supports jointly-funded development projects, with the Swedish Government providing approximately SKr 500 million and an equal amount of project development finance is coming from the business sector. There is also support for basic and goal-oriented research at higher education institutions and research establishments.

A wide range of on-going support programmes has spread awareness of the possibilities of the use of advanced manufacturing technology and strengthened the infrastructure for IT applications. For example, by 1987 the National Industrial Board (SIND) was supporting the extra costs to the firms involved of operating 17 flexible manufacturing system demonstration plants showing all aspects of advanced process applications, computer numerical control, flexible manufacturing systems, CAD/CAM, computer integrated systems, monitoring and control systems. There are also a number of training, demonstration and co-operation centres aimed at improving the skill level of small firms investing in advanced manufacturing technology.

The Work Environment Fund has been examining all aspects of best practice organization and skill development associated with advanced manufacturing technology. This tripartite body, consisting of government, labour and employer groups, implemented a 5-year Development Programme through 1982-1987 to spread knowledge of best-practice use of advanced technology combined with new forms of work organization as widely as possible.

The extensive system of co-operative research institutes and the regional development funds also supply advisory services to enterprises in such areas as demonstration of new systems, assistance with technical problems, and training and skill development to make applications more effective and efficient.

United Kingdom

The United Kingdom was one of the first countries to introduce government programmes to diffuse micro-electronics more widely through manufacturing industry. The Micro-electronics Application Project (MAP) of the Department of Trade and Industry was begun in 1978 with the aim of encouraging manufacturing firms in the United Kingdom to apply micro-electronics in their products and in their production processes. MAP was mainly targeted at small firms with less than 200 employees in established industries where the scope for applications of micro-electronics had not been fully exploited.

There were four parts to MAP. They consisted of:

- Increasing industrial awareness of the benefits and implications of applications;
- Providing assistance to develop training courses in micro-electronics techniques;
- Supporting micro-electronics consultancy. The costs of independant expert advice on the feasibility of applying micro-electronics were subsidized; and
- Providing project support to firms developing applications of micro-electronics technology.

Some £85 million was allocated to this programme.

The early phases of MAP focussed on increasing general awareness, with heavy reliance on professional associations to conduct broad-based information activities. Subsequently, consultancy support was designed to help firms examine the feasibility of applications, and project development support has developed new applications. Most of the funds went to project support for the development of new applications by individual firms.

With the launching of the Enterprise Initiative in 1988 there has been a shift in emphasis by the Department of Trade and Industry away from direct support for individual firms towards collaborative research and development at the pre-competitive stage. But part of the Enterprise Initiative (the Manufacturing Systems Initiative) aims at drawing the attention of potential users, particularly small and medium enterprises, to the scope and opportunities offered by advanced manufacturing technology.

The Manufacturing Systems Initiative is operated on behalf of the Department of Trade and Industry by the Production Engineering Research Association. This association supplies small and medium enterprises with advice and technical assistance in the planning and introduction of advanced manufacturing systems. Half of the cost of five to fifteen days of consultancy to explore the potential for using advanced manufacturing technology is subsidized through the scheme. In special assisted regions and special urban regions the Department meets two-thirds of the cost of consultation. This initiative is a follow-up of the earlier diffusion and application programmes typified by MAP.

EEC Programmes

The European Community has a range of programmes which support the development of advanced manufacturing technology. For example, the BRITE programme (Basic Research in Industrial Technologies for Europe) is specifically designed to spread new user applications of advanced production technology more extensively through established industries. There is a heavy concentration on basic manufacturing technologies (automated assembly, computer controlled production, robotics, sensors). ESPRIT (European Strategic Programme for Research and Development in Information Technology) is focussed on pre-competitive research in micro-electronics and information processing and embraces industrial research projects to develop advanced manufacturing technology (CAD-CAM/CIM), often by supplying firms. The BRITE programme focusses particularly on the lagging sectors and countries and on supporting smaller firms, whereas most of the ESPRIT expenditures and effort have gone to large firms. The Pan-European EUREKA programme also has projects aimed at increasing competitive and more directly commercial research to develop applications of advanced manufacturing technology.

These programmes - particularly BRITE - are paying increasing attention to the general infrastructure and environment for small firms and to consultancy and training activities designed to expand investments in human resources and human capital formation. There has also been increasing attention given to firm-based training by the European Community to complement efforts to increase the level of firm-based and firm-financed training in the schemes and programmes in various European countries.

5. Key Features of Programmes

These policies and programmes to support production-oriented applications are clearly different from each other. However, there are a number of features which are of common general interest when considering government actions to promote industrial diffusion of production technology.

Out-reach

Most programmes reach a very large number of firms, particularly small and medium sized firms. Awareness campaigns at the beginning of programmes and demonstration projects at their end aim to increase knowledge of opportunities and benefits of effective applications.

Simplicity

Most programmes are relatively simple to administer and to deliver.

Funding

Funding is relatively low compared with sectoral R&D expenditures and investment expenditures. But schemes focus attention on new areas and mobilize corporate interest in small firms in intangible investment (R&D, software, training).

Technological Institutes

Established government-backed technological institutes can usefully complement and implement information, awareness and development schemes, particularly if they supply market-driven consultancy services.

Market Orientation

Most schemes have a strong element of market control and direction, often involving extensive use of consultancy.

Focus on Intangible Investments

Product development, software, and most importantly, investments in skill development and upgrading are vital features of these programmes.

A relatively low level of resources is going into these programmes compared with the expenditures of industry. However, by being carefully focussed to reach as many firms as possible, by having simple administration, and by operating in conjunction with technological institutes, industry and professional associations, these programmes are very effective in delivering information, awareness and consultancy services. Another important feature is that demand-driven shared-cost consultancy is used to deliver technological and advisory services. Finally, increasing intangible investments in training, software, market exploration, research and technology acquisition is a key feature of all of these programmes.

6. Summary

Advanced manufacturing technologies have a high potential to achieve gains in industrial flexibility, quality and productivity. But high levels of applications are concentrated in a limited range of industries and countries and in large firms. This concentration is even more marked when the technology is more highly integrated and more advanced.

There are a number of common constraints hindering more widespread applications. In particular these are the need for more effective human resource management when introducing AMT, the development of new skills, organizational adjustment to flatten hierarchies and increase shop-floor responsibilities, and better coordination of production activities and links with suppliers and purchasers. The industrial environment in which firms operate is an important determinant of the rate of uptake of AMT, and of its effective utilisation.

Governments have an important role to play in shaping this environment, particularly in maintaining or promoting a strong market-driven technological infrastructure - in such areas as awareness, information, consultancy and technology supply - and in training and the supply and upgrading of skills in conjunction with in-firm and firm-financed efforts.

References

OECD, Government Policies and the Diffusion of Microelectronics, Paris, 1989.

OECD project on "Technology, Flexibility of Manufacturing and Industrial Relations", Working papers, 1988, 1989.

COMMENTS ON PRODUCTION ORIENTED INFORMATION TECHNOLOGY POLICY IN JAPAN AND EUROPE

Mamoru Mitsugi
Executive Manager, Fujitsu Limited, Tokyo

Correct evaluation of the impact of information technology has an important bearing on business policy decisions and the projection of future business. The information technology impact will differ from that of the other technical innovations man has experienced in the past. Today I am going to talk about the impact of information technology. First, I'd like to refer to the Kondratieff wave, which diagrams the four major social waves that have occurred since the nineteenth century (Figure 1).

The age of canal networks:
In the 50 years starting with 1790, the use of canals reduced transportation costs, broadened the market for products, and strengthened the ties between rural and urban communities.

The age of electric railroads:
In the second half of the nineteenth century, the invention of the steam engines contributed to development of a railroad network and to machine industry modernization.

The age of power networks:
In the last part of the nineteenth century, use of electricity progressed and the availability of electric energy encouraged the development of industries.

Figure 1

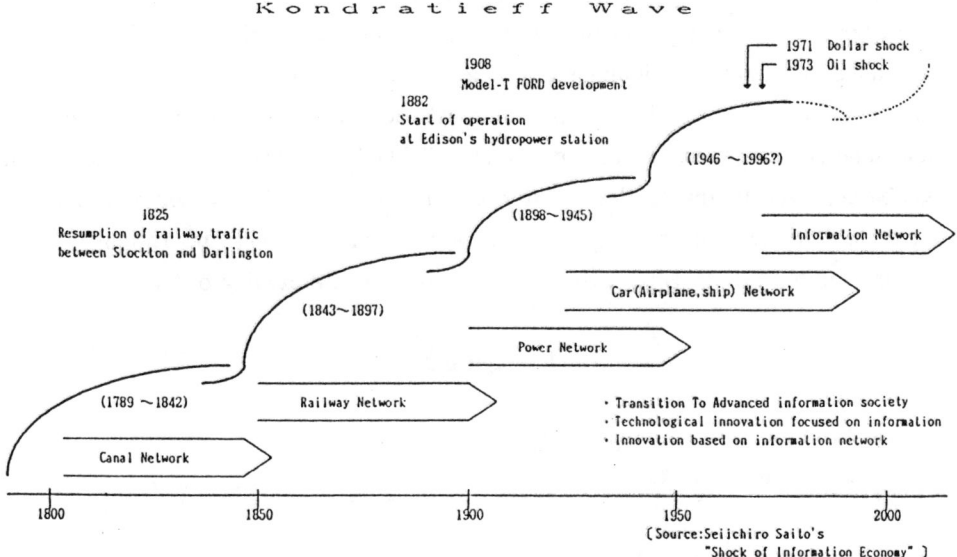

The age of large-scale transportation networks:
In the early twentieth century, overland, maritime, and air transportation networks were developed. Since the end of the Second World War, the development of global transportation networks has made good progress.

These waves in economical activity are the result of the technology acquired in the past 200 years. They all have had an enormous and homogeneous impact on society.

The information technology that we are acquiring will bring about another wave, and the age from now until the twenty-first century will be characterized by that wave. But the wave will have an individual and heterogeneous impact on the society, unlike the previous waves. Let us examine the relationship between the social waves already explained and the transition of the industrial structure. Figure 2 shows that in the United States a labor power transition from the agricultural sector to the industrial sector occurred in the past and that the power is now shifting from the industrial sector to the services and information sectors. Although this tendency is also observed in Japan, the rate of labor power transition from one sector to another is much higher in Japan than it is in the United States. Previous waves have resulted in the development of industries that produced tangible products. Those industries continue to supply products characterized by mass production and uniform quality. In the age of information oriented society, however, intangible products such as services and software will be the main products. More and more products will be produced so that each meets an individual's requirement such as personality, individuality, and heterogenity. The age will be characterized by this tendency. Information technology will be used as a powerful social tool to achieve the requirements of the times. It must be recognized that information technology is powerful enough to destroy the existing order in the world.

Figure 2

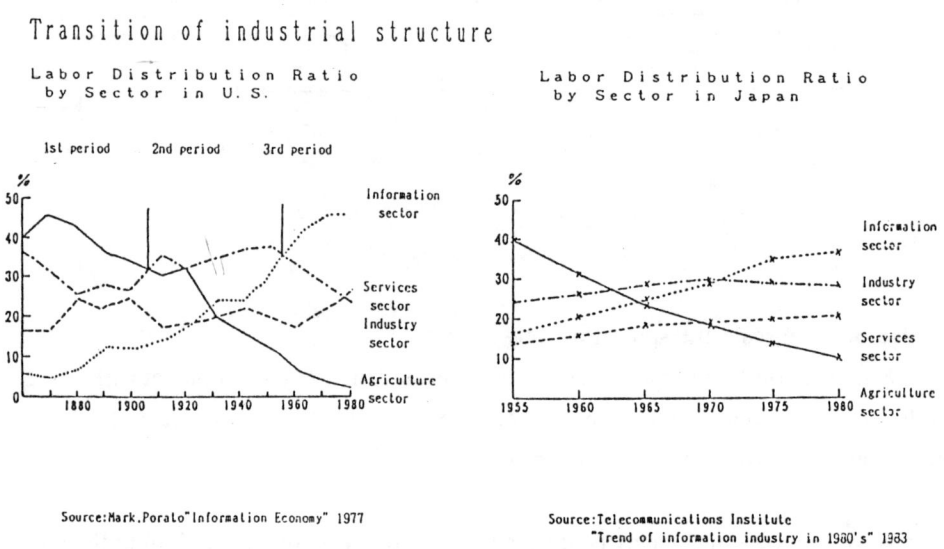

Next I'd like to explain the trend of corporate strategy in Japan in the environment in which information technology is progressing (Figure 3). The strategies common to all industries are to catch up with the rapid appreciation of the yen, to accept the business opportunities brought about by the easing and abolition of the governmental regulations that framed the conventional order, and to deal with the consumer market that is being broadened with the increasing disposable income of individuals. Of corporate strategies, the foreign strategy is to promote globalization, the interindustrial strategies are to strengthen the ties between industries and to integrate industries, and the marketing strategy is to promote rationalization and differentiation. Improved information technology will function as an infrastructure in executing these corporate strategies. Business restructuring is indispensable to the further growth of a company in the twenty-first century. Strategical use of information technology is the key to the achievement of the restructuring.

Through the following three slides that show examples of the impact of information technology, I'd like to show your how great the impact is.

Figure 4 shows the transition of world computer shipments. Since 1984, the quantity of personal computers shipped has continued to exceed that of traditional computers. Traditional computers include large-, medium-, and small-sized computers and minicomputers. World computer shipments still shows this tendency, and the difference between the two groups will increase. The components of a traditional computer, that is, the computer itself, the basic software that controls the computer, and the input/output devices are generally developed, manufactured, and sold by the same manufacturer. Those of a personal computer, that is, the computer itself (semiconductor chips), the basic software, and the input/output devices are supplied by more than one company. The personal computer market is an open market, and personal computers are freely tailored to multiple applications, unlike traditional computers. Since information technology is expected to function as an infrastructure of the society, it is important that personal computers be universal, general, and nonmonopolitic. I'd stress that an innovation, which is indispensable to achieve the age of information oriented society, is progressing in the computer field and that the innovation does not prevent the universal use of computers just mentioned.

Figure 3

Recent Changes in Business Environment and Corporate Strategies

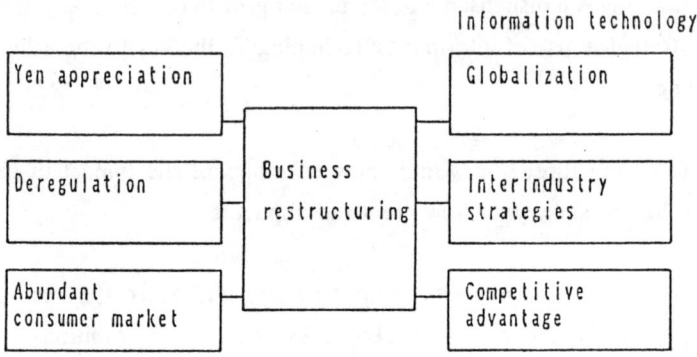

Figure 4

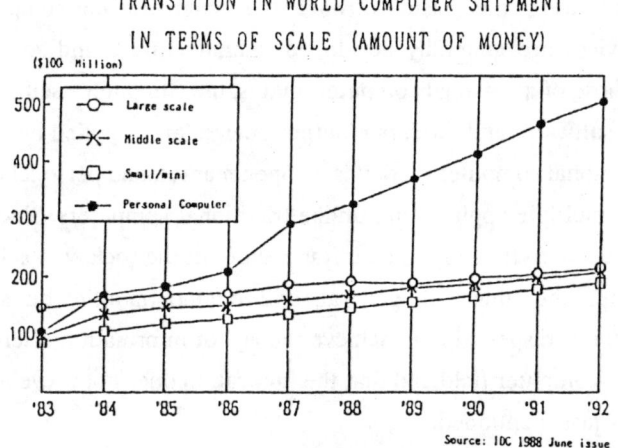

Figure 5 shows the progress of a company that made an inroad into an existing business and established its own business in a short period. In 1976 the Yamato Transportation Co., a company of medium standing started a revolution. Door-to-door parcels delivery were either railway parcels handled by the Japan National Railways or postal parcels handled by the Ministry of Posts and Telecommunications. In Japan there were no private transportation companies that handled such parcels. Yamato made an effort to establish its basic policy under existing regulations. That policy was for Yamato, a private company to establish a new market, and to deliver parcels anywhere in Japan within 24 hours by using a physical distribution system supported by computers, and to gain the customers' confidence through reliable transportation. As shown in Figure 5, Yamato overtook existing competitors within eight years after it established the business. This is the result of low cost, speedy service, reliable delivery, and a network that covers all of Japan. Yamato has justified its customers' trust in the company by using information technology as a means of delivery parcels reliably. I think this example clearly demonstrates that information technology is powerful enough to destroy the existing order in a short period.

Figure 5

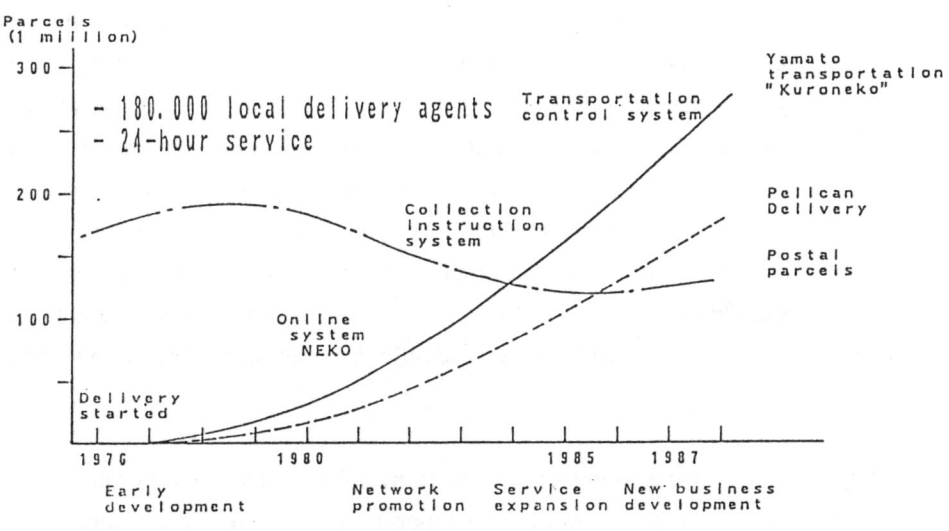

The example in Figure 6 shows how the use of information technology helps a company develop business and how a company placed under an obligation of technology can offer valuable information to others. PHARMA is a voluntary pharmacy chain that has 200 subsidiary pharmacies in Japan. In the first stage of the business, PHARMA collected orders from the pharmacies, sent them to the wholesalers, obtains the merchandise from them at preferred prices, sorted the merchandise according to the orders, and distributed it to its pharmacies. By dealing with PHARMA, the manufacturers and wholesalers received orders in a lump, and reduced shipping costs because PHARMA sorted the merchandise for distribution. The pharmacies obtained merchandise at preferred prices because PHARMA consolidated the orders from drugstores. The lower half of Figure 6 shows the interesting financial design made by PHARMA, although the explanation is omitted. Although PHARMA started the initial business in this way, it soon stopped handling merchandise. PHARMA assured the manufacturers and wholesalers that the 200 pharmacies would order merchandise from them only through PHARMA, and established a system that enables the manufacturers and wholesalers to check every day the movement of merchandise in the pharmacies. In a conventional system, it is difficult for the manufacturers and wholesalers to check the movement because it spent too much time controlling the amount of stock so that articles could be shipped according to the orders from each pharmacy. The new system eliminated this difficulty. Simultaneously, an improvement enabled member pharmacies to use their personal computers for ordering by electronic mail. Pharmacies get ideas for improving everyday business while doing it. They exchange their evaluations of customers with each other through a communication network. One pharmacy gets an idea for selling off-season articles. When customers buy them enthusiastically, the other pharmacies take up the idea. One idea generates another; a chain reaction occurs. Information is used independently of the instructions based on the manual unified by the PHARMA head office. Each pharmacy not only receives information from the head office but transmits information to the other pharmacies.

Today I presented these examples to support my opinions that correct evaluation of the impact of information technology has an important bearing on business policy decisions and the projection of future business and that new technology will have an impact that differs from that on the technology man has acquired up until now. I believe that information technology will be a powerful tool to achieve a society based on individuality and humanity.

Figure 6

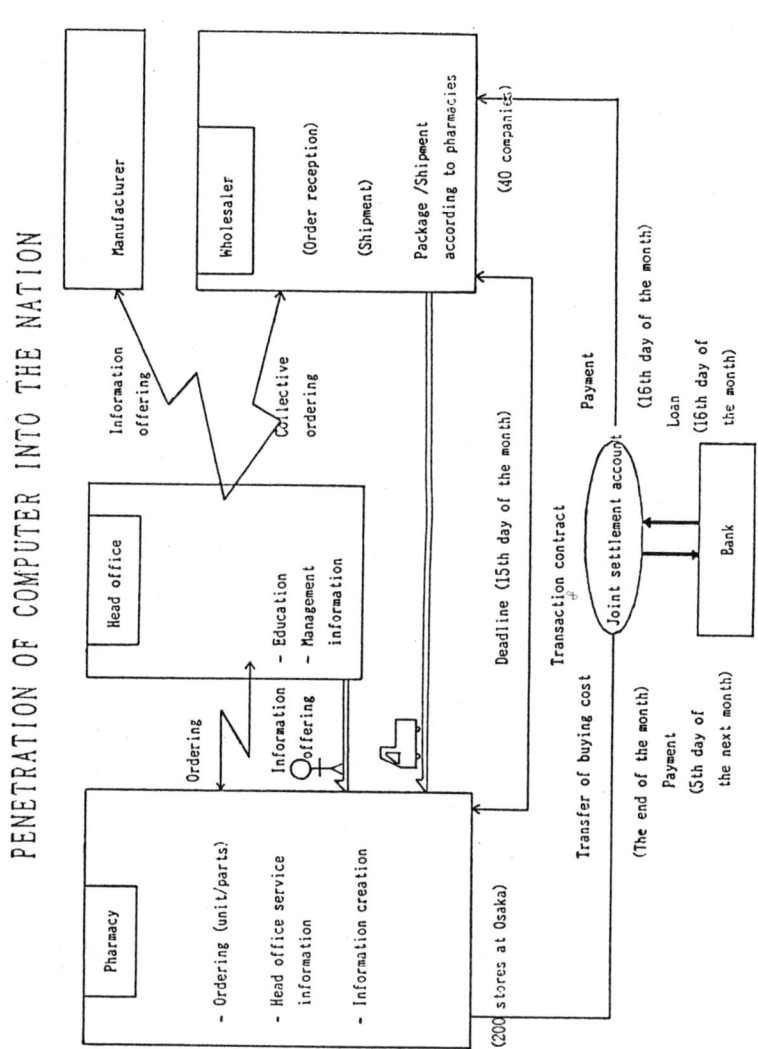

IV. EUROPEAN-JAPANESE COLLABORATION

"Collaboration between firms - an overview"

"Collaboration between firms - case studies"

"Scenarios of 1992 and consequences for Euro-Japanese relationship"

EURO-JAPANESE COOPERATION IN INFORMATION TECHNOLOGY

Hellmut Schütte
INSEAD, Fontainebleau

1. Background and Framework

1.1 Agreement and Objective

At the end of September 1987, the author was entrusted by the Japanese Government, represented by the Japanese Delegation to the OECD, to carry out a study of the "European-Japanese Cooperation in Information Technology". The project attempts to collect data on industrial cooperation between Japanese and European firms and to analyze this data with regard to the benefits expected to be derived from, or already brought to the partners and their countries of origin.

The study's objective is to contribute to the better understanding of the workings and the constraints of international cooperation in a field which is of utmost importance to both Japan and Europe. It should also give an up-to-date description and analysis of the dynamics of European-Japanese cooperation in information technology which are rapidly developing, and as such difficult to follow by outsiders.

This article represents a condensed version of a report submitted in February 1989.

1.2 Definitions and Methodology

According to our definition, information technology consists of the computer and office automation, the electronic component and the communication sectors, and comprises of the development, production and marketing of related products and services.

Consumer electronics, as well as factory automation, although technologically closely linked to the IT-sector, are excluded, as is the application of information technology for military purposes.

Data collection has been done based on a search through material available in both academic and journalistic publications on the topic. It has been supplemented by various interviews with a number of company representatives and government officials both in Europe and Japan.

Since official statements and press reports do not necessarily disclose the real feeling and intentions of the parties concerned, interviews with company and government officials were seen as important and have, in general, revealed information not publicly available, and of great relevance.

During the period from September 87 to January 89, the author has been in direct or indirect contact with almost all major players in Europe and Japan in the field of information technology.

2. International Cooperation

2.1 Changes in International Business: The Stage

Up to a few years ago, discussions in the field of international business mainly focussed on the multi- or transnational companies. With these firms competing either among each other on a global scale, or with regional and local firms in limited areas, there was concern about their growing power in particular vis-à-vis national governments. These political bodies felt restricted in their sphere of influence by sovereignty, while multinational firms could move their resources easily across borders.

Within the very large firms, issues of fostering innovation and entrepreneurship, while keeping control and internal coherence, dominate the agenda of top management. Cooperative agreements were seen as second best solutions, often required by governments, especially in developing countries.

This has recently changed. Even very large and diversified companies realise that in cooperating with other firms, risks can be minimised, costs reduced, new markets or segments entered, or, in more general terms, revenues can be enhanced. Medium-sized and small firms are following their lead. Negotiated cooperative agreements across borders have thus grown almost explosively over the last decade both in number and importance. Today the leading global firms in several industries find themselves involved in a number of coalitions with different partners, and consider themselves members of an ever-changing network of international relationships.

Cooperative agreements are not limited to the classical joint venture in which two or more partners invest equity to achieve a common goal in a separate legal entity. Cooperative agreements comprise all efforts of independent partners to work with each other over a long period. It therefore includes everything beyond spot transactions i.e. buying and selling without further commitment, and up to mergers and acquisitions, where independent firms evolve into unified organizations. Joint research projects, OEM arrangements and distribution agreements thereby fall into this category.

A clear distinction between cooperative agreements and "deals" for short-term gain does not exist as it depends on the willingness of the partners to actually work together. A similar argument can be used regarding the importance of such agreements for the partners. There is an obvious difference between a long-term supplier-buyer relationship for nuts and bolts or paperclips, and an alliance which influences the overall competitiveness of one or all of the partners involved. Such latter agreements are referred to as strategic alliances and are the focus of this report.

Since cooperative agreements are not bound to any legal form, cover a wide variety of projects, and often do not identify the real intent of the partners, reliable statistics do not and cannot exist.

Moreover, there is a problem of definitions. For the Japanese,"cooperation", especially in the context of "industrial cooperation", also includes 100% foreign-owned investment, seemingly because it links the economies of different nations.[1] In this report we do not follow this wider definition.

Since, in many cases, the partners in a cooperative agreement are in the same business, competition and cooperation exist side by side. This competitive cooperation makes the management of joint efforts extremely difficult. To succeed in a joint undertaking, the partners need to share knowledge. At the same time, they have to protect their knowledge in order not to jeopardize their competitive position.

Graph 1 shows competition and cooperation as alternative modes in business. If, however, the only objective of the individual firm is to win over other firms, then cooperation is only a derivative of competition and, as such, limited.

---

[1] L. Turner "Industrial Collaboration with Japan", Euro-Asia Business Review, July 1987, p. 11-26.

Graph 1

	Business	Government
Competition	Improve quality/service Increase scale Lower costs etc.	Sponsor national R&D Protectionism
Cooperation	Joint research Joint manufacturing Joint marketing	

2.2 Developments in Information Technology: The Game

Information technology is one of the three core technologies having a significant impact on the world until the end of this millenium (the other two being biotechnology and new material science).

Military applications make information technology a key strategic resource for governments which also represent major customers for the industry and, at the same time, set the rules through a number of regulations, particularly in the area of communications.

The industry has produced some very large firms such as IBM in computers, and AT&T and NTT in communications, but also many innovative firms which rose from garage-type operations into sizable companies within a very short space of time. All of them are facing a rapid rate of change, decreasing product life cycles, rising R&D expenses, a proliferation of converging technologies, products and services, and increasing globalisation of their businesses.

These factors, one may argue, make international cooperation among the players not only an option, but a must. From the point of view of the industry we would see the following reasons for going into cooperative agreements:[2]

---

[2] F. J. Contractor and P. Lorange, "Why Should Firms Cooperate? The Strategy and Economic Basis for Cooperative Ventures," in: Cooperative Strategies in International Business, Lexington Books, p. 3-28, 1988.

1. Risk reduction
    Failure in R&D
    Being too slow/too late

2. Economies of scale/rationalization
    Production in countries with comparative advantage
    Lower costs from higher volume
    Concentration on key products/services

3. Fostering technological competences
    Technological synergies
    Specialization and complementation (horizontal cooperation)
    Subcontracting (vertical integration)
    Access to public research

4. Overcoming and building market barriers
    Utilizing complementary marketing networks
    Offering complete product ranges/systems
    Overcoming investment/trade/procurement barriers
    Co-opting potential competitors.

Obviously, the reasons for cooperation are manifold and overlapping. As the market demands increasingly complete solutions to computing/communications problems, competitors find it increasingly difficult to be both horizontally (with a broad product/service range) and vertically (from R&D to marketing worldwide, from key components to application software) integrated.

In order to connect computers with each other, communication systems and equipment are needed. In order to function, communication systems need computing power to facilitate switching. Both sectors rely on electronic components such as semiconductors and microprocessors as major accelerators in their development. The underlying convergence of technologies leads to a convergence of products which in turn leads to a convergence of those companies who aspire to offering "information technology solutions" rather than products and services of limited value. Further growth of the large firms may be one answer to this trend; mergers or acquisitions are other solutions. Cooperation within the industry is an alternative for the information technology industry.

2.3 Europe, Japan and the USA: The Players

All competitors, even international ones, are shaped and influenced in their strategies by their home country. No firm can yet claim to be truly global and thus to be independent from a national culture or national government.

The major European firms in information technology have long enjoyed government protection and preferential treatment for procurement purchasing. This has produced national champions which suffer in the broader international arena from the fragmented market in Europe, and thus the lack of economies of scale. The over-regulation in some countries has slowed down innovation, which in turn has led the companies to lobby against too rapid technological changes from which their faster competitors could benefit. However, strength in some niche markets and in software has remained and a revival of the industry is in the making inline with the European Commission's programme for Europe 1992.

Japan's leading firms were not known internationally when their European and US competitors were already globally represented in the fifties and sixties. Their entry came along with the change of the industry from electro-mechanical technologies to electronics. As such they are "late-comers" in the establishment, admired for their achievements, especially in production technology, and feared for their growth momentum and determination. Fostered by an industrial policy which called for concensus, collaboration, and at the same time competition, the new rules of inter-firm cooperation are not new to them. Particularly vertical integration is carried out through a sophisticated, cooperative subcontracting system, in contrast with European and American firms who rely primarily on their own resources.

This wealth of experience in managing relationships is exclusively derived from the Japanese environment and internationally transferable only to alimited extent. Even after several years of experience abroad, the Japanese firms still cannot match the expertise of their foreign competitors in dealing with the international business environment.[3] The track record of Japanese firms in computers and telecommunications (in contrast with mass-produced components) is also less impressive. While this may be due to protectionistic policies in telecommunications, in the computer field the

---

[3] K. Ohmae, "Companies without countries", McKinsey Quarterly, 3, 1987.

underestimation of software led some years ago to some of the very few Japanese international market failures, especially in personal computers.

A similar cooperative spirit among firms or between firms and the government cannot be found in the USA, except in the defense area. This important segment has provided the US firms with massive research funds and contracts. Otherwise competition is tough, resulting in high performance fluctuations of firms over time, and quick changes in market shares among competitors. Winning and losing seems to be close to one another in the US, as are high profit and high losses. Mergers, acquisitions, bankruptcies, meteoric rises - all these are the consequences of a generally volatile market in which customer loyalty is less known than in Japan or Europe.

While the economic power of the USA has relatively declined over the last two to three decades, this may not necessarily apply to the information technology sector. The largest and the most profitable IT companies are still American companies, who are market leaders in the US and in many other countries, where they successfully compete with national champions. Only Japan represents an exception, but even here IBM achieved sales of more than Y1 trillion in 1987 and a profit of Y170 billion.

Their heavy investments abroad and their local manufacturing in many countries make them rely less on exports from the USA. Thus, the judgement of the strength of the American IT sector from trade statistics alone may be misleading.

Undeniable, however, is the decline of the US' competitiveness in mass-produced components which has led to some degree of dependence on Japanese supplies even in defense-related industries. The controversial semiconductor pact between Japan and the USA demonstrates the complexities of international government agreements.
Together, Europe, Japan and the USA form the "Triad Powers" in which the bulk of purchasing power of the world is accumulated. While competition is increasingly global in industries such as information technology, the closest competitors are still perceived as coming from the same country/area. This means that American firms consider other American firms as their main rivals, European firms other European firms, and Japanese firms see other Japanese firms as their most serious competitors. In order to succeed against one another globally, competitors have to be strongly represented, not only on

their "hometurf", but also in the other parts of the triad.[4] Should the resources for this undertaking not be sufficient, alliances with other firms from other parts of the triad are a viable option. This explains why cooperative agreements are not only concluded with partners close-by, although geographical proximity and cultural similarity may facilitate communication and thus increase the probability for success. The change from local or regional competition to a global scenario in the information technology industry could be called "geographical convergence of the market". It leads probably more to market-driven cooperations, while technological convergence leads primarily to technology-driven cooperations.

Firms which have taken into account both trends and become globally spread and technologically integrated firms at the same time, do not yet exist. Through cooperations, some major players move into the direction of becoming global IT alliances such as Olivetti-AT&T-Toshiba and Bull-Honeywell-NEC.

Graph 2

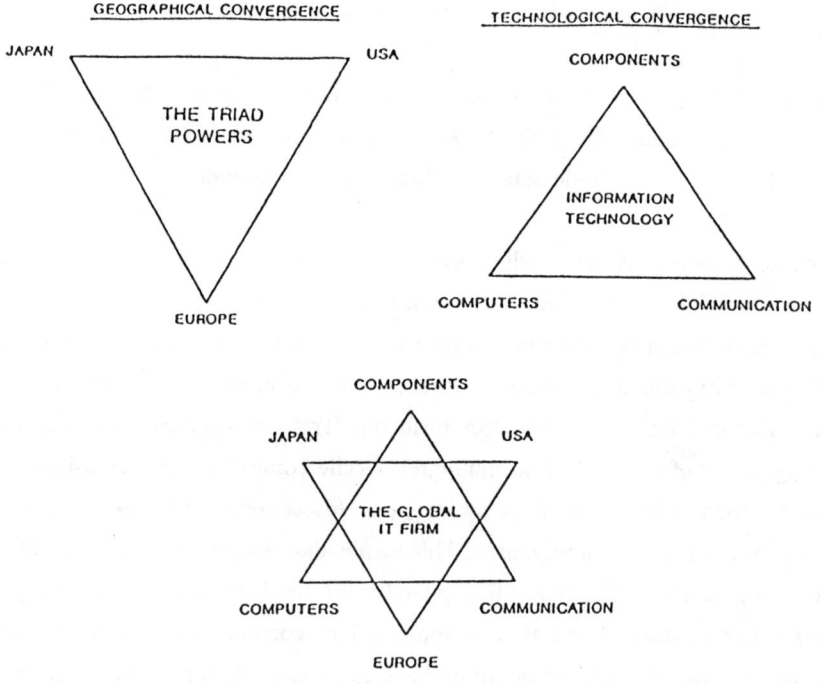

---

[4] K. Ohmae, "Triad Power", New York, 1985.

3. Cooperative Agreements between Japanese and European Firms

3.1 Characteristics of the Agreements

Our research has identified 45 cooperative agreements between Japanese and European information technology firms which have been active or newly concluded over the last 3 to 4 years. They span the range from licensing to OEM deals to joint ventures and involve all of the major Japanese and European companies. They are multi-product and international in scope, or local and uni-product, and are transacted on a pan-company basis or only on behalf of a single division.

- Sectors

Cooperative activity is most pronounced in the components, computers and, to a lesser extent, the telecommunications sectors. There are a scattering of agreements involving the major automobile producers in the robotics and factory automation area, and a few examples of agreements with software producers, although neither of these two sectors are a focal point of cooperative activity at present.

- Products

Agreements have concentrated on main frame computers, integrated circuits and facsimile machines.

It is interesting to note that the focal product areas are the ones in which Japanese companies have achieved a strong degree of competitiveness, if not superiority, in the marketplace. This applies to a lesser degree to mainframe computers, although the Japanese strength in computer hardware cannot be denied. Agreements involving these products are frequently marketing or OEM agreements which help the Japanese firms sell their products in Europe and/or allow European producers to complete their product line(s).

Some cooperative agreements span two or three sectors and are created to develop or market a hybrid product. A hybrid product would be one which combines the technologies from two separate sectors, such as telecommunications and components.

- Companies

Ventures between two small or even two medium-sized companies are rare, perhaps because of the limited international outlook and experience of those firms. The majority of agreements of any importance have been concluded between the largest and most important producers in the industry. The second most prevalent grouping is between a major world-competitor and a small/medium-sized national company which is specialized in a certain skill area or product, and has gained a degree of recognition in those areas.

- Size

Looked at as a whole, the vast majority of Euro-Japanese cooperative agreements are rather small in scale, with low volumes or covering one national market, and/or are limited to a single product or product group. There are very few attempts being made either to cooperate globally or to develop complementary product strategies which avoid head to head competition between the two partners in various world markets. The NEC/Bull arrangement, a potentially global collaboration, may develop into one of the few exceptions.

- Scope

Many cooperative ventures start out as short term purchasing or marketing agreements whose life-span is eventually determined by the quality of the relationship over time, as well as by external factors which make it more or less desirable for two companies to continue to cooperate. A straight forward licensing agreement, such as that between ICL and Fujitsu in 1981, can set the stage for a longer term relationship which is fairly extensive and mutually advantageous for both.

One factor adversely influencing the continuity of many cooperative agreements is the fact that most accords involve a single product or product group. The present pace of technological change is resulting in rapid product obsolecence. Once the technology or the product is obsolete, then the "raison d'etre" of the cooperation can be brought into question. A new agreement on a new range of products must be negotiated which may or may not include a technology which the two companies wish to share.

3.2 Categories

Viewed as a whole, the cooperative ventures which this study has identified fall into one of four categories. First, there are those agreements which concern the Japanese marketplace and involve joint development, production, marketing or distribution in or for that market. Second, there are similar agreements in or for Europe. Third, cooperations are listed which deal with transfer technology, and, lastly, there are those agreements which are broad-based, potentially global inscope and/or cooperative on a corporate-wide basis.

a. Agreements for Japan

Japanese	European
Y-E Data	Olivetti
Matsushita	Philips
Kyocera	Philips
Toppan Printing	Philips
Fuji	Siemens
Canon	Siemens
Marubeni	Siemens
NMB Semi-conductors	Thorn EMI/INMOS
Mitsui	ESS
Denki Kagaku Kogyo	Air Liquide
Sanyo	Acorn
Mitsui	Sinclair Research

There are twelve cooperative agreements that fall into this category. European firms enter such agreements with Japanese firms with one of two objectives in mind: either, the accord is considered to be an easy way to break into the reputably difficult Japanese market, or the company intends to actively profit from Japanese manufacturing expertise and efficiency.

In the first case, by tying up with a well established Japanese company, a European firm can benefit from the existing contacts and sales support of their Japanese partner, and avoid the large investment required for the establishment of an independent operation. The importance of long-lasting buyer-seller relationships in Japan cements the European firm to the Japanese partner and makes any strategic or structural changes of this kind very difficult.

The Japanese firm enters these kind of cooperative ventures and benefits from them as it is able to offer its customers a greater variety of products and perhaps a different technology than that which is presently available on the market. Such an arrangement may also permit marketing expenses to be spread over a larger range of products.

In the event that two companies decide to pursue a cooperative venture in Japan over the long term, then this accord can form the basis for a broader and technologically cooperative relationship. Such has been the case of Philips and Matsushita. The Matsushita/Philips accord is one of the oldest agreements which is still very active and two-way cooperative.

A second type of cooperative agreement, for manufacturing in Japan, takes advantage of Japan's recently acquired manufacturing expertise, due to very large economies of scale and high productivity in production processes which require a large number of manufacturing steps. Both of these criteria apply to memory chips and consumer electronics.

As a rule, products produced to order in Japan for European firms do not find their way into the Japanese market, but are exported and incorporated into the European companies' final products. The borderline between such agreements and OEM-sales of Japanese products by European firms in the European market is fine. OEM agreements mainly cover standardized products sold by the Japanese partner in other markets.

b. Agreements for Europe

<u>Japanese</u>	<u>European</u>
Seiko	Olivetti
Kyocera	Olivetti
Hitachi	Olivetti
Hitachi	BASF
Hitachi	Comparex
Sony	Logitek
Canon	Ferranti
Canon	Plessey
Canon	Siemens
Toshiba	Siemens
Toshiba	Telic-Alcatel
Toshiba	Rhone Poulenc
NEC	GEC/Marooni
Fujitsu	Swedish Telecom Adminstration
Aster Intl.	Micro Peripherals
Matsushita	Quick-Rotan
Matsuchita	Nixdorf
OKI Electric	SGS-Thomson

In one way, the same rational which is used to explain Euro-Japanese cooperative ventures in Japan can be used to explain Euro-Japanese ventures in Europe. For the Japanese firms, they represent a less expensive, faster and easier way of entering the European market. There are, however, many more agreements for the European market, and for every agreement being signed for Japan, there are two being signed for Europe.

First of all, this is due to the fact that the Japanese are more substantially committed to the European market than the Europeans to the Japanese market.

Secondly, the fragmented European market remains a difficult one to conquer for outsiders facing established and strong national firms which enjoy government support. A cooperative agreement with such a firm can overcome barriers and convert a potential member of the anti-Japanese lobby into a Japanese supporter. This applies not only to marketing ventures, but also to assembly/manufacturing operations which have encountered increasing criticism for appearing to be disguised imports and have been labeled "screwdriver" plants.

Lastly, when examining European based cooperative ventures, one finds that European companies enter such agreements hoping to have access to Japanese technology or to their high quality products. This is generally not the reason given by Japanese firms for entering a cooperative venture either in Europe or in Japan. The Japanese, who have greater respect for and interest in American technology, enter a cooperative agreement in Europe quite simply to have access to the European market. For the Europeans, a production plant in France for the manufacture of the newest model of facsimile machines brings with it not only the promise of higher sales and profits, but also that of technology transfers.

There are basically three types of accords presently being reached between Japanese and European firms in Europe. The first is a marketing or distribution agreement, the second is a manufacturing or licensing agreement, and the third is an OEM deal. For the most part, they are all initially rather small in scope and have limited specified time frames, unless they are already part of an overall relationship which has been established between two firms.

As most of the Japanese already have established networks in Europe, marketing and distribution agreements with other European firms are either small - thus not addressed by this report - or are concentrated on only one or two national markets.

The second group, manufacturing and licensing agreements, is on the rise in a response to stiffer local-content regulations. They involve manufacturing or manufacturing together with distribution. The Rhone-Poulenc/Toshiba arrangement is an illustrative example. It is in the form of a joint venture for the production of Toshiba's plain paper-copiers in France and for the sale of that and related office automation equipment into France.

Such an agreement evidences little true cooperative activity between the two firms and is, rather, a way for Toshiba to avoid protectionist policies and comply with local content regulations.

The third group, OEM agreements, allows for the incorporation of Japanese products into European companies' product lines and for these products' eventual sale in Europe. Such agreements can cover a whole product or any one of a number of components of that product. As such, the borderline between a company with which one has an OEM agreement and with which one has a supplier agreement is rather thin. Even if products of that nature are modified for the European partners, it is the marketing side of the added-value chain which is important for the OEM-agreement and not so much the origin of the product.

All of the OEM agreements in our list involve computers or computer peripherals or some parts thereof. In the case of Olivetti/Kyocera, OEM sales cover small-sized computers; BASF/Hitachi, high-end memorytape units, and Hitachi/Comparex, mainframes. The present popularity of OEM agreements within the computer sector is not all that surprising, as it is a sector in which completed product lines are rapidly gaining importance. A main frame producer cannot easily provide, over night, a complete range of related products and thus buys what it needs from other, often foreign, producers, in order to keep clients and to maximize use of its sales and distribution network.

The publicly announced OEM deals are probably only a portion of the total number of agreements reached between Japanese and European firms. In an industry which feels increasing pressure for technological renewal and advancement, the supply of "standard" products may not merit the word "cooperation", even if contracts cover extended periods or represent a major reason for the purchasing company's competitiveness. There are also companies which are not anxious to admit that a certain portion of one of their major product lines is actually being produced by another company, either for reasons of company image or national pride.

While initially OEM agreements may have met short-term objectives, they also have the potential for serving as a basis for the continuation or expansion of the firms' relationship over the long term. With a successful OEM agreement in place, there is little motivation for either party to duplicate the efforts of the alliance partner; both firms are free to explore and expand operations in other areas. In turn, a success relationship fosters its own expansion and can lead partners to cooperate in not just one or two, but in many aspects over time.

c. **Technology Transfer**

<u>Japanese</u>	<u>European</u>
Toshiba	Siemens
Toshiba	Alsthom
Fuji Electric	Thomson
Hitachi	Lucas Ind.
Mitsui	Intelligent Terminals

Apart from joint development projects, technology can be shared by transferring it from one firm to another. Contrary to cooperative agreements which are largely long-term, this process normally takes place during a limited span of time. The partnership between firms is, thus, transient in nature, except if the transfer of technology is part of a broader cooperative agreement called strategic alliance (see below).

The basis for the transfer is the sale of technology. As this can normally not be done by handing over blueprints, it requires the cooperation of scientists and engineeers from both partners in joint meetings and training sessions, joint setting up of facilities and launching of test runs etc. During these undertakings, the actual flow of know-how takes place.

Technology transfer agreements are not always reported, appear in no trade or investment statistics, and rarely attract as much attention as the agreement between Toshiba and Siemens in the megabit chip. Most of those listed above represent the flow of technology from Japan to Europe such as in the field of transistor modules from Fuji Electronics to Thomson, and deal with production rather than product technology. The agreement between the British company Intelligent Terminals and Mitsui is an exception as it comprises of the transfer of software technology for structuring artificial intelligence systems from Europe to Japan.

d. Strategic Alliances

Japanese	**European**
Canon	Olivetti
Toshiba	Olivetti
Fujitsu	ICL
Fujitsu	Telefónica
Fujitsu/Fuji	Siemens
NEC	Bull

This group of agreements represents the core of broad-based accords which are truely cooperative and longterm in nature and approach. They involve the active participation of both companies in some step of the development/production/sales process and most often a sharing of technological information. The accords are negotiated and supported by the very top management levels of the companies and can encompass the activities of several divisions. The strategy behind the accords is a longterm one with at least some emphasis on the global coordination of operations and markets.

The possibilities for the integration of the two companies' technologies often leads to a decision to develop a new group of products based on the expertise which the two firms have in the technologies involved. However, such forms of cooperation do not exclude the simultaneous pursuit of other activities such as OEM or licensing arrangements. In a well-developed relationship, the two companies are likely to have a number of joint development projects, involving two or more divisions, in addition to a series of supply and/or licensing agreements.

The dividing line between true strategic alliances and other agreements seems to be determined by the willingness of firms to cooperate in new technologies and, in some cases, on a multi-national basis. Under a number of different cooperative agreements, a company may be willing to share with another a technology which is known and already produced by a variety of companies; however, this same firm may not be willing to share, or cooperate in the development of, a brand new, highly competitive technology unless such a cooperation is part of a strategic alliance relationship. Similarly, a firm may have a joint operation with another for a particular national market, be it the Japanese, Malaysian or Norwegian; yet, these same two firms may never consider cooperating on a global basis and their operations may never pass the borders of a single country, unless the firms are strategic alliance partners.

Most of the companies listed above have important agreements with more than one company. This is not unusual and largely the norm. Corporate management takes the decision to enter into cooperative agreements as an alternative to or complementary mode of expanding the operations on its own. In implementing such a strategy, it may cooperate with one other firm in various fields, but it may also tie up with a number of different firms in different fields at the same time. Often we witness a majorstrategic alliance between two firms being accompanied by a host of other, less important, cooperative agreements with other firms. However, some firms such as Olivetti, Fujitsu and Canon have been able to develop major alliances with a deep level of cooperation simultaneously with several partners.

Canon is a good case in point. Canon is in the process of securing its position in global markets and in a broad range of technologies. It has chosen to do so by entering into a number of strategic alliances with firms which have a level of expertise in areas where Canon is weak. By combining Canon's own strengths in the photocopying area of the office automation sector together with European and American companies' expertise in other areas of the same sector, Canon hopes to eventually carve a place for itself in the highly integrated office automation market of the future. At the same time, these alliances are providing Canon special access to national markets where import regulations are formidable or risk to be formidable in the near future. The company is thus using stategic alliances and cooperative ventures as one way of assuring the firm's future growth and expansion.

3.3 Quantitative Analysis

All of the agreements discussed above represent for the participating firm the contribution of one or many resources at the firm's disposal. The type of contribution made to the agreements, simultaneously, a reflection of its partners wants and needs, and of its own expertise in a certain skill area or its comparative advantages from being from a certain nation or having penetrated successfully a certain market. With this in mind, we have classified all of the agreements according to the contribution each party is making to the cooperation. We have chosen as contributions technology, manufacturing (or the product itself), and marketing or distribution capabilities. Where none of these resources are supplied or exchanged, financial compensation is paid in lieu and listed separately. Each number in Chart I below represents a contribution by the partners in one area. Multifaceted relationships have more than one mark. For example, in the Kyocera/Philips agreement, both firms are contributing technological knowledge (one mark in the Tech/Tech box), the firms are jointly manufacturing the product (a second mark in Manu./Manu. box), but the products are only being sold in Japan by Kyocera, thus a third mark in the Japanese Dist., Marketing/European Financial Compensation box.

The strategic alliances identified in Part 3.2.d, all fall in the middle of Chart I with predominantly joint technological development, joint manufacturing and joint marketing or distribution (box 1, 6, 11).

The large number of agreements which involve joint technological development or exchange is note worthy. While the majority fall under the umbrella of a strategic alliance, the remaining are agreements between Japanese and Europeans to jointly develop a particular technology or product. There are more than a few of these types of agreements. This supports the general hypothesis that the exchange of technological information is a major motivation for cooperative agreements.

The relatively small number of agreements for the Japanese market (box 10), in which the Europeans provide the products or the manufacturing expertise and the Japanese the marketing or distribution expertise, can in part be explained by the fact that a number of such agreements are structured as joint ventures, and thus, in our chart, they appear under joint production and joint distribution/sales. Otherwise, we can comment that the rationale for their creation lies in the closed nature of the Japanese market which makes it more interesting for a European firm to enter this market under the auspices of a marketing/distribution agreement with a Japanese firm.

Chart I

Quantative Analysis
Contribution of Partners to Cooperation

European Companies Japanese Companies	Technology	Production/ Manufacturing	Marketing/ Distribution	Financial Compensation
Technology	(1) 16	(2)	(3)	(4) 5
Production/ Manufacturing	(5) 1	(6) 12	(7) 15	(8) 1
Marketing/ Distribution	(9)	(10) 7	(11) 9	(12) 1
Financial Compensation	(13) 3	(14)	(15) 1	(16)

Having said that, it must be pointed out that there are many agreements which combine only European marketing capabilities and Japanese manufacturing expertise (box 7); their number far outweighs the number of cooperative technological exchange agreements (those not covered by a strategic alliance). They are principally the OEM or OEM-type arrangements discussed in Part 3.2.b, above. Their relative abundance in comparison with similar OEM or distribution accords for the Japanese market, is certainly a distortion. The Japanese, finding it difficult to sell directly into Europe, have entered into cooperative marketing/distribution/OEM agreements which are at least for the time being more effective, and more favorably viewed by government authorities than their own European based sales networks. On the chart, when we take away the multiple markings for some of the strategical liances, the resulting distortion in favour of box 7 - Japanese manufacturing and European marketing - is even more pronounced. This has been done in Chart II.

Chart II

<u>Principal Contribution of Partners to Cooperation</u>

European Companies Japanese Companies	Technology	Production/ Manufacturing	Marketing/ Distribution	Financial Compensation
Technology	(1) 6	(2)	(3) 1	(4) 5
Production/ Manufacturing	(5) 1	(6) 6	(7) 15	(8)
Marketing/ Distribution	(9)	(10) 6	(11) 5	(12) 1
Financial Compensation	(13) 3	(14)	(15)	(16)

All in all, these charts support the comments made in III. 2. above. There are four basic groups of agreements: those relying on European marketing expertise and Japanese manufacturing expertise, mostly for the European market; those designed to allow Europeans to sell in the Japanese market; those through which technology is transferred; and those agreements which are part of a strategic alliance agreement. The two first groups of agreements are entered into order to profit from another firm's expertise in a certain skill area or market. They are particularly valuable when the skill area or market is one which would require considerable investment to master and which would not necessarily generate the desired return to the in experienced firm. In other words, the cooperative agreement serves as a convenient expediant in the normal course of business affairs. Transfer of technology agreements are of transient nature.

Strategic alliances are different. Those which we have identified in this report, in contrast to OEM, marketing, manufacturing or licensing agreements, cover the full range of joint technological development, joint manufacturing and joint marketing and distribution. More importantly, they are the result of a deliberate policy of the participating firm of growth or globalization through strategic alliances. Of all of the agreements discussed in this paper, it is this last group of Euro-Japanese agreements that truely merits the name of strategic alliance. They are broad-based and technologically cooperative. They are at least potentially global and they are longterm.

4. Strategic Alliances: Experiences and Perceptions
4.1 International Agreements: A Comparison
a. Statistical Indications

By examining available statistics on cooperative agreements we can see that there are largely fewer cooperative agreements between European and Japanese firms than between either of these two parties and the Americans. Information from FOR, a data base of accords in information technology created by Montedison, shows that there were 81 agreements contracted between Japanese and European firms over the period 1982-86 versus 128 American/Japanese agreements and 253 EEC/US agreements. Similar surveys come to the same result.[5]

Moreover, while there is spectacular growth today in inter-European agreements and was an increase in such general agreements of more than 7 times between 1983 and 1986,[6] the growth in the number of Japanese/European accords is negligible. It is certain that the increase in inter-European agreements has been fueled by the EC programes ESPRIT and RACE and by the approach of 1992 and the European union, yet, this does not necessarily explain the lack of cooperative venture activity between Europe and Japan. It cannot be attributed to a lack of interest in foreign partner ventures because the number of international cooperative accords as a whole has risen during this period and, in particular, the number of US-European agreements has risen from 32 ('83) to 49 ('86). Nor does the lack of growth appear to be the result of a public manifestation of anti-Japanese sentiment, along the lines of the "buy US" campaign in the United States.

---

[5] FOR, "Joint Ventures and Inter-Company Agreements: An Introduction to a Comparative Survey in High Technology Sectors," a paper presented at a conference in Lucca, Italy on Technical Cooperation and International Competitiveness, 1986. See also Reseau, Draft Report for the Industry Committee, OECD.

[6] Financial Times, "Keeping Europe on the IT Map", May 18, 1988.

The question therefore is, what motivates a company to enter into an agreement with one company rather than another. More specifically, why is it that Japanese and European firms more often choose to enter into agreements with an American firm rather than with a European or Japanese firm, respectively?

b. Partner Selection
<ins>Technological Expertise</ins>

In selecting a partner for a cooperative venture, firms have to identify the strengths of those who are potential candidates for an alliance. In terms of technological expertise, American companies' strength in innovation makes these firms attractive partners for cooperative alliances both to the Japanese and the Europeans.

The Japanese, for all their expertise in product perfection and in manufacturing, continue to lag in break-through technologies and are keen to link up with partners in the development of latest technology. Being large firms themselves, they suffer from well-established bureaucracies which slow them down in an industry which is fast moving and constantly changing. Smaller American firms, on the other hand, suffer from a lack of manufacturing and marketing resources, but provide an environment in which innovation flourishes.

A cooperative agreement between the two firms, if carefully managed, can plug the small firm into the large resources of the bigger partner and, thus, provide benefits for both. In such a case, the smaller firm becomes a "sub-innovator" similar to a subcontractor in other industries. European small firms are less prepared to take over such a role in a cooperation. They shy away from agreements with the Japanese and seem to be reluctant to share their technology with them.

Vice versa, the Japanese do not demonstrate enthusiasm for European technological know-how either and have not pursued agreements with small European firms. Present agreements with large European firms do not seem to have been contracted in order to access their technology but rather their marketing network.

As for the Europeans, they have recently become aware of their weaknesses in the R&D area and are striving to regain earlier strengths. Cooperative agreements with the Americans are seen as an excellent way of initiating this process as the technologies which are transferred can rapidly put them on an equal footing vis-a-vis the rest of the industry.

Now here documented, but well understood, is that the Europeans perceive the Japanese as being less willing to share information or resources with alliance partners than the Americans. The Japanese are takers or absorbers of information whereas the Americans are sharers or just plain talkative.

The Americans themselves are also anxious to gain access to new technologies and appear ready to try a number of sources. On an individual basis, European firms are often viable candidates for cooperative agreements, often because of their expertise in a particular area.

Recently, Americans' respect for Japanese technology has risen. The highly publicized "Japanese threat" in the US has probably served to fuel Americans' interest in the Japanese because it has focussed public attention on the extremely viable technological challenge that Japan is posing. This same Japanese challenge is little or less perceived by European firms operating in fragmented and more protected markets.

Manufacturing Expertise

The Japanese are today leading in manufacturing techniques and efficiency. For this reason, both the Americans and the Europeans are interested in learning more about Japanese manufacturing methods. The forming of cooperative agreements is one way of doing so - the Americans view such agreements as an excellent way of learning; the Europeans are more reluctant.

Instead, the Europeans are studying Japanese methods at arms' length. In the interim, the Europeans are "farming out" production to the Japanese in areas where European industry is uncompetitive. A strategic alliance for the purpose of learning about Japanese manufacturing methods is perhaps a last alternative and not a very appealing one. The Europeans are not so hungry for manufacturing knowledge that they are willing to share either market access or technological knowledge in return.

The Americans view Japanese manufacturing expertise with much more probing interest. It represents the first time in decades that a nation has bypassed American technological superiority on a grand scale. Perhaps this fact alone explains the near obsessive interest which many Americans have in this topic today.

There are volumes and volumes of literature on the US market on the Japanese success story, examining their methods from every angle. In addition, there are Japan tours for manufacturing executives; exchange programmes whereby American firms receive Japanese employees, and Japanese firms welcome American employees; or consultancy projects such as in the steel industry through which Japanese manufacturing expertise is transferred to the United States.

Last, but by no means least, cooperative ventures and strategic alliances have been formed in line with the proverb "If you can't beat them, join them". Unable to out-manufacture the Japanese, the Americans are now joining with the Japanese in order to learn directly from them in a cooperative environment. The NUMMI-project of GM and Toyota is a good example of such venture. The Americans are most anxious to learn what the Japanese have to teach them and are willing to exchange technological experience or market access for that information.

Market Access

The third major reason for which a company choses to enter into a cooperative agreement with another is to have access to new markets. These can consist of new market segments in an existing national market and/or of additional national markets, normally represented by the partner's home market or market strongholds. For the partner who receives products for sale in new markets, the agreement represents a horizontal integration in the sense that it enables it to offer a broader product line.

Both the Europeans and the Japanese are attracted by the American market. It is the world's largest borderless market and is homogenous in nature. There is also a perception that this market is in excellent economic health and will continue to grow for some years to come.

Some of the same could be said for the Japanese market and, indeed, many foreign firms have entered into cooperative agreements in order to have access to the Japanese market. Yet, when compared with the American market, the Japanese market is less appealing to most Europeans, despite the fact that in terms of economic buying power,

Japan is no longer behind the US and is ahead of many European countries in terms of GNP per capita. Part of this can be explained by the problems encountered by Western firms in the area of information technology in dealing with the Japanese language, and more specifically with the switch to the Japanese writing of Katakana and Hiragana and its final conversion into Kanji. This requires major efforts in software and hardware development and represents a formidable entry barrier surmountable only by fully committed firms.

The European market is attractive in size, but fragmented. In the information technology sector, the direct and indirect influence of national governments on purchasing decisions is strong, at least stronger than in the US. This requires a differentiated marketing strategy for each market, a difficult task for outsiders to master within a limited time. So far, Japanese subsidiaries in Europe have found it difficult to sell their own products under their own brand names, through their own distribution channels. Cooperative agreements have proven to offer a good solution to these structural barriers, particularly OEM agreements.

The Americans are also attracted by Europe, perhaps more so than the Japanese. They are looking to 1992 and the enhanced possibilities for American products in a standardized, unified European market. Markets in which American firms are not active today, can be accessed through already existing nationally based US subsidiaries.

4.2 Asymmetries in Partnerships
a. Competitive Cooperation

In part 2.1 it was briefly stated that international cooperative agreements are often concluded between competitors, a fact which renders the successful negotiation and management of such competitive cooperations, for both or all partners, extremely difficult.

Observations of alliances between competitors have so far shown that the incongruity of objectives of the partners, differences in competences contributed to the partnership, and the diverse ability to learn from another are important factors leading to failure.[7]

---

[7] Y. Doz, G. Hamel, C.K. Prahalad, "Strategic Partnerships: Success or Surrender? The Challenge of Competitive Collaborations", revised AIB Conference Paper, 1986/87.

Failure in this respect is defined as the premature break-up of the partnership, and/or the emergence of one partner as a clear winner over the other.

From this, one can conclude that competitive cooperation should ideally be based on very similar objectives, competences, and learning abilities. Such a situation, however, does not and will not exist. Competitors operate in different environments, and, thus, have their own individual strategic logic. They have different historical backgrounds, different strengths and weaknesses, and different corporate cultures. Even if all these characteristics could be the same at the time of the initial agreement, they would change over time and move into different directions.

Differences are, as such, not problematic. In fact, if partners would contribute precisely the same resources and competences, the cooperation would, at best, produce scale effects. Synergies, on the other hand, require complementary competences which are therefore much more attractive as a starting point of a cooperation. It is only when differences are considerable and structural, i.e. not related to a passing phenomenon, that they threaten the success of a partnership. The threat may come from one partner benefitting more from the joint undertaking than the other, or from a shift of negotiation power from one partner to the other.

Considerable and structural differences between partners which determine the outcome of a cooperative agreement we call asymmetries. Our research and discussions with executives in the IT-sector have shown the existence of a number of asymmetries between European and Japanese firms which are either explicit, implicit or based on different management systems.

b. Asymmetries
Explicit asymmetries

When partners in an alliance openly acknowledge that they are making a different kind of contribution to their undertakings or have a different status in the venture or different obligations, explicit asymmetries come into being. In the Euro-Japanese projects in the IT industry, such asymmetries are apparent when the Japanese partners are provided with access to the European market, while the European partner secures supplies from Japan on a long-term basis. Access to the Japanese market is seldom given or not demanded in exchange. The European partner benefits from cost savings or the broadening of its product range, while the Japanese partner expands its foreign markets without transferring manufacturing activities abroad. This enables it to accumulate manufacturing experience, a process which generally leads to lower production costs and a strengthening of the overall competitive position of the Japanese partner. The European partner, on the other hand, works on the last parts of the value-added chain, i.e. marketing and sales, and eventually on system integration for the specific product or product range. It is doubtful that this activity can fertilize other parts of the firm in such a way that the partner's overall competitive position is strengthened.

Even if such cross-fertilization is achieved, the long-term benefits for the European partner from selling Japanese equipment are questionable. If it is very successful in penetrating the market, the Japanese partner will sooner or later decide to go it alone and set up a distribution network based on the reputation gained with the help of the European partner. Such a development is neither new, surprising or unique to Europe or Japan. It touches on the very nature of distribution agreements between firms and does not merit the comparison with the Trojan horse so often depicted by Western politicians and writers.[8]

The more products are sold under direct or indirect OEM agreements in such scenarios, the more feasible it becomes to switch to own marketing strategies under one's own name, and the less the Japanese producer depends on his European distributor. On the other hand, by gaining more manufacturing expertise, the Japanese partner will not only be able to reduce his cost and improve the quality, but it will be increasingly capable of developing related new products which attract the European partner to purchase even more from Japan. It will thus transfer more manufacturing activity to Japan and become even more dependent on the Japanese supplier. This ever-expanding asymmetry, called "an extended dance of death"[9] is inherent in all market based cooperative agreements aimed at the European market. It provides an in-built threat to the European partners in all of those alliances and, as such, a risk in the relationship between Europe and Japan.

---

[8] See for example: R.B. Reich and D.D. Mankin, "Joint ventures with Japan give away our future", Harvard Business Review, March/April 1986, p. 78- 83.
also: Barrie G. James, "Trojan Horse: The Ultimate Japanese Challenge to Western Industry", Mercury Books, London 1989.

[9] See again R.B. Reich and D.D. Mankin p. 85.

K. Ohmae's concept of the "Triad Powers"[10] requires future global competitors to be present in Japan, Europe and the USA. In obtaining access to Europe and the US without getting access to the Japanese market even through alliances, European and American competitors are reduced to regional players, with the only global players being the Japanese. Such a development may not be inevitable. European firms, however, have not been successful in demanding reciprocity, a term now frequently used in trade talks and reflecting today's perceived need to obtain market access through political pressure rather than, or in addition to, negotiations at the firm level.

Implicit asymmetries

Implicit asymmetries are not written in cooperative agreements, but provide the motivation for the firms to associate. They are based on the firms' strategic intent or vision, and are rarely openly spelled out. Even if an interpretation appears to be easy, due to an obvious strategic intent, the existence of a "hidden agenda" cannot be ruled out. As interviews show, the purpose of strategic alliances is differently assessed by the partner firms concerned, and even by individual managers working together for either one or the other firm.

The explicit asymmetries of market access versus manufacturing expertise described above have lead to the assumption that Japanese partners use cooperative agreements as a way to expand and to reach global leadership, while European partners see them as a rescue anchor to stem decline.[11]

Such an interpretation seems justified since, in most markets, Japanese firms are fast growing latecomers who are taking market share from long-established moderately growing or stagnating European (or American) competitors. The example most frequently cited in this context is that of the alliance between British Leyland/Rover and Honda.

European executives in information technology, however, do not agree to the existence of such implicit asymmetry. While acknowledging the shift of key manufacturing activities to Japan and their own role as market access providers, they consider software and

---

[10] See part 3.3.

[11] See again Y. Doz et al.

system integration the key to their customers and do not mind their Japanese partners producing the hardware. The apparent weakness of the Japanese firms, at least abroad, in software, and the increase of software expenses versus hardware in total IT-costs reassures them of not being "hollowed-out" by their Japanese partners. In arguing this way, they assume that the Japanese will not be able to overcome their software problems in the foreseeable future and thus, will not be able to erode their European customer base. Different business cultures and language difficulties are cited in support of this view.

It is probably for this last reason that Europeans do not feel misused by their Japanese partners as proxies in the global battle with IBM. Such an allegation can easily be put forward by believers in the "Japan Inc." concept who can point out that all major European computer firms are tied to Japanese partners and face IBM as their most important competitor in their national markets. With an overall market share of 50% in Europe, IBM has no need to cooperate with European companies, either in the hardware, or in the software area. The European firms, on the other hand, believe in their marketing strength and their software competences. They look for partners in need of or depending on those strengths and providing other expertise such as in manufacturing. Following this logic, Euro-Japanese alliance should provide an ideal "strategic fit".

Two questions, however, remain for the future. One is the impact of the wider usage of standardized software systems such as UNIX on the industry which so far has extensively used firm specific software as a way of differentiation and as entry barriers for competitors into the territory of existing customers. Even a partial lowering of these entry barriers may re-emphasize the value of hardware as the most important competitive weapon. Secondly, the importance of chip technology for both the computer and the telecommunication sector must be considered with regard to the continuing trend towards higher integration, to the opportunities to transfer software onto chips, and to compensate software weaknesses with greater hardware power.

Managerial asymmetries

Managerial attitudes, systems or cultures are formed by the environment in which an organization operates as well as by individuals or groups of individuals. They are implicit, and influence managers' decisions substantially, often unconsciously. If one looks at firms in groups such as the Japanese IT-firms and the European IT-firms, the influence of individuals can be neglected and the impact of national culture on managerial behaviour can be studied.

Much has been written on Japanese management, and despite many contradictions and exceptions to the rule, there is an acknowledgement of certain differences in managerial culture between Japan and the West, the latter often mistakenly identified as American management. A European managerial culture as such does not exist, as the behaviour of managers differs significantly from country to country, or at least between those from the Northern and the Latin countries.

The assessment of managerial asymmetries between Europe and Japan therefore cannot be very specific and must contain generalizations, but it may nevertheless provide us with valuable insights into the "inner workings" of Euro-Japanese strategic alliances.

One of the striking features of Japanese management is the role of information as a strategic resource. It puts emphasis on collecting diffusing and analyzing information systematically. Information in Japan is shared internally and is a property of the organization. Information in European firms is often obtained by chance, not diffused, and used to strengthen the position of the individual in the organization. Related to this is the inherent Japanese urge to learn continuously from others which has no equivalent, neither in the US nor in Europe.

Both aspects are vital for cooperative undertakings between European and Japanese firms. If in an alliance, new knowledge is emerging or existing knowledge made available to the partners, and only the Japanese side is interested in collecting and diffusing it, the benefit for this partner will invariably be much greater.

This process is aggravated by the fact that Japanese firms have not much hesitation to adapt foreign know-how while in European firms the "not invented here" syndrome often leads to the rejection of new ideas from the outside and, as a consequence, to unnecessary delays and/or development costs.

This asymmetry in fertilizing or leveraging other activities of the firms provides the partners in an alliance with very different benefits and can lead - over the life of a joint undertaking - to significant shifts in competitive position, even if the direct benefits from the alliance are equally divided between the partners.

The long-term approach to business is another characteristic of the Japanese firm, often contrasted with the short-term outlook of Western firms geared towards quarterly or yearly results. This is an area where European firms certainly differ from American ones, and are to some extent, more similar to their Japanese partners. Asymmetries exist nevertheless. Constant organizational learning in the Japanese firms combined with a strong strategic intent to expand globally have resulted in an endless process of new product developments, matched by the European partners neither in volume, depth nor speed. It is especially the latter aspect which seems to be important in the fast changing information technology sector which requires from competitors today economies of scale, of scope, and of speed.

c. Management and Perceptions

Marketing/manufacturing based strategic alliances between Europe and Japanese IT-firms show a greater degree of asymmetry mainly due to explicit arrangements. This would argue in favour of joint R&D based cooperative agreements.

These joint undertakings, however, tend to create more problems in defining common ground and destination than the other ones. New developments by definition lead into uncharted waters. The targeted output is difficult to specify, as is the required input of resources and time.

Projects of this nature are ambiguous, and require constant adjustment to meet the needs of the partners and the task, as well as to the changing environment. The Japanese are known to be able to cope well with uncertainty and to react with flexibility. Not all European firms have this capacity.

The management of alliances requires full attention and the will for constant bargaining and re-bargaining with one's partner. Under these circumstances, excellent managers are needed on both sides to steer the partnership through the complexities of inherent instability.

The outcome of a cooperative agreement may be judged by comparing costs and benefits, but can rarely be accurately measured due to the multifaceted character of the projects. Perceptions of the outcome therefore vary from person to person, especially when taking into account the effects of organizational learning and the leveraging of benefits through the organizations of the respective partners. This is naturally a subjective process made more difficult by the fact that benefits may not only be perceived in absolute but also in relative terms, i.e. in comparing one's own benefits with those obtained by the partner.[12]

European managers interviewed somehow admit that their Japanese partners benefit more from cooperative ventures than their own firms. Reasons given are mostly emotional and range from accusations of unfair practices by their Japanese partners to the admittance of their own failure in managing these complex relationships. The latter perception is more frequently found among managers directly involved in partnerships with Japanese firms. The Japanese managers who were interviewed were less open in their judgement, but showed general disappointment and tended to belittle the competences of the European partners.

This provides a dangerous breeding ground for using outside pressures and unfair practices to strengthen the bargaining power within the partnership.

---

[12] Y. Doz and A. Shuen, "From Intent to Outcome: A Process Framework of Partnerships", INSEAD Working Paper, n° 88/46.

EXPERIENCES OF A JOINT VENTURE
(ENDRESS + HAUSER / SAKURA)

Klaus Riemenschneider
Endress + Hauser (International) Holding AG, Reinach

Ladies and Gentlemen,

I am very happy to have the opportunity to contribute as a representative of the industry to this conference. Although I was warned by the organizers of the congress not to mis-use my time for publicity purposes, I can't avoid to introduce the company and our Japanese partners not only with words but also using some transparencies. I really believe that this is necessary to understand my conclusions and reasonings much better.

Endress + Hauser has become an established name in industrial measuring technology in the course of 30 years. From a small South German business specializing in electronic level measuring instruments, it has grown into a homogeneous group of companies with manufacturing sites in Germany, Switzerland, Italy, United States and Japan, assembly units in UK, Korea and India and as well a worldwide sales and service network through 18 company-owned sales outlets.

Even though level measuring technology continues to be an essential part of our business, flow, moisture and throughput measuring instruments, measuring systems for water analysis, as well as recording instruments and systems are increasing in importance.

The question of what has led to the extraordinary success of this family of companies can be answered as follows:

The Endress + Hauser group offers practical solutions to a large variety of industry branches, aims at being an innovator and is very quality conscious.

For those of you that need some statistical data, I want to mention, that we are wholly family owned, that we employ worldwide 3000 people, more than 30 % of our staff are graduated engineers/technicians and we achieved a turnover of approx. US $ 250 Mio.

We are a truly cosmopolitan company. Our shareholders are Swiss, we concentrate a major part of our activities in the center of Europe, near Basle, where the Rhine river makes a sharp turn, an area whose importance had already been recognized by the Romans and which has under the visions of 1992 not lost its appeal.

Let me now explain you the industry branch that we are in. This branch is called internationally the M+C-industry, which means measurement and control of industrial processes. It is an industry that is a small part within the Electronics Industry (approx. 10 %) and is a truly internationally operating industry. European, American and Japanese companies compete heavily and keep market shares in each other's territory. The fact that such control instruments are used in any industry and since all developed countries have to look for automation and security for their employees and the environment, technology, enginuity and quality are the determining factors for a buying decision of the customer.

Control products go as parts into all kind of industrial machinery, into petroleum and aerospace industries, into electric, gas and sanitary industries, into rubber and plastics, into paper, food, chemical and into the primary industries as mining, cement etc. Process control manufacturers are typical medium sized firms highly specialized or part of larger electrical companies operating world wide (i.e. Siemens, Toshiba, Fuji, ABB, Honeywell etc.). The biggest company worldwide has sales of less than 1 Bio US $.

The industry uses for its products typical "high-tech-technologies" for the sensing side and for the amplification and transmission of the signals. Latest electronic semiconductor technologies as well as physical or chemical research results keep the industry busy to develop permanently new products to improve our life quality.

Endress + Hauser has therefore adopted a theory that all three key market-areas, Europe, United States and Japan, have to contribute to allow manufacturing of products, that can be applied to an utmost extent in a global marketing concept. However, we are still far away from this dream, since there are dozens of tariff and non-tariff barriers in the way. Don't get me wrong, those do not just exist between for instance Germany and Japan, they even exist between Switzerland and Germany or in some instances even within Germany.

To overcome such problems, we started already as a very small company in the early 70's to look for a partner in the Far East. We had at this moment approx. 300 employees and as a rapidly growing company very little cash to buy us into the Japanese market. In those days the Japanese electronic industry was still closed to foreign ownership above 30 % and we therefore looked for some minority in terest. We were dealing through one of the Shosha Trading companies, that was handling our export business from Europe. As you all know, those Shoshas handle all products from French wine to aeroplanes and it was always for us a secret, how they were able to sell such sophisticated instruments that need in-depth application know-how not only of the instrument itself, but also of the customers "cooking process". I don't want to talk about the role of "Shoshas" in Japane's industry, but from several years of experience with such companies, I believe that they have really made a big contribution to the miracle of the Japanese industry since World War II.

This Shosha, handling our products together with German beer, approached us one day and brought us together with a small Japanese manufacturer of precision-mechanical measuring devices for the petrochemical-industry. This company faced severe problems because of a monoculture of products. They were looking for diversification and we were looking for a partner that had the potential to trade our products more efficiently than the trading-house.

After long negotiations over approx. 1 year, we succeeded to give them a license to manufacture and sell a part of our product range for the Japanese market. We didn't ask for a great amount of cash for the patent rights, but we asked for a shareholding in the company. This naturally was also in their interest, since the financial situation of the company was, as many small Japanese companies in those days and still today, not very rosy. We were once of a sudden in 1971 a shareholder with an equity interest of 25 %.

Starting with that date, we travelled each year approx. two to three times to Japan and we trained every year 5 - 6 Japanese technicians in our European factories. As a minority shareholder we had basically not much to say and we really were always frustrated, when we attended a shareholder meeting in Tokyo, where we didn't understand the proceedings and admired the unbelievable consensus.

Our products made very little progress and we started to be very inpatient. The results of the company were very disappointing and we thought several times about selling the shares. We were, however, scared to do so, because we felt that we had transferred already too much technology and that we would have educated a competitor. We therefore decided to express to our partners our interest to gain control over the company or to desinvest completely.

When our partners realized our increased interest, they presented suddenly two consecutive years of losses. We were told that a Japanese competitor in their traditional business was actively trying to eliminate our shareholding company by dumping prices on the domestic Japanese market. They were distributing order forms to customers with the remark, please fill in your desired price.

At the same time, we experienced, that the company was increasing its staff with several elder gentlemen with excellent records and coming from leading positions of well-known Japanese companies.

We were told by our partners, that those new managers would have the necessary business contacts to the industry to quickly improve.

The results of the company, however, got worse and worse and we were really surprised how loyal the Japanese banks and the company's suppliers were and how they continued to support such an unsuccessful operation.

The company was really in a dead-lock and additionally the employees went on strike because the bonus couldn't be paid as the average of the companies in this particular area of Tokyo outskirts. Now, the situation was completely hopeless to us;

- bad products with very low margins in a monoculture and a competitor trying to kill our partner
- little progress to adopt and penetrate into the license technology that we provided
- a sales net that was dependent of Shoshas
- an age structure among the employees to exceed 42 years
- a fixed salary structure with no flexibility to be changed
- unhappy employees because of low bonus payments, strikes and once of a sudden the decision among them to form a closed shop

- a management that was backed-up by obviously very well reputated gentlemen in three positions (production, maketing and R&D)
- a terrible banking situation, roll-over credits as long-term financing and payment-- terms to key customers of more than 5 months
- the impossibility to find fresh people on the Japanese labor market to build up a sound sales net and to form needed product management
- a majority shareholder in SAKURA (listed at the Tokyo market) that was under those circumstances still looking for the distribution of dividends to keep face towards its own shareholders
- a manufacturing facility in a sunshine-area, where expasions or modifications were very difficult to be approved by the authorities
- a 600 zubo piece of land that was just rented and that we always considered to be company owned and that was due for contract renewal with the landlord for another 30 year's period
- a president of our partner company that was enthroned by his father as his successor, without having the recognition of the employees
- a natural hesitation and resistance towards foreign owners and influence among company employees.

Those were some of the problem areas that we faced in 1979, when we decided to attack them with a typical Japanese concept: patience and doing everything step-by-step embeded in a long term strategical plan.

We had to go through a terrible time and we were very often inclined to give up.

Let me try to work out some of the findings and experiences over those years to stress a little bit the cultural differences and the problems to understand each other because of fundamental misunderstandings. I have tried to put our experiences in some general context and where ever possible, into general remarks. I have chosen some topics that I felt do be of importance and that are worthwile to be passed on to others that still want to take the challenge.

The Role of a Trading House

For any foreign company planning to sign up a sales agent to market its products, it is an alternative to entrust this function to one of Japan's major sogo shoshas, the giant trading companies that per form an extraordinary range of business functions including the financing of distributors. Today, the most famous ones as Mitsui, Mitsubishi, Sumitomo etc. have changed already their basic character and they operate as manufacturers with hundreds of subsidiary companies within their empire. And additionally, today they often turn out to be already handling products competitive with those of a new-comer to the Japanese market. Increasingly, therefore foreign companies must turn to other channels.

Lining up a sales agent, no matter how prestigious, does not, of course, guarantee success in the Japanese market.

Many negative examples in the recent years indicate, that it is still today a much easier approach to the market if it can be done with the initial help of a sogo shoshas. The direct way is much more difficult and costly. The sogo shoshas still can provide a conduit for foreigners into the market. Today, there are about 8000 mostly one-room trading companies in Japan but 60 % of its imports pass through the hands of the nine biggest ones. They have 1100 offices overseas.

The Entry by Technical Licensing and Know-How Transfer

This method to enter the Japanese market is naturally not that easy anymore. The Japanese industry has today reached a technology, that is totally comparable and even in many industries superior to that of Western enterprises. The desirability of joint ventures has increasingly come under challenge. Japanese companies are by no means as enthusiastic about this concept as they once were. Today they are inclined to say: "We don't need your technology any longer. Or at least we don't need to pay so high a price for it."

Joint venture companies between foreign and Japanese partners were the rule in the past and there were very few wholly owned foreign enterprises in Japan. Most of them were entirely the product of historical accident.

In general one can say, that the form of joint ventures posed problems and many of the most successful joint ventures have been dissolved in the last few years. The joint venture era has come to an end.

Historically it was an ideal form of an investment. Not only government restrictions were the reason why this form became the most common pattern.

In many industries the joint venture turned to be the best solution to overcome distribution problems. A foreign company entering the market can't get a competitive cost position against established competitors. The new-comer has traditionally a narrow product line and cannot spread the costs over a full line. Even the big companies like Coca Cola, Nestlé, Nabisco, Del Monte and many others had to experience this fact. They had to use established Japanese food companies' distribution systems.

There are naturally other factors that contribute to the fact, that the joint venture approach is drawing to a close. The joint venture is an awkward compromise of conflicting interests. It is harder to satisfy two or more masters than it is to satisfy just one. The problem of conflict of interest between partners is more severe, as it is usually the case, when the partners are in the same industry or even in the same business within our industry. Not surprisingly, but very obvious both partners try to benefit from each other and each one is looking to gain the experience and the position of the partner that has been established already. Unfortunately, this also means that if the venture expands and if the partnership expands into world markets, the parties of the venture come into conflict with each other.

Although this needs not to be the case, there are very few ventures in the industry that we are working in, in that did overcome those obvious problems. In our industry there is a very clear tendency of companies that once were very open to discussions of possible joint ventures, have as a matter of policy decided against entering into new ones.

In the electronic industry there were quite a few break-up cases of ventures in the last years. However, those separations appear in all cases to have suited the purposes of both partners and the clarification of clear ownership has cleaned the air. In the electronic industry, in contrast to the more traditional industries and despite the fact that this sector is considered to be of primary interest to the Japanese government as strategic industry, it is more penetrated by foreign investment and ownership. The list of wholly owned or majority-owned foreign operations in electronics in Japan is a long one.

The Japanese "Bullying" System of Senior Employees

Another operational problem that makes the joint venture solution difficult, is the personnel issue. It is simply not possible to recruit first-class experienced managers from the open labor market in Japan. It is already difficult for a foreign firm to recruit youngsters to fill lower ranks, but it is almost impossible to find factory managers, sales managers and other senior personnel to manage such a Japanese operation. The Japanese joint venture partner is therefore considered to be a source of supply of key personnel.

This solution is full of hazards and frequently a matter of disputes in a joint venture. Usually the Japanese partner discharges its less able staff because of its system of permanent employment and may take the occasion to send some of them off into the venture, allowing the foreign partner to share those costs of incompetence. Such personnel inherited from the Japanese partner will always remain a follower of the Japanese partner and never become a supporter of the venture. Frequently those "borrowed" people are managers, that are affected by what is considered a part of the Japanese retirement system. At a certain age they are driven out of positions where they have gained a lifetime of experience. In recent years, Japanese courts had several times to decide, whether the common practice of early "retirement" of managers at the age of 55 or drastic salary cuts of up to 60 percent, by using them in lower ranked positions or in smaller subsidiary companies, are legal or not. No standard opinion has been formed yet. Companies try to drive out middle-age and elderly employees to give younger people the opportunity for promotion. Although the official retirement age has been extended to 60, it is almost unusual to reach this age in the position that the individual had before. The instances of transferring senior employees to subsidiaries and related companies are still increasing and the age of those being transferred is getting younger. Companies are even saving personnel expenses by sending employees at subsidiaries back to the head office at the same salaries that they were making at the lower paying branches. Bullying of senior employees is in today's Japanese environment a serious problem.

Although I am going to mention life time employment several times in my paper and although I am aware that it is sometimes overstated, I am certain, that this fact has a great influence with big consequences over the entire Japanese economy. The Japanese system is build on growth and also the employment situation can just be managed if growth is achieved.

There is very little statistical data available, how many Japanese employees have a life time employment guarantee. However, in order for older employees to keep rising in hierarchy, there must be a constant inflow of younger staff. This is naturally only possible by permanent expansion and this is again a reason why Japanese companies jump much quicker on new products, inventions, into new areas as Western companies. This also relates to overseas ventures. The life time employment has obviously advantages for exporting, because an employee will not hesitate to accept an overseas assignment that might even be beneficial to his career.

The system also gives management a completely different horizon. Since they will be with the company for at least 35 years, they plan ahead and do the necessary long-term decisions. They recruit personnel which may not be needed immediately, but may be necessary for future projects to go into effect. Although this might be costly, Japanese companies live with this fact and this might be a reason for a relative disconcern about profits. This policy could never be exercised in our world, since our managers are judged on much shorter cycles i.e. annually or even quarterly and contracts with top managers are usually term contracts by intention.

To close the circle of my arguments, I also tend to justify the Japanese eagerness towards manufacturing with the before-mentioned reasons.

The search for market share is a result of the Japanese conclusion, that attainment of economies of scale is another factor of permanent growth badly needed by all Japanese companies. One more reason for the superiority of Japanese companies lies in mass production products. Only in those areas investments can be justified where large scale sales are attained.

In industries where small quantities or customer-tailored products are the determining factor, Japanese industry has very little advantage over their competition in the West.

Japanese companies are graded by prestige and respect, which are related to size, number of personnel, amount of assets, turnover and especially market share. Companies permanently fight to be among the top ranking companies in their market environment.

The Importance of Quality and Service - The Behaviour of a Japanese Customer

Japanese customers are the toughest and most quality-conscious in the world. This statement I could underline. Any foreign company has underestimated this fact and had to learn, that Japanese standards are high.

Western companies try to brush Japanese complaints about Western quality away, but I think that we must admit openly, that the average Japanese industry product is better. Even the least expensive product needs a certain perfection to be sellable in the Japanese market. You all know the zero-defect-attitude of Nippon manufacturing companies. Total quality control, quality circles etc. are Japanese intentions or practices.

A Japanese product must be perfect, all the way through packaging. Japanese are obsessed not only with product quality but also the way the product is packaged. The aesthetic style and manner of presentation characterizes the product as well.

But not only the packaging will ensure or increase commercial success in Japan. Far more than Americans or Europeans, Japanese are also very demanding in good service. This starts with prompt delivery and the accuracy of papers. Japanese can be very bureaucratic and stubborn. The rigid insistence on keeping to precise schedules of delivery is very often neglected by Western companies. Japanese customers are used to precise planning of domestic companies and don't give any credit to the foreign enterprise.

Some foreign companies have realized this fact and give the Japanese market special attention. I know a German car manufacturer that provides in Tokyo a spare parts service that they don't have in Germany.

Japanese companies are also very flexible in providing warranties. They are very generous and use the provisions of warranty periods very flexibly. It is therefore advisable to investigate what is more effective: To compete on the basis of an outstanding service or on lower cost to the customer. Japanese prices must therefore cover a lot of things, that need additional compensation.

The Japanese customer is in general willing to pay for those additional standards that he requires. Most of the markets are less price sensitive than in the Western world. Although one has to differentiate between products, this remark is valid for quality articles. Only in day-to-day consumption articles, the Japanese looks for the cheapest. Another very important demand of a Japanese customer is price stability. Constant price increases, as common in the Western world, are just impossible to enforce in the Japanese market. Prices must be justified to the customer in a degree of detail that is completely unknown in the West.

It is not unusual in investment goods to remain prices unchanged for a period of 5 - 6 years.

The Policy of Banks

The typical Japanese company has a profitability that is far below its Western counterparts and still has the creditability from its banks. Something that we just don't understand. There are fundamental differences in policies between Western and Japanese firms. Japanese companies are happy with a return on sales of 1 % after tax, whereas Western corporations reach about 5 %. Although recent surveys have indicated that the gap is no longer appropriate, I can tell you that it is the case in the industry we are in.

Additionally Japanese companies accept a much higher debt ratio than Western firms. The traditional lower cost of capital of the Japanese companies provides them a little advantage. This is used by the Japanese industry and in 1984 for the first time since the invention of the transistor, the total capital investment into the semiconductor field in Japan surpassed that of the United States. This caused concern to the US industry, since this gap will furthermore increase in the next years.

From my own experience in corporate financing I know, that Japanese banks really accept debt ratios where a Western bank would ring the bell.

The financial policy of Japanese banks is very difficult to under stand. Western balance sheet criterias would exclude lending money, when Japanese banks start to negotiate. I don't want to enter into the discussion how Western and Japanese balance sheets might compare. However, Japanese companies have very close relationships with their banks and financial institutions. Such relationships are frequently underlined by a shareholding of the bank in the customer company. Time deposits, compensating balances etc. are means of satisfying the banks. Even small Japanese companies have at least three banks where they deal permanently with. This policy usually exerts unnecessary influence of one particular bank on the corporation.

Japanese banks permanently shift and refinance long and short-term money. For a Western management sometimes not very transparent, but common practice.

The Japanese Company as a Competitor

When I talked earlier about our problems with a domestic competitor that had the intention to kill us, I must remind you that there are numerous examples in the Japanese industry for such a behaviour. Just several years ago, we all experienced a dramatic fight in the motor-cycle industry between Honda and Yamaha. The result was, that Yamaha suffered enormous losses and had to dismiss people from the payroll.

To avoid bankruptcy, the company had to dispose assets and finally surrendered in 1983.

It was a long-term well prepared plan by Honda. Honda won this battle because two thirds of its sales came from other activities, which continued to prosper in those days whereas Yamaha's growth potential was heavily on motor-cycles.

This aggressive pricing policy even with suffering tremendous losses is a part of the Japanese market environment. Japanese companies look for growth and are made to meet real competitive threats rather than abstract financial criteria.

The Japanese Finance System - Accounts Receivable

Small Japanese companies need to finance their accounts receivable, since the average payment period of a customer easily exceeds 150 days. One reason for these unbelievable delays are the long distribution channels. This again is a reason why smaller companies can't sell direct and have to use agents or trading companies. Note payables (drafts) are in today's Japanese economy the most popular means of payment.

It is therefore very obvious, that Japanese investment goods prices include an interest percentage that usually compensates for 6 months delay. In our Japanese company the majority of customers pay with 2 months after shipment with a 120 days note.

This Japanese business practice might be one of the reasons, why the corporations really like the export business when they get cash payment against documents.

I have stated once in a discussion, that I got the feeling that Japanese companies need the export business for liquidity and the domestic business for profitability.

The Myths and Misunderstandings in Japanese Shareholdings

How powerful is the Japanese shareholder? A question that is justified after knowing the aggressive pricing and low profit situation of Japanese corporations. High rates of profit retention, liberal use of debt ratios to fund growth and special banking relationships do additionally weaken the position of the average Japanese shareholder.

In contrary to the Western world, Japanese companies pay dividends to reassure shareholders that the company is healthy. The common practice calls for a dividend of approx. 10 % of the par value stock. All Japanese companies try to pay this and will even borrow or sell assets to do so because missing this payment is just not possible. If a company fails to do this, it will lose face and its creditability. Japanese shareholders have a right to a dividend. Beyond this, they have very few rights. The management of a Japanese company is usually much more free than in the Western world.

Aggressive pricing, high profit retention, low dividends and aggressive use of debt are the mechanisms of Japane's industry to grow faster. The welfare of employees, shareholders and the management is improved by continuous growth.

Small non-institutional shareholders are overshadowed by big shareholders, usually banks and insurance companies, trading partners of the company, customers and suppliers, whose interest in the company is not principally that of shareholders but of business associates. The amount of small shareholdings of suppliers and customers, even very often competitors is in comparison to the Western world remarkable. Japanese shareholders therefore invest as a means to doing business with companies.

We all know the theory about the six large combines known as Zaibatsu. Today they are mostly loose alliances in which member companies co-operate only to a limited extent and there is scarcely an attempt at central direction.

Although I don't want to underestimate their importance in the over all Japanese economy, I think that it is just not a correct judgement to say: They form "Japan Incorporated".

The Japanese market place is very competitive, although one might be able to trace a big portion of the industry belonging to the big Zaibatsus.

The Role of Company Unions in a Small Company

Japan has a rate of organization of close to 40 % and with this exceeding the rate in the US and comparing with Germany. Peculiar to the Japanese situation is the dispersion of this power among thirty thousand separate union organizations. More than 90 % of Japan's organized workers are so called members of enterprise unions. Unions compared to the Western concept of crafts or industries are rare exceptions.

Enterprise unions have distinctive characteristics, i.e. only regular employees can be members. Management members are excluded, blue and white collar employees form one organization. In Japanese unions the idea and practice of separate bargaining is not existent. The practice of decision making through majority vote is coupled with the concept of egalitarianism. Union officers are elected from the employee list of the enterprise. Professional union leaders are therefore almost not existent in Japan.

It is needless to say, the system for decision-making in Japanese company unions includes much administrative inefficiency. The process is excessive and time-consuming. I have experienced such bar gaining sessions and I must admit, that I got impatient and irritated. The more urgent and important a problem is, the more likely the negotiators are to postpone discussions in order to consult with their Union committee.

A considerable part of the manpower, time and energy of Japanese unions is spent planning, preparing and recording the countless meetings required to produce policy decisions. However, I was always told that this is essential for maintaining solidarity. The spring wage offensive of last year was a very complicated one in our company. This is the time when the leadership capabilities of the top management are displayed. A leader's intuition, analytical skill and judgement become crucial; he must assess such factors as mood surrounding the negotiations, the relative bargaining power of the union, the ability of the union to follow a long strike etc. It is beyond description how long it takes and how formal those sessions can be. Such campaigns can easily last 3 weeks.

However, despite those inefficiencies, the Japanese union movement has been very successful. Union membership has permanently increased, wages have risen at a speed superior to those in Western industrial nations. Job security has increased along with an overall improvement in working hours and conditions. Hence, the Japanese movement has been a huge success.

We have a closed shop in our company and it is therefore very complicated to do anything without the consensus of the unions. In comparison to the German participation laws, it is more difficult to deal with a Japanese union's committee.

Non-Tariff Barriers

There is almost every day a complaint in the European or American press about hidden barriers for foreigners. If we are honest, we must admit that there are also within Europe thousands of hidden barriers and we have just recently experienced, that the European Community has given up the illusion of harmonization.

I can report about some obstacles in my industry, but they are in reality not any bigger than those within Europe or United States. We don't have any problems with Japanese customs. Product approvals and testing sometimes cause complicated procedures, but again in general are reasonable. One basic difference we have experienced, regulations are occasionally unclear, don't exist in writing and tend to change frequently.

Japanese authorities like the flexibility, which leads Japanese bureaucrats to give specific advise or just hints about what to do rather than laying the rules down in general words that are accessible to all.

Very often it is the Japanese attitude to handle things on a case-by-case basis in direct consultation with a particular party and little concern for a general solution.

The systematic prevention of imports, as it is often stated here in the West, is in my opinion not true and by no means reflecting the reality. There are naturally hundreds of fundamental differences that one has to understand, digest and accept. Many of those are just manifestations of another way of doing things.

Japanese Distribution System in the M+C Industry

This system, which is very often presented in articles as a major barrier to foreign entry into Japan, has less relationship to the customers we serve in the process instrument world. The multilayered distribution system is primarily associated with consumer products.

Japan is full of sales people and there are industries where there are ten times more salesmen per customer than in Western countries. The Japanese distribution world is also very competitive.

In our industry, we sell either direct to the end user or we sell through agents. However, those agents in Japan are very commercially orientated and normally have excellent relations to customers in a certain industry or in specific companies. They treat their customers much better than in the Western world, to obtain their loyalty which can often override the strictly business approach. Japanese customers are not only attracted by innovative products but also like personal relations.

The importance of entertainment and the permanent treatment by sales people are key elements of Japanese business. Unstable supply and changes of sales personnel are very often enemies No. 1 to successfully do business in Japan.

Those agents have usually no protection for a geographical area. There can be several of them covering a territory. Some of the business is done on a reselling basis and in those cases the agent is free to charge customers' prices at his discretion. He acts as a reseller and therefore also as a "bank" towards his manufacturing supplier. In other instances he might act as a manufacturer's representative as in the United States and receiving a commission.

Employed company salesmen are usually acting out of the company. Real field sales people as in the Western world are very seldom. A Japanese salesman wants to do his own quotations and doesn't want to leave any part of the job to be done to anybody besides himself, to satisfy his assigned customer a hundred percent. Sharing of responsibility in these aspects are unusual in an usually very much team orientated environment.

The employed sales people are remunerated on a fixed basis and it is still very uncommon to pay individual commissions, bonuses or incentives. The individual merit part rather than the strict seniority order is still a privilege of foreign-affiliated companies. Japanese companies are only slowly adopting Western practices.

In our own company we have experienced, that individual incentives were refused to accept or they were spend with their colleagues for entertainment purposes. It is against the Japanese spirit of team and it must therefore really be seriously considered if it is worthwhile to be introduced. The opposite effect can really happen.

Let me conclude that part as follows: There is no way of making offers by mail or simply by displaying goods. There is a need for repeated personal visits and a lot of patience. This may result in a sale or it may not. And it may take months before knowing it. Japaneses do not like the one shot deal and are looking for long relationships. They want suppliers who can be counted on indefinitely. Initially the margin with a particular customer may be tight but it is certain that this must not be the case forever. Those findings are clearly biased against any new-comer. No matter how much cheaper or better his goods are.

The Family Managed Japanese Company

Japanese companies are usually organized in the form of an incorporation. The cooperative system in business is the typical Japanese style. The anonymous company, by which it is meant that the company is named after the work it aims to carry on, or to use an artificial name creation, instead of having the names of persons involved in it, is the common practice. The relationship between the employer, the employee and related companies is that of a partnership, aiming co-existence and co-prosperity, to let all the members share profits as well as development as human beings. You all know how much the Japanese company interferes into the private affairs of their employees and on the other side how much the employee expects to be treated that way.

Life time employment and pay-by-age practices are certainly more characteristics of larger firms. Smaller firms are usually not sound enough to do this. A company which offers security of tenure and a promise of automatic salary increases to its employees makes a considerable commitment for a very long period. You practically can never cut back your work forces. Large companies usually employ numbers of temporary workers, which lack the security and can be dismissed when times are hard. A second way in which large firms can adjust is by curtailing orders to the small firms which act as subcontractors to it. These small firms have no alternative but to lay off or dismiss their workers. Big firms are stable and their workers enjoy security partly because small firms are weak and their workers' positions unsafe.

When we entered into our venture company, the company had another shareholder having approx. 40 % of voting power. This stock market listed company was run by the founder family, having shares of approx. 15 % in both, the mother and the daughter company. Our joint venture company was run by a son of the owner family. This sounded all logical to us and we were very happy that such a family with recognition and influence was our partner. However, it took us several years to realize the fact, that a Japanese family-run company has many disadvantages.

Private companies or founder family managed companies are in Japan a part of the entire system. They cannot act differently than their bigger competitors. Their founders are often more forced into expansion than the relatively bureaucratic companies of larger size. The individualistic inventor-entrepreneur does practically not exist anymore in Japan. Family run companies must act as all other members of the economy. They can't look for optimization of profits because the traditional roots in culture, since recognition of an individual is much more based on other elements than money, which in Japanese fundamental thinking is only a result of vulgar merchandising.

Conclusion

We are now since almost 10 years majority shareholder (90 %) of a formerly totally Japanese style family-managed small company in the Tokyo area.

Today, we employ 260 people and we achieve annual sales of US $ 26 Mio. We are profitable and presently in an investment plan execution not only to build a new sales headquarter near Shinjuku, where a square meter of land costs US $ 8000, but also into a manufacturing facility in the Yamanashi district on a piece of land of 8000 m^2 of surface. It was a long way to gain all the experiences that I have mentioned in my paper before. The Japanese market is a dynamic economy, that nobody can neglect. The basic conditions of this country are ideal, although the Japanese economy is a very strange mixture between a planned, almost socialistic system, and the liberal economy that we are used to.

Many managers of foreign companies in Japan have warned their country fellows not to try it at all or to come with a long-term commitment, with a lot of money to invest into the market first. Hundreds of new Western firms came in the last years as an annual average, however, after three or few years more than half withdrew in costly frustration.

A new-comer must learn everything about Japan before he comes, the homework has to be done first. Business in Japan differs in a number of highly important respects from doing business in other parts of the world. Acceptance of this fact, even if it is sometimes difficult to swallow, is the key to prosper in this difficult market.

By looking backwards, I must say that we would do it again, but certainly differently. The success of the Japanese economy and the continuing strength of Japanese companies in the world prove, that the Japanese methods are by no means inferior to what we apply in the Western world. Japanese companies are well managed and deserve to be studied. We should start to recognize this fact. Japanese corporations' success can only be assessed, if one understands the total system. The Japanese Kaisha is a product of the economy and their effectiveness is controlled by the effectiveness of the economy as a whole.

Today, Japanese companies are setting the standards in worldwide competition, costwise, technologywise, qualitywise etc.

Isn't it a shame that the organizers of this conference had really difficulties to find European companies that were willing to talk about their experiences in a venture in Japan?

My paper was aimed to be a contribution to the inevitably arising questions of any multinational European company, if it has to go to Japan one day.

I personally have witnessed in those years since our entry into SAKURA in Japan, that there was more economic growth and the creation of wealth than the world has ever seen anywhere else or before. The Japanese market is a challenge!

SCENARIOS OF 1992 AND CONSEQUENCES FOR EURO-JAPANESE RELATIONSHIP

Jürgen Müller
German Institute for Economic Research (DIW), Berlin
and INSEAD, Fontainebleau

1. Introduction

Even though the European Community (EC) has been formed in 1958 and its economic integration has progressed steadily since, the concept of achieving a more or less unified single market by 1992 has created an additional impetus for further integration. The major emphasis of the policies aimed at completing the single European Market by 1992 rests on the removal of the Community's remaining internal market barriers. But the link of this policy to external trade is obvious. The more the Community moves towards becoming a cohesive economic block, the greater is its ability to behave in a consistent unified manner vis-à-vis the outside world. Some have therefore expressed the fear, that the realization of a unified single market may lead to further external barriers in line with the "Fortress Europe" concept.

In this paper these tendencies will be analyzed in more detail, specifically with respect to products and services in the area of information technology. In the second and third chapter the relevant background documents pertaining to these industries, namely the EC's White and Green paper, will be discussed and their likely effects analyzed. Chapter 4 reviews the development in the Japanese market and the Japanese trade policy in the area of information technology products and service. The potential areas of conflict, particularly in the area of trade in hardware are discussed in chapter 5, before the gains from joint problem resolution are analyzed. Chapter 6 completes the analysis with an outlook and an agenda for action.

2. The Goals of a Single European Market in Telecommunications Equipment and Services

2.1 The Evaluation of the Single Market Concept

Since the formation of the Community by its six original member countries - Netherlands, Belgium, Luxemburg, West Germany, France and Italy - in 1957 several policy initiatives (like reducing import tariffs, removing intra-Community technical barriers etc.) helped to keep the dream of a united Europe alive. But the double recession related to the oil crises and the enlargement of the Community to a 12-nation market in 1986 (by which time Spain, Portugal, Denmark, the UK, the Irish Republic and Greece had joined) brought with it many new problems and the process of integration was slowed down. Together with the recession after the second oil crisis, increased nationalist protectionist policies emerged. In the information technology in particular preferential procurement policies, which relied to some extent to disparate national technology standards, led to only a limited degree of integration, especially in the more publicly sensitive areas of public sector procurement. The persistance of closed national market has been further strengthened by stringent testing and certification requirements for equipment attached to the network. Even in the areas outside of the telecommunication monopolies integration was slow.

It is against this background that the commitment towards a progressive completion of a single market by 1992 arose. Lord Cockfield, Vice President of the European Commission and one of the driving forces behind the attempts for a single unified European market, tabled in 1985, with the agreement of the EC's heads of government, a White Paper (COM (85) 310) with 300 reforms, that forms the basis for the current effort. In the White Paper the costs of physical and technical frontiers are indentified as basic obstacles to completing the internal market. The main advantage of reducing these technical and administrative frontiers is seen in the greater integration of markets, in other words making them more competitive while at the same time allowing increasing specialization and utilization of economies of scale.

2.2 The Myth of 1992

The real significance of 1992 lies much more in the effective PR campaign than in the programme itself. The campaign of marketing 1992 has been enormously successful in alerting the public and especially the entrepreneurs to the potential of a unifired European market and the opportunities for European ventures. It has restored self-confidence in the European ideal, which was fast slipping in butter and wheat mountains and lakes of olive oil. To quote Lord Weinstock "nothing new has happened except that this time these joint projects work. 1992 has changed things. People have woken up."[1] Thus, even if objective reality has not changed very much, the manner in which it is perceived has, and the spirit in which programme implementations are carried out has also. In a way, it is already apparent that some opportunities will be seized which were not taken before, not because there official obstacles to them, but because business horizons were to national in outlook. Furthermore, the spirit with which past Directives are now being implemented indicates a much greater sense of sincerity than in the past, for example in the case of public procurement policy or financial market liberalization (Centre for Business Strategy 1989).

How far the process will actually go is difficult to say. The idea of creating a single market of 320 million people is certainly misleading as a guide to the real degree of economic integration to be achieved. Europe is much too heterogenous in its cultures, its institutions and its demand patterns. What is likely, therefore, is that trade liberalization will primarily affect supply, through increased integration, but differences in demand will continue to persist. From an economic perspective, 1992 is therefore more about the creation of greater product diversity within more competitive national markets. The major effects will therefore derive from wider product variety as a result of integration, and the greater degree of competition through the liberalization of the traditional national regulatory structures. Telecommunications equipment and services is of course an area in which market entry has in the past been inhibited, either by domestic regulation or public procurement policy, so these effects will be of special interest here.

2.3 The Major Policy Aspects of the Green Paper

The Commission's 1985 White Paper covers many industries and market regimes, from buildings and automobiles to such service sectors as banking, insurance and telecommunications. Of more specific interest is the EC's Green Paper on the development of the

---

[1] Financial Times, December 30th 1988.

Common Market for Telecommunication Services and Equipment (COM (87) 290 final) since it focuses exclusively on one specific subsector of economic activities. The purpose of the Green Paper was to initiate a wide ranging discussion on the issues of completing a common market and to help in the establishment of a coherent Community-wide framework for the ongoing changes of the present system of telecommunications regulation.

The issue of greater market integration seems to apply particularly to telecommunications equipment, while in telecommunication services provision economies of scale are more or less realized at a national level. Except for the UK, we have usually only one operator and one physical network, if one ignores the sizable networks of public utilities and the military (there are several network operators in Italy, Denmark and Portugal, but their responsibilities are strictly delineated according to geographic or functional lines). Increased integration in telecommunication services could therefore only arise on a limited scale but the harmonization of the different regulatory procedures and an increased availability for competitive offerings could have important economic effects.

2.4 The Likely Effects of the Green Paper's Policies in the Telecommunications Equipment Market

Telecommunications equipment is used to construct the network infrastructure for telecommunication services. It usually consists of transmission and switching equipment, as well as customer premises equipment (CPE) which is needed to have access to such networks. These three product categories make up the most important market segments of the equipment market, in addition to a small set of miscellaneous products. Table 1 gives an overview over these four markets. It shows the dominance of central office equipment with almost half the market volume, depending on the definitions used. Other market studies use a slightly different product delineation, but all come to similar size magnitudes. The interesting point in connection with the Green Paper is that the majority of products fall under public procurement rules, while only part of CPE equipment and some switching and wiring in private networks is really sold in a more or less open market.

There are three influences, which are likely to be felt as a consequence of Green Paper policies:

- the first relates to increased Community-wide standardization,
- the second to an increasingly open public procurement policy (extending the earlier EC Directive 77-62 and its more recent Recommendation 84-550) and
- the liberalization of the CPE market.

Concerning the first effect, standardization, the greatest influence will be felt in central office equipment, where at the moment a number of different non-compatible European switching systems exist. In assessing the likely effect of the EC's policy, one has to compare the EC's current role in standardization efforts compared to those activities already carried out by internal standard setting bodies. The setting up of a European Standards Institute (ESTI) and the support by the Commission of more open network interfaces (also the support of OSI standards in public sector procurement) will lead both to rationalization and competitive effects. Rationalization effects are here mainly due to increasing lot sizes while competitive effects arise because more competitors can now compete in larger integrated markets that were previously separated. The EC's recent estimate indicates that savings in the neighbourhood of 5 to 10 per cent of the current European CO switching market of about 5 bn ECU may be possible, thus saving the PTTs eventually .25 to 50 bn ECU per annum. The competitive effects could increase this number in the long run (EC, 1988, chapter 10).

Table 1

Telecommunications Equipment Markets in the
Principal OECD Countries, 1984 (in Mill. US$)

	public switching	private switching	public transmission (incl. broadcast)	CPE
World Market	10000	9420	14590	6495
France	730	251	650	448
West Germany	457	492	690	400
U.K.	687	361	460	250
Italy	710	129	400	131
USA	2850	5400	5220	2830
Japan	627	808	1520	316
Canada	327	210	210	72

Source: Rausch (1987, p. 20)

The other two product groups, transmission and CPE equipment are already more standardized, so the effects of the Green Paper standardization efforts are likely to be smaller. Nevertheless there might still be dynamic competitive effects.

More important is the effect expected from more open public procurement policies in line with the EC Recommendation 84-550. This Recommendation foresees that 40 to 50 per cent of public contracts are to be opened by 1992 (compared with 10 per cent of all tenders today). If this recommendation is implemented and used in a strategic way, i.e. applied mainly to the non-standardized, semiclosed procurement markets, sizable savings might be possible. The EC's estimates are as high as 15 per cent or 3 bn out of a total budget of 17.5 bn ECU (EC 1988, chapter 10).

Already there is a great deal of restructuring taking place in the European central office equipment industry: Alcatel has taken over all the ITT facilities in Europe; Siemens has acquired the European operations of GTE and formed a joint company concerning its U.S. activities; L.M. Ericsson has taken over CGCT in France; AT&T has made cooperation agreements with Philips and STET, the Italien holding company for Italtel and SIP and GEC and Siemens have jointly taken over Plessey. Nevertheless, in order to carry out the radical restructuring in the industry, which is necessary to achieve savings of this kind, we would expect considerable political opposition to such rationalization policies. If public telephone operators (PTOs) nevertheless were able to adapt the aggressive procurement rule envisaged under EC's Recommendation 84-550, recourse would probably be taken by national governments to extra funding from public sources in order to maintain some of the activity and employment in the industry on a regional basis. As a consequence, the 3 bn ECU savings mentioned above represent pershaps only the maximum price reduction possible.

The reason why such rationalization effects are probably not realistic in the short run (i.e. by 1992) is because of the political opposition to the necessary restructuring that would by needed to achieve the kind of competitive price levels currently being achieved in the U.S. The reason is that economies of scale effects take place both in software production (spreading roughly 1 bn US $ development cost over a given market plus US $ 0.1 bn annual updating and modernization efforts) but also in the actual hardware production and assembly. European CO manufacturers, who often only produce one to two million lines of CO equipment per annum must compare their production cost with AT&T's seven million access lines per annum (in a single plant) or the four to five million lines produced by Northern Telecom, the other large North-producer. Even if European plants also produce large private branch exchanges, for which some components, software and testing tools of CO equipment production can be used, the European production scale is by comparison still small, suffering from a cost disadvantage that is equivalent to 20 to 30 per cent, when comparing a plant of seven million lines capacity p.a. to one of one million lines p.a.

That European production scales of this size are not possible is indicated in Table 2 which shows the distribution of CO manufacturing plants across W.-Europe. Some of the firms have often more than one plant per country, with the smaller countries actually accounting for only very small market.

Table 2

The Presence of Major Central Office Equipment Suppliers
in Different European Countries (EC and EFTA) 1986

	B	DK	E	F	UK	IRL	I	NL	P	D	A	CH	S	N
					EEC							EFTA		
Ericsson		xx	xx	xx	xx	xx	xx	xx				xx	xx	
GTE							xx							
Alcatel	xx	xx	xx	xx		xx	xx	xx	xx	xx	xx			xx
ATT-Philips								xx						
GEC-Plessey					xx									
Siemens	xx							xx		xx	xx	xx		
Italtel							xx							
Northern/STC					xx						xx	xx		
Teli													xx	

1) refers to actual plant sites; excludes Greece

The economies of scale in the production of transmission equipment are less pronounced, especially as off-the-shelf components can be used for part of the transmission applications. Significant scale effects exist however in the production of cables (both copper and optical fibres) and standardized microwave components. Satellite receiving dishes, traditionally part of transmission technology, are now becoming actually part of CPE, as they are more and more found in the CATV home owners market.

Despite these large benefits that could arise from specializations, we currently find, at least in the public procurement area of transmission and switching and to some extent also in CPE, highly protected national markets within each EC member country. There is little intra-EC trade, but a fair amount of exports to countries outside the EC. Total imports account for much less than 10 per cent of final demand, a further confirmation of the national orientation of these markets (and of these imports, more than 50 per cent come from the U.S. and Japan rather than from Intra-European trade).

2.5 Reasons for a Lack of Market Integration

The reasons for this peculiar "closed" market structure are threefold:
- selective procurement and certification policy,
- incompatible standards and
- "input specificity" (goods and services specifically customized to the user's specification, for example to allow compatibility with previous investment in a complex network system).

Selective procurement policy is related to the insistance of national governments - for industrial policy reasons - on maintaining a "technology base" in such an advanced manufacturing sector as telecommunications equipment. Foreign suppliers have therefore no chance to enter. Restrictive certification policy and incompatible international standards are sometimes also used as instruments of such a "technology-home-base" policy. But often these policies are also related to a specific technology orientation of an administration, often in close accordance with domestic manufacturers who use their influence in certification and standard setting to raise entry barriers to outsiders.

"Buyer or input specificity" is especially relevant for CO equipment. Given the high adjustment cost of moving from one type of switching system or standard to another, it is of course difficult to open national markets quickly to suppliers of different systems. The degree of buyer specificy is less strong for transmission equipment and CPE, because the interfaces between different types of equipment have already been more or less internationally standardized, allowing smaller specialist suppliers to survive in different national markets.

As a consequence, while we believe that the restructuring in the CO area and partly in transmission will move rather slowly, also because the Community at the moment does not have strong enough policy tools for implementation (the 40 to 50 per cent rule is only contemplated to be used by 1992) stronger adjustments in the private markets, including CPE are expected. The likely dynamic implications of such a move are illustrated by the recent growth in the liberalized U.S. and UK CPE markets. As a consequence of private purchasing, depreciation rates dropped considerably, simple handsets were replaced much more frequently than before, leading to a significantly larger turnover. Similar tendencies, perhaps less dramatic, occured in the market for private branch exchanges (PBX). Nevertheless it is in this market, where AT&T has recently filed an anitdumping petition with the Department of Commerce, against manufacturers from Japan, Korea and Taiwan (AT&T 1988). Instead of the projected import penetration for CPE equipment of 20 to 23 per cent, which was predicted by the International Trade Association in 1984, total annual import penetration has in some market segments risen above 50 per cent. A similar picture emerges from an analysis of the UK, where imports in the CPE sector, and especially that for mobile handsets, have increased dramatically after opening these markets, with many of the imports coming from either the U.S. or the Far East.

These observations suggest that if the Green Paper recommendations were implemented fully, considerable structural rearrangements would result, with significant long-term benefits to users. These positive results must be seen against the adjustment cost to producers and the fear of the loss of regional or national technology bases. It seems therefore likely that national industry objectives and differentiated equipment standards will continue to play a role in this adjustment process. The full fruits of integrating the European telecommunications equipment market can only take place if some common agreement between the governments concerned can accompany this restructuring, for example about where centres of R&D and the relevant national technology bases ought to be located (as in the case of the Airbus Consortium).

To sum up the expected effects on the equipment side, we find significant savings as a result of moving towards a single European market in telecommunications equipment. The reasons are insufficient exploitations of scale and specialization economies as a result of limited national markets and the insufficient competive pressure because of protective procurement and certification policies. These implications must not be seen as a threat but rather as a potential. The threat has already been outlined above and is reinforced by the ongoing restructuring. The potential on the other hand is often forgotten. It lies not only in increasing the available market area which would make certain marginal applications profitable, which would otherwise have to be foregone, but also in stimulating the competitive pressure in each of the different submarkets for equipment, service provision and network utilization. Increase competitiveness means a painful restructuring for some, but it also means lower prices and an increase in application potential for others. This has important demand expanding effects, which are often forgotten on the equipment producers side.

3. Completing the International Market for Telecommunication Services

3.1 Expected Effects

Improving the performance of the market for telecommunications equipment would already result in lower telecommunication cost. But the performance on the service side can be increased further through more effective service provision, fewer restrictions on network utilization and the availability of additional, Community-wide standardized services. These effects may be due to

a) lower cost per given output and

b) better network utilization through more rational pricing.

The recommendations of the Green Paper (points A-G of the Green Paper) may produce these two effects. The main recommendations, which concern us here, are

- the provision of competitive "non-reserved" services by private firm (proposition C),
- open network provision on the basis of nondiscriminatory terms (proposition E) and
- a more liberalized market for CPE (including receive only earth stations) in combination with
- more Community-wide standard setting (proposition F).

Important are also the insistence on stronger antitrust rules (propositions H and I) and the recommended separation of regulation from operation (proposition G). This should give support to those competitive activities that are permitted to take place in competition with the PTOs.

While the scenario of full network service competition, as practised in the U.S. and eventually envisaged in the UK, seems unlikely to be repeated in the rest of Europe, the threat of competition through nonreserved services and marginal network services (such as mobile and satellite services) might be enough to increase productivity levels of the PTOs in the area of reserved services.

How large such productivity effects are is difficult to know. Productivity comparisons are difficult to carry out but we are currently undertaking such an exercise in an elaborate comparative productivity study at the DIW. Initial results suggest that significant productivity differences between the European PTOs exist, perhaps as a consequence of differences in the production technology used and the degree of X-inefficiency allowed to take place within an organization, but also as a consequence of important outside (political) constraints on the PTOs that prevent a movement to the least cost frontier. Such movements are especially important over time, i.e. if some administrations are able to achieve continuously higher productivity records. If this is combined with scale effects that can be realized with network use, the more efficient growing networks will be able to pass on these savings at lower average costs to their users than the more slowly growing, less efficient networks.

3.2 Better Network Utilization

The second effect mentioned above relates to the effect of a more rational tariff policy, when the recommendations of the Green Paper to move tariffs closer to costs take place. Since current telecommunication tariffs diverge significantly from cost (see Table 3) greater network efficiency is not only achieved through lower cost per given output, but also through better network utilization as a consequence of a more rational pricing structure. As a consequence of current tariff policy, the price signals to the users of the telecommunication networks are often severely distorted, causing the users to make allocatively inefficient decisions. They also prevent the dynamic productivity effects of potential entrants, whose services are prohibited because of the danger of creamskimming through arbitrage.[2] But this prohibition of arbitrage has other side effects. Innovative services that may have been developed "inhouse" by larger enterprises or between their subsidiaries or cooperation partners (for example in the case of airlines, banks etc.) can be sold to third parties only under certain restrictions and sometimes not at all. This implies not only significant barriers to entry for the socalled value-added network services (VANS) that are based on telephone networks, but also discriminates against small and medium sized users who cannot develop or utilize these services inhouse because of their small scale.

While the dynamic benefits that are being lost as a consequence of current tariff policy are difficult to estimate, the static welfare losses, measured on the basis of consumer surplus[3] foregone, are already quite sizable. A move towards cost oriented tariffs would probably result in welfare gains of 10 per cent of current call revenue, i.e. 4 to 5 bn ECU. If in addition, productivity could be increased by a further 0.5 per cent and this differential growth rate be maintained thereafter, further actual savings of 2 to 3 bn ECU p.a. may be possible.

What is interesting to the outside observer is that these two effects, i.e. increased productivity and a move towards cost oriented tariffs, are really only stated as a policy goal of the Green Paper, without the proper implementation tools or directives. As long as PTOs retain their more or less public structure, and competition in network services across the Community does not arise, these benefits are unlikely to take place. The number of potential losers (mainly the workers of the PTOs) are even more influencial than those in the equipment firms and often organized better, so that the political resistance to such moves will be very high. It is interesting to see how cautious the Germans, the Italians and the French are moving in this connection despite their lip services to fully embracing the goals of the Green Paper. Only if the regulatory framework of the Commission can be strengthened with the goal to also increase performance and if the PTOs are released of some of the infrastructure policy tasks by shifting them to more direct policy tools (taxes, subsidies, personnel retraining) will the kind of rational tariff and operating policies result, which will yield the benefits we outlined above. In other words, the likely effects of the Green Paper for telecommunica-

---

[2] This refers to the incentive that any potential service supplier would want to enter mainly in the lucrative long distance market, thereby "skimming" the cream needed to subsidize the deficit services - rentals and local calls.

[3] The consumer surplus is how much buyers would have been willing to pay over and above what they actually pay for a service.

tion services could be of a sizable magnitude. But the policy problems involved in getting there are so large that the full technology potential of the information technology can probably not be realized within the current institutional framework of the Commission.

Table 3

Major Tariff Variables in the EC (1986)
(in ECU, includes VA charges where applicated)

Country	Connections	Monthly Rentals		Local Call Tariffs (LC) (3 min)	Call Area Size[1]
		Households	Business		
Great Britain	150	9.00	14.02	0.21	221
Italy	151	4.48	11.54	0.20	9
Belgium	116	10.50	10.50	0.14	78
Ireland	235	11.20	15.10	0.14	78
Luxembourg	58	5.78	5.78	0.12	n.a.
France	36	5.67	13.82	0.11	120
West Germany	31	10.80	10.80	0.11	135
Denmark	189	9.88	9.88	0.10	n.a.
Netherlands	97	9.81	9.81	0.06	5
Portugal	66	7.98	7.98	0.05	1
Greece	199	2.23	2.23	0.03	5
Spain	83	6.66	7.03	0.03	n.a.

	Tariff for Trunk Calls		Intern. Calls (3 min)[2]		Intern. Leased Lines[3]	TC1 LC	TC2 LC
	up to 100 Km (TC1)	max. Dist.(3min) (TC2)	From	TO			
Great Britain	0.56	0.56	1.94	2.12	1162	2.7	2.7
Italy	1.62	1.72	2.92	2.16	3500	8.1	8.6
Belgium	0.69	0.69	2.22	2.10	1625	4.9	4.9
Ireland	1.26	1.26	2.88	2.30	1878	9.0	9.0
Luxembourg	-.--	-.--	1.41	2.10	1702	-	-
France	0.85	1.59	1.85	2.10	1541	7.7	14.5
West Germany	1.00	1.66	1.67	2.13	2352	9.1	15.1
Denmark	0.36	-.--	1.37	2.31	1312	3.6	3.6
Netherlands	0.26	-.--	1.75	2.09	1743	4.3	4.3
Portugal	1.19	-.--	2.88	2.40	2889	23.8	23.8
Greece	0.97	1.15	2.73	2.33	2582	32.3	38.3
Spain	0.60	1.07	3.15	3.15	2481	20.0	35.6

[1] measured in thousands of exchange lines
[2] average peak charges from a country to EC members and vice versa
[3] monthly rental and connection charge in $ for eight private circuits to adjacent country and two transatlantic.

Source: Telefonica, Revista T, No 16, Oct. 1987; DIW for International Leased Lines, IBM 1987 for International Calls: European Commission, XIII 1178 (1988)

4. Japanese Policies Concerning Telecommunications Equipment and Services

4.1 Policy Focus

In Japan too, the importance of information technology has led early on to specific policy objectives. For example, the remarkable achievement of Japan's export plan, developed at the Ministry of International Trade and Industry (MITI) in the form of the "Industrial Rationalization White Paper" of 1957, has for some western countries been a model of how to nurture the new information economy. However, this blueprint to "informatize" the national economy has undergone significant changes over the last decade. After reaching its primary objective of eliminating the telephone service shortage and providing nation-wide automated dialing in 1978, NTT had to shift its objective. As full market saturation was reached, the rate of new subscriptions fell off sharply, combined with the threat of network bypass from alternative carriers. Two subsequent events have accelerated the departure from the traditional model of the public telecommunication sector controlled by the MPT. One was the American attempt to open the traditionally very protected public procurement market of NTT, which resulted in the first agreement of the American trade negotiator with NTT in 1979 and led to subsequent rounds of renegotiation and further opening of the equipment market.

The second event was initiated in the comprehensive telecommunications reform legislation package that was submitted to the Japanese Diet in March 1984, mainly as a result of the 1982 report of the Administrative Reform Commission which has studied the inflexibility of state monopolies, associated bureaucratic inefficiencies and excessive union influence (Kato, 1983).

4.2 Opening up the Equipment Market

The American effort to open up the Japanese telecommunications equipment market to international trade had, of course, commenced earlier through pressure of the major industry associations and business groups, who wanted the increased access of the unregulated information sector to the traditionally regulated public monopoly service sector. Together with the first three year NTT procurement agreement, covering the period 1981 - 83 and the subsequent enlargement in 1984 (including the now famous $12 million contract for a Cray super-computer at NTT) the respective shares of total NTT purchases from the four major traditional telecommunications equipment suppliers fell dramatically.[4] The analogy to the "open door" policy that was initiated by Commandore Perry in 1853, prior to the Meiji Restauration from 1868 is suggestive: the traditional policy regime was weakened and beset by increased challenges to its authority and ultimately its legitimacy. In a way, the control through the MPT was eventually replaced by the more pro-competitive influence of MITI, which nevertheless pursued, as we shall see below, a very aggressive industrial policy.

4.3 Opening up the Service Market

On the network side the ultimate legitimacy of the network monopoly was equally challenged. The telecommunications reform legislation, which was submitted to the Diet in March 1984, redefined the character of regulation, and opened competitive access to the growing information and communications market in Japan. NTT was restructured and privatised and the huge public voice and data communications sector opened to private competition. The monopoly of KDD over the international telecommunication sector was broken as well, with the introduction of a domestic competitor (International Telecom Japan Inc.) and a second competitor (International Digital Communications) with strong British and American influence.

The effect of this restructuring has been much more fundamental than the gradualist approach of the EC's Green Paper. Network competition is now taking on a serious dimension with three major terrestrial carriers, some regional carriers (mainly from the electricity industry) and a number of domestic satellite carriers (Müller, 1987). Even though the MPT has only gradually released its influence and still keeps a protective hand over NTT through its interconnect agreement and the licensing of new competitors the behavioural change initiated is significant. The effects of opening up the equipment market have been accelerated through the competitive pressure which now exists on NTT. It can no longer afford to give preferential treatment to its traditional "court" suppliers, but it must aim at procurement conditions that are similar to those of its competitors. As a consequence, some of the industrial policy aims, which have been carried out through NTT in the past, have had to be replaced by other policy instruments. As a consequence of this and the extraordinary export performance of the

---

[4] Oki Electric's share fell from 27 per cent in 1979 to only 14 per cent in 1983; NEC share declined from 16 per cent to 8.6 per cent; Fuijitsu's share from 15 per cent to 8 per cent and Hitachi's from 2.3 to 1.5 per cent, i.e. a reduction in the combined share from 60 to only 32 per cent; Fuchs, 1984, p. 131.

Japanese telecommunications equipment industry, the anticipated restructuring has been much less severe than what is envisaged on the European side. This has partly to do with the much longer competitive history in the Japanese CPE market, which gave domestic firms a lead-time in adapting to a new more aggressive market environment, and the booming home market for informative products. To some extent perhaps Japanese companies too have been very successful in exploiting the economies of scope between computer and telecommunications applications (C&C) and developed market niches, in which their relevant company's size allowed them cost advantages without the scales necessary in the CO market. By comparison, it is mainly in the market areas outside of CO equipment, where the Japanese have emerged as very sucessful world suppliers while some restructuring in the CO side perhaps remains.

5. Areas of Conflict

5.1 Japanese Trade Surplus and Administrative Reactions

The trade imbalance which triggered the American effort towards opening up the Japanese telecommunications equipment side finds its parallels in the Community's attempt to rectify the trade imbalance with Japan in the information sector. The problem seems to be that the Japanese continued to be "too" sucessful. This is partly related to their own industry structure, which is often forgotten both in the U.S. and in Europe. It is the lack of raw materials, which necessitates a trade surplus on the manufacturing side. The other reason is the traditionally high propensity of the Japanese to save, which limits the absorptive capacity of the home market while stimulating foreign lending.[5] Furthermore, the Japanese preference for domestically produced consumer and investment goods, and the unsatisfactory performance of imported goods in distribution outlets, which are not fully owned by foreign producers make a successful penetration of the Japanese market difficult. As a consequence, Japan has been faced with a number of challenges to its trade policy, that led to a number of international agreements on voluntary export restraints, often as a consequence of dumping complaints or accusations of unfair and injurious trade policies (Grewlich 1988). What comes to mind, to quote Grewlich, are catchwords like "telecommunications, semi-conductor agreement, the Toshiba case, Airbus, high definition TV etc.".

---

[5] This absorptive capacity seems to have been greatly increased in the last couple of years, however.

5.2 Export Restraints and Antidumping Threats

The effects of the 1986 voluntary export restraint agreement in chips with the U.S. are well known. It not only raised profits and prices in the U.S. sector, but resulted in a significant shift of trade to Europe. Similar effects probably took place as a consequence of a similar agreement for car imports, but that lies outside the scope of the present paper. The EC, to some extent, has pursued a similar policy, sacrificing short-term gains to the consumers in the hope of maintaining a long-term viability of domestic industry. This policy does not only cover voluntary export constraints, for example in the case of video recorders and automobiles, but increasingly more punitive tariff levies as a consequence of dumping charges. In 1988 for example the Council of Ministers applied such tariffs for electronic typewriters, printers and photocopiers. Today, the EC uses its antidumping regulation as a formidable trade weapon that tends to restrict severely the trade relations that have emerged in the area of information technology products (Hindley, 1988). Local content rules are furthermore being strengthened, so that even substantial assembly in Europe does not allow Japanese manufacturers to circumvent dumping charges (the rules of origin have been redefined: in the past, the Commission has defined country of origin of a good as that where "the last substantial transformation or operation that is economically justified is performed", now the make reference to that country where "diffusion - the operation that make the integrated circuit intelligent" takes place, thereby increasing the barrier to entry further.[6] It is quite clear that the view which was expressed in the Commission's document on EC-Japan relations in March 1986 still holds today: "...the sense of responsibility and strong leadership evinced by present government in Tokyo have not done away with the multilateral structural imbalance which threatens the foundation of postwar cooperation and represents a veritable time-bomb within the trading system" (EC 1986, p. 6). Such statements, which stand for many, are a sign that Japan's trade surplus with the EC is politically unacceptable in Europe, especially as much of it is in high technology manufacturing products such as electrical, electronic and other machinery, appliance and transport equipment (Bell, 1987). It seems that the EC is following the unhealthy example of the U.S. in "solving" its trading difficulties with Japan through tough protective measures.[7]

---

[6] Financial Times, Feb. 7 and Feb. 10 1989.

[7] See the 100 per cent tariff charge on colour televisions, desk top computers and machine tools that followed the Chip Pact of 1986, Financial Times, 31.3.1987.

5.3 Controlling Standards

Quite a different policy tool, namely that of standards, has been used to protect European producers of brown goods, i.e. in the area of television and video recorders. Standards had already been used in the past rather successfully to protect European equipment producers.[8]

Standards are again being employed with respect to high definition television (HDTV). The policy of the Japanese producers has been quite different from that of the Europeans. They essentially and early developed an HDTV standard, that was non-compatible with existing systems, but would have been introduced through the studio site first. This standard was almost introduced world-wide at the international meeting of the international standard setting body CCITT of the ITU in Dubrovnik in 1986. At the last minute, however, the Europeans led by Philips, Thompson and Bosch and coordination help from the European Commission prevented such agreement and engaged on a tour de force to establish their own backward compatible system under the auspices of the Eureka project;[9] a similar policy is now pursued by U.S. manufacturers where the American Electronics Association has tried to set up a U.S. consortium to stop the demise of the American equipment production industry.[10]

5.4 Excessive Specialization and Dependence or International R&D Races

It is useful to stop for a minute and think about the underlying factors behind the current trade difficulties. We agreed early on, that the reasons behind the EC push for a unified single market lay in the hope of reducing further barriers to trade and thereby increasing specialization and competitive effects. If these effects are to work within an EC framework, they also ought to work in an international framework. This static picture, however, ignores one fundamental issue, that seems to worry both the Americans and the Europeans. The successful "targetting" of export industries by the Japanese, which relies on scale and learning effects on the one hand, and increased

---

[8] Telefunken, which had development the PAL standards used in most Europe to exclude Japanese competitors from marketing large screen TV sets for years, because it controlled the patents on the PAL television systems (Brown 1987).

[9] The Economist, October 1, 1988, Brown 1987; EC 1988.

[10] Computer Week, January 16, 1989.

R&D efforts to achieve technology leadership on the other (while at the same time spreading R&D costs over a larger market) may result in the eventual elimination of certain sectors in the home market. The disappearance of the European phototechnical sector on the one hand, and the enormous shrinkage of motorbikes on the other seems to confirm this point. The dynamic benefits might therefore lead to some form of predatory behaviour, where the emerging monopolist is able to raise prices to monopoly levels and make up for initial losses obtained in acquiring market shares.

This popular scenario ignores import reaction functions of the domestic industries. Furthermore, they may also be different depending on the industry structure involved. If we look at the work on research and development rivalry (starting with Scherer, 1967) increased competitive pressure on both production cost and R&D effort can have two effects:

- submissive reactions coupled with a slow down in R&D and eventually discontinuation of production or
- accelerated R&D and competitive improvements.

The first policy may not be exclusive of the second however. When such rivalry is symmetric, so that no firm has an irrecoverable head start or other advantage, the effect of enhanced competition may stimulate all participants to more expansive R&D efforts (even if only as a "fast second"). With asymmetric rivalry smaller firms may remain submissive but not necessarily forever. Unless they lose their strategic position permanently (because of enduring "first mover advantages") such first generation laggards may not be caught napping in subsegment competitive rounds but may sustain an aggressive R&D pace (Scherer, 1988). Such theories may explain the behaviour of firms in Japan, as well as in Europe and the U.S. The submissive hypothesis is certainly supported by the advent of the Japanese leadership in transistorized radio and solid state TV sets, the export performance of numerically controlled Japanese machine tools etc.

On the other hand, the emergence of some of the other Japanese sectors on the world market has more to do with a catch-up strategy in the increasingly aggressive international R&D race. For example, the Japanese came very late to the international car market, but gained enormously in the small car segment as a consequence of the second OPEC oil shock of 1979/81. The subsegment quota limits led to extraordinarily rapid product innovations into the much higher margin luxury cars which are now making their appearance in Europe as well. The rapid growth of Japanese chip exports (particularly in 16 K dynamic RAM) was a result of a catch-up project, started with MITI's VLSI R&D projects in 1975. By 1980 Japan captured 40 per cent of the U.S. market and has now an equally important position in Europe. Plain paper copying machines show a similar catching-up phenomenon being repeated by the performance of Japanese (and Korean); as do digital computers and PC's, taking advantage of IBM's PCs open architecture which came in the 1980s (Scherer, 1988, p. 8). Recognizing the changing competitive fortunes of industry in a dynamic setting gives one therefore a much longer term view in which in addition to the submission and extinction hypothesis, hypothesis of accelerated competition is also plausible, coupled with important economic benefits for both sides. Against this background, the antidumping measure pursued by the EC, often pursued in the interest of consumers or the interest of the Community seems to ignore this point.[11]

6. Gains of Joint Problem Resolution

We have earlier argued that the liberalization of the European telecommunications market, both for equipment and services, as envisaged by the Green Paper, offers more an opportunity than a threat, especially if envisaged in the long run. Given the short-run orientation and impatience of policy making (Noll and Owen 1983) it is unlikely that the EC will move very fast in this field, given its limited instruments and the need pursue consensus policies. Superior product performance and entry by the Japanese producers should therefore be seen as an additional policy tool that is to be supported and not hindered in the process of achieving the implementation of the long-term productivity effects of the IT revolution. This however requires a steady hand on the policy side not one of conflicting signals to potential entrants. The gains would thereby be a "win-win" result or a "positive-sum" game. Similar to what has been argued in the assessment of the free trade agreement between the U.S. and Canada (Scott and Smith, 1988), it demonstrates that trade relations, which are characterized by recurrent disputes about subsidies and countervailing and antidumping duties must be managed at a higher level of priority than that which is usually given to such disputes. What is needed is a higher level international framework for bilateral economic relations, in which extensive new rights and obligations will have to be established and enforced. Furthermore, a

---

[11] To quote Stegmann (1985, p. 473): "The basic drift of the antidumping policy of the EC is the same as it has been in the U.S. and Canada: antidumping measures are employed (deployed) as instruments of "commercial defence" to protect the interests of import-competing producers. The interests of the latter appear to be trated as identical with the Community, unless other interests mount sufficient political pressure to prevent the same position of antidumping duties."

consultative and dispute settlement procedure should be introduced, which helps to preempt the occurrence and reoccurence of some of the disputes and more expediously resolves others that might crop up in the process.

The elements of dispute resolution, which are envisaged under the Canada-United States Free Trade Agreement might be a useful model on which to restructure the European-Japanese relationships (Horlick, Oliver and Steger, 1988, in Schott et al.). These procedures not only foresee the binational penal dispute settlement but also the setting up of a bilateral trade commission and the possibility to send not resolved disputes to a binding arbitration panel. These recommendations go further than those currently available under GATT procedures and have the additional benefit of comprising a different, more influential panel membership. They also work much faster so that the framework, in which trade takes place, is more quickly stabilized. The effects of such policy ought not to be only seen in the relations between Europe and Japan or between OECD countries in particular, but also the potential they offer for trade with Third World countries. If two advanced nations, like the EC and Japan, cannot liberalize trade and reduce restrictions on services and investment, what hope will there be for the benefits of such development vis-à-vis third countries?

References

AT&T 1988: Press Briefing by Gus Blanchard, AT&T General Business Systems, Dec. 20, 1988.

Brown, W.A. 1987: The Campaign for HDTV, Euro-Asia Business Review, Vol. 6, No. 2, April, p. 3-11.

Cecchini, P., Catinat, M. and Jacquemin, A. 1988: The European Challenge 1992: The Benefits of a Single Market, Wildwood House, Aldershot.

European Commission 1984: Council Recommendations of 12 Novembre 1984 concerning the first phase of opening up access to public telecommunications contracts (84/550/EEC; O.J. L298/51), Brussels.

European Commission 1985: Completing the Internal Market, White Book of the EC and the European Parliament (COM (85) 310), Brussels.

European Commission 1986: EC-Japanese Relations, COM (86) 60 final, Brussels.

European Commission 1987: Towards a Dynamic European Economy - Green Paper on the Development of the Common Market for Telecommunications Services and Equipment, COM (87) 290, Brussels.

European Commission 1988a: Research on the "Cost of Non-Europe", Basic Findings, Vol. 10: The Benefits of Completing the Internal Market for Telecommunication Equipment Services in the Community, Brussels.

European Commission 1988b: "The Economics of 1992", European Economy, 35, March 1988.

European Commission 1988c: Commission Directive on competition in the markets in telecommunications terminal equipment, 88/301/EEC, Brussels.

European Commission 1988d: Proposal for a Council Directive on the Procurement Procedures of Entities operating in the Telecommunications Sector, COM (88) 378, 11 October 1988, Brussels.

European Commission 1989a: COM (89) 325, Revised Proposal for a Council Directive on the establishment of the internal market for telecommunications services through the implementation of Open Network Provision (ONP), 10 August 1989, Brussels.

Foreman-Peck, J. and Müller, J. (Eds.) 1988: European Telecommunication Organisations, Nomos, Baden-Baden.

Fuchs, P. 1984: Regulatory Reform and Japanese Telecommunications Revolution, in: Center for Industrial Affairs, Harvard 1983-84 Review, chap. 8, Cambridge.

Grewlich, Klaus 1988: Positive Sum Game USA-Japan-Europa, Aussenpolitik, III, p. 216-233.

Hindley, Brian 1987: Dumping and the Far East Trade of the European Community. In: Regulatory Trade Measures and the Concept of Unfair Trade, Trade Policy Rearch Centre, London.

Kato, Hiroshi 1987: The Japanese Economy in Transition, Tokyo Keizai Shinpasha, Tokyo.

Müller, Jürgen 1987: Liberalisierung des japanischen Fernmeldewesens: Ein mögliches Modell für die Bundesrepublik Deutschland? In: DIW-Wochenbericht 23/87.

Müller Jürgen 1988: Der Europäische Binnenmarkt im Fernmeldewesen - Auswirkungen einer verstärkten Integration. In: DIW-Wochenbericht 29/88.

Noll, G.R. and Owen, B.M 1983: The Political Economy of Deregulation, American Enterprise Institute.

Richardson, Lewis F. 1960: Arms and Insecurity, Pittsburgh and Chicago: Boxwood and Quadrangle.

Scherer, F.M. 1987: "Research and Development Resource Allocation under Rivalry", Quaterly Journal of Economics, Vol. 81, p. 359-394.

Scherer, F.M. 1988: International R&D Races: Theory and Evidence, Swarthmore College, Swarthmore.

Schott, Jeffrey and Smith, Murray G. (Eds.) 1988: The Canda-United States Free Trade Agreement: The Global Impact, Washington, DC.

V. THE FUTURE WORLD MARKETS FOR INFORMATION TECHNOLOGY

"Future world market for information technology products"

"Impact of information technology on East-West relationship"

"US influence on Euro-Japanese relationship"

FUTURE WORLD MARKETS FOR INFORMATION TECHNOLOGY

*William H. Melody**
St. Antony's college, Oxford University, Cambridge

1. Introduction

Forecasting is a dangerous business. The best forecasters either look sufficiently far into the future so that they can never be caught out by comparisons with reality, or they provide forecasts of sufficient generality that almost any trend of developments can be rationalised as fitting under the umbrella forecast. I shall concentrate on the structural changes occurring in the global economy, and examine how these changes are likely to influence the size and structure of future world markets for information technology (IT).

At the outset it must be recognised that future demand for IT will be directly influenced by those larger forces affecting global economic development. Also, the demand for IT products is a derived demand, governed by uses and applications, increasingly in the provision of economic and social services. Of equal importance to noting those factors that are likely to influence the expansion of world markets in IT is noting those factors that are likely to constrain them.

2. Major Trends

The Increasing Significance of Telecommunication

In the evolution of the computing industry, the transition from a primary focus on data processing to tele-processing is reaching a mature phase in the developed economies. IT continues to be integrated more intensively into the production processes of many industries, including manufacturing, agriculture and natural resources. The integration of IT into the services sector is still at an early stage of development. The establishment of new markets in information and communication services, i.e., the commodification of information, is at a very early stage of development. With respect to research and development on newer technologies, including biotechnology and new materials

---

* As of July, 1989, Director, Centre for International Research on Communication and Information Technologies (CIRCIT); Visiting Professor at the University of Melbourne and at Monash University.

technologies, IT (or more precisely, the information and communication processes that IT makes possible) is a fundamental component.

One important factor influencing the growth pattern for IT in future is the changing structure of the telecommunication sector. The telecommunication system provides the indispensible infrastructure for the provision of many services that employ IT. Revisions of telecommunication policies and regulations now underway - at national, regional and global levels will play a major role in determining the efficiency and responsiveness of the telecommunication infrastructure to future opportunities. The telecommunication sector is increasingly being recognised as strategic to economic development in virtually all countries. For most transnational corporations, telecommunication is no longer just an expense of doing business. It is a key to efficiency, competitiveness and the quality of the services and products that can be delivered.

In addition, telecommunication has become the key factor in extending the limits of markets to global dimensions in many sectors of the economy. It has reduced the significance of spatial constraints, thereby increasing commercial sensitivity to modest comparative advantages among different locations.

Innovation and Diffusion

R&D and invention will remain important in future in preparing the ground for technological improvements. But the size and structure of future world markets will be primarily determined (1) by the innovation process, i.e., applied improvements of known technologies, and (2) by rates of diffusion of known technologies across industry sectors, countries and strata of the population. This is perhaps best illustrated by the explosion of facsimile service in recent years. FAX is a very old technology. Market growth has been made possible by the application of compatible (but certainly not new) technical standards to the global telecommunication network. The diffusion process will be the dominant factor influencing the size and structure of future world markets in IT products and services.

The barriers limiting diffusion of technologies and services are seldom technical. Rather, they arise from institutional, organisational, cultural or regulatory constraints. Yet relatively little is known about the nature and significance of diffusion processes in IT, as is illustrated by the disappointing experience with videotex and other IT based services.

A Shift From Supply-Push to Demand-Pull

The demand for information and communication technology products is dependent upon uses and applications in satisfying fundamental needs for information and communication. The success of many IT products and services is often explained by a fundamental shift from firms pushing supply onto the market to consumer demand pulling the product into the market. With increased attention and resources devoted to the exploration of demand and market opportunities, there is increased potential for more rapid and effective diffusion. Nevertheless, diffusion will remain a matter of fundamental concern for IT products and services. For example, it is questionable as to how fast, and to what extent ISDN will progress from a technology in search of a market, to a vehicle enabling the most efficient satisfaction of information and communication needs.

This shift in emphasis toward diffusion will be associated with a shift in market emphasis from hardware to software. In some developed countries, investment and revenues in software already have exceeded hardware. In addition new applications can be expected in terms of improvements in user-friendliness in an increasing variety of IT applications, as a result of increased attention to the human side of the human/computer interface. New markets in "information" services will not only be characterised by an explosion in the number of global data bases, but also the opening of new applications that will affect products such as CD-ROM, desk-top publishing, and specialised communication network activities.

With growing dependence upon telecommunication networks and information transfer processes, there will be increased attention to concerns about security, diversity of sources of supply, quality control and control of access. This is not only to secure payment,(e.g., pay TV), but also to limit access, (e.g., global data banks). There is already a growing concern about the receipt of large numbers of undesired FAX messages.

3. Key Factors Influencing Market Growth

Effective Management of the Global Economy

In the future global economy the significance of information and communication will increase. The economy will gradually begin to justify the label of an "Information Economy". There will be increased recognition that the problem of enhancing knowledge and understanding is not simply an issue of information shortage. In fact, a major issue will be coping with information overload. The implications of managing in an environment of information overload have only begun to be explored.

One of the characteristics of the future information economy may be increased instability caused by massive reaction to certain instantly communicated information. The stock market crash of October 1987 may be an illustration of what could become a much more common occurrence.

The direction and structure of economic growth in future will be fundamentally affected if peace breaks out and military influence upon the global economy is drastically reduced. This would open the way for a massive reallocation of resources toward civilian and social activities. It would place an even greater emphasis on the processes of innovation and diffusion, on service applications, and on the need to understand more about human and social demands. The effectiveness of international technology transfer would become an even more important determinant of IT market growth.

The implications of regional trading sectors now forming in Western Europe and North America, and potentially in Asia/Pacific, Latin America, Africa, etc., will carry major significance. The establishment of regional trading agreements can serve to erect barriers to trade with the outside world, or as a step toward a more dynamic global economy.

Perhaps the greatest potential market for IT is in developing countries. If these economies acquire the institutional conditions conducive to balanced economic development, they could represent an enormous untapped IT market. However, this will require resolution of the crippling debt crisis, and creation of conditions where the effective demand necessary to facilitate development is made possible. It will also be necessary to develop imaginative new ways of overcoming the foreign currency problem. If these more fundamental economic issues can be successfully addressed, an enormous market for IT products and services could be unleashed.

Finally, a much better understanding of the future global information economy will be essential to its sound management. This will require fundamental improvements in the accounting classifications and statistical systems for measuring activities in the information economy. Improvements in the fundamental concepts and theories for analysing the future economy will be essential to an understanding of its functioning and its implications. Assessing economic productivity in the information economy and in the IT sector is only one area where current economic thinking cannot satisfactorily explain current practice. Resolving the increasing problems surrounding invisible trade, including "black holes" in trade statistics is another. Our inherited economic theories unfortunately explain the economy less effectively as it evolves toward the future information economy.

Effective Management in the Information/Communication Sector

The effectiveness of policy and regulatory structures in the IT sector will establish the basic framework within which the sector develops. The implications of telecommunication policies are now extending to the computer and information content industries and to the services sector generally. There is an increasing integration of technologies, products, services and applications.

Experience is demonstrating that a separation of policy-making functions from operating functions in many countries will bring about more effective performance of both. In addition, an increasing diversity in the uses and applications of information and communication systems is requiring a liberalisation of historic telecommunication regulation. Yet, at the same time there is a need for an updated framework of policy and regulation at national, regional and international levels. These issues are now under active discussion in most countries, ITU, GATT and other international agencies. Mr. Butler has drawn attention to the new ITU Report, "The Changing Telecommunication Environment: Policy Considerations for Members of the ITU" (Geneva 1989), which specifically examines these important issues.

The point to be stressed here is that the policies and regulations established in the telecommunication field will have major implications for the size and structure of future IT markets. They can provide either a major stimulus or a major restraint for future market growth.

Knowledge for Policy Makers

Ironically, in an age of sophisticated information and communication, we understand less about the information economy than we do about the older industrial economy. Our experience confirms the conclusion of the Canadian economic historian, Harold Innis, who observed many years ago that "Major improvements in communication make understanding more difficult". (The Bias of Communications, page 31)

Policy makers must work in an environment of very limited knowledge and considerable uncertainty. Although magic solutions to the problems of policy making will never be possible in the real world, the knowledge base for understanding policy options and their implications can be raised substantially. But this requires an explicit commitment to policy research as part of the policy making process.

A number of people attending this Conference are part of research efforts now under way in the field. This research will have to be expanded significantly if policy analysis is to be informed, and the policies actually selected are to open new opportunities for economic development and not restrict them. Market success is ultimately determined by an in-depth understanding of the economic, social, cultural and policy implications of the evolving global information economy. Knowledge always has been the most important factor in economic development. It will become an even more important factor in the information economy of the future.

THESES ON THE CONDITIONS OF FUTURE WORLD MARKETS FOR INFORMATION TECHNOLOGY PRODUCTS

Brigitte Preißl
German Institute for Economic Research (DIW), Berlin

Information technology (IT) products include a broad variety of goods and services for the production, storage and transmission of information. Some of these goods and services appear in a sequence - e.g. networks and value added services -, others are complementary or can substitute for each other. The analysis of IT markets is further complicated by the fact that goods and services are linked together in networks resulting in complex information and communication systems. Thus not only the development of markets for single goods has to be observed, but complementary, simultaneous and synergetic processes cause a strong interdependence in the performance of individual markets. The different sections of the information technology market follow different paths of evolution. Thus, analysing future markets for information technology products implies a great deal of simplification. Much has been said in discussions on information technology about the size of the global market and its future growth and trade potentials. Less emphasis has been laid upon the structure of the IT market and the distribution of its potentials within the world economy.

The market for IT products shows some specific features which suggest that its expansion on an international level will take a different form and provide chances and problems which are different from those of other goods and services. Some of these features are: IT is a key technology which influences all sectors of the economy and provides a high potential for the development of innovative goods and services. Large economies of scale occur for certain products. High research expenses and considerable amounts of investment (especially for communication infrastructures) are required. Regulatory conditions differ from product to product and from country to country. Often supply and/or demand is controlled by state monopolies. Services based on IT products show a relatively high tradeability, i.e. they can be produced and consumed in different places. Information and communication technologies grow together and exhibit synergetic effects.

The "world market" consists of groups of countries with different economical and political characteristics. It comprises industrialized, developing and less developed capitalist countries as well as industrialized and non-industrialized socialist countries. Geographically and economically the following blocks can be identified: Europe, Japan, USA; Asia, South America, Africa; Socialist Europe, Soviet Union, China. These groups and blocks are not homogenous units, and, often even within one country there is a broad variety of economic potentials. For example industrialized countries in Western Europe have different sectoral structures, and Japan and the U.S. differ in terms of world market orientation. The economic problems of the Soviet Union can be compared only to a limited extent with those of the German Democratic Republic. The structures of the future IT markets will reflect these diversities.

International trade depends on economic policies dealing with protectionism, balances of payment disequilibria and debt crises. IT markets will be affected significantly by these limiting factors.

The following paper contains 12 theses concerning selected problems of supply or production (1 - 6) and demand or adoption (7 - 12) of IT goods.

1. IT goods can be divided into four categories with different patterns of internationalization due to their production characteristics

The extreme dynamics of the market for IT products are reflected by short amortization periods for large research and development investments and short product cycles. Therefore it can be expected that producers will have to react more flexibly to technological pushes. Like other goods, IT products will show traditional product cycles. Complex research-intensive products will go through experimental, pilot and mass production phases. However, as can already be seen in present developments, only in a small part of the IT market mass production will prevail.

Four typical groups of IT-products and production processes can be distinguished:

A rather unsophisticated mass production - based on high research expenses in previous periods (e.g. microchips, personal computers, telephones);

B sophisticated production of single items with high research content (e.g. satellites, electronic switching systems);

C   middle and large scale production of software and services requiring skill and new qualifications (e.g. customer-oriented programming; value-added services);

D   production of large single units requiring some technical know how and high capital advances (e.g. telephone and cable TV networks).

In the production processes of type A considerable economies of scale can be achieved. Here the size of the market is the major limiting factor and competition for market shares is strong. High R & D (research and development) expenses can only be amortized with large scales of production. It is estimated that certain high tech telecommunication products can only be produced efficiently, if the world market is shared by only 8 to 11 producers. It is likely that these producers will have their decision centers in economically advanced countries. The tendency to transfer mass production to low wage countries might be counterbalanced by automatization and high quality requirements which can only be met with intensive input of qualified personal.

Products of type B will most likely be produced in technically advanced countries. Competition within this group of countries is already fierce. Production costs as well as technical and time schedule reliability are the most important variables to be taken into account on these markets.

New patterns might arise, however, in group C. Countries which offer cheap manpower with basic skills in programming and data handling will attract routine software production and data processing activities. Here especially newly industrialized and some Eastern European countries have got comparative advantages.

For the production of type D IT goods technological know how will come from countries with experience in information/telecommunication systems. Besides industrialized countries in Europe and America these may well be industrializing countries like Brazil and even China. Such projects are usually carried out in cooperation with local construction firms.

There is no evidence that the international division of labour in most of these processes in groups A to D will differ between IT and other goods. Changes in the international division of labour may arise, however, from the fact that IT increases the tradeability of services. This will eventually lead to more trade in services[1] and to bigger shares in international trade for countries that already have a well developed services sector.

However, shifts in production locations and trade flows accompanying the growth of markets for IT products, will not reverse traditional patterns and trends in the division of labour between industrialized, third world and socialist countries.

2. **The integration of a global market for IT goods depends on deregulation efforts in national IT markets. The nature of IT as an important strategic technology and as a mean to transform cultural identities will cause reluctance towards deregulation in some countries**

The production of IT-based services for national and international markets requires efficient communication infrastructures. These were traditionally provided by large state or privately owned monopolies. For reasons of technical suitability and economic efficiency in many industrialized countries deregulation processes were initiated introducing competition and various new forms of market regulations on the different levels of telecommunication sectors. Government participation in the supply of IT goods and services will continue to be quite typical in R & D and in infrastructure activities, despite considerable deregulation and privatization efforts. National interests will prevail over economic liberalism in prestigious high tech projects as well as in projects which require a well distributed network of infrastructures created by an investment policy which is not exclusively guided by profitability considerations. Nevertheless, countries with (more or less) competitive telecommunication markets put pressure on others to deregulate their telecommunications systems in order to establish conditions for free flows of information between countries including free access to national markets for firms which provide services of information transmission. To a certain extent the future of IT markets will depend on the spread of deregulation processes worldwide. Some countries are reluctant to open telecommunication markets for national and international competition because IT infrastructures are of considerable military and strategic importance and thus should be under governmental control. Others are hesitant, because free markets favour the strongest competitor. A domination of American, European or

---

[1] The terminology is not always clear. Sometimes "trade in services" is used for the execution of a service in one country by a firm which is based in another country. Here it is meant in a more strict sense as carrying out a service in one country for a customer who is located in another one.

Japanese firms in domestic markets which is seen as the most probable outcome of deregulation is considered as a non desirable result by many countries. Especially the distribution of information over the globe threatens the cultural identity and heritage of countries which do not belong to the dominant suppliers of news, software, videos, tv programmes or movies.

In a deregulated environment private IT service providers have a tendency to limit their activities to those communication lines with the highest data exchange traffic. This can already be observed today, as by far the most busy lines are the north-atlantic links between Europe and the US. Routes between these regions and third world countries are less likely to be served (Langdale 1989).

3. **International trade regulations will be formulated to liberalize the worldwide flow of information. Here first results have been reached by the GATT negotiations on trade in services**

IT creates challenges for trade regulation. Whereas the GATT rules were mainly conceived for trade in physical goods, a free flow of information and services needs a different framework. Considerable work remains to be done to reach generally accepted agreements for the international trade in IT-based goods and services. The negotiations will have to take into account legitimate objections (expressed mainly by smaller countries) concerning cultural domination which might be accentuated by what is quite innocently called "free flow of information". Other objections are derived from needs to protect military and political interests by defending existing state monopolies and regulation in information and telecommunication sectors. Third world countries (e.g. Brazil) which promote the domestic IT market by supporting local producers of IT equipment and IT services are trying to limit imports of IT goods. They have strict rules about activities of foreign firms in data processing. Their attitude towards international trade in IT-based services is rather restrictive and tends towards protectionism.

Another group of countries like South Korea, Singapore and India have been successful as service exporters. Their position in the GATT negotiations for service regulations is necessarily with the supporters of trade liberalization (cf. Langdale 1989).

Trade regulations for IT goods which have been established by western countries to stop the supply of strategic technologies to socialist countries (Cocom list) are a powerful obstacle for the development of international trade in IT products. These barriers might be reduced in connection with measures to promote mutual trust and understanding.

4. **In the aera of the transnational firm national boundaries become less important. national economic policies will be partly substituted by new forms of competition and cooperation between large firms**

Given the existence of large transnational corporations it might no longer be adequate to talk about competition between countries. The dynamics of the IT markets result from decisions of multinational firms about their global activities.

One consequence of the internationalization of economic activities is the emergence of international joint ventures which can - to some extent - evade protectionist national policies. Another way to overcome or avoid tariff barriers is cooperation among firms (cf. Riemenschneider in this volume and with respect to 1992: Féaux de la Croix 1989). In a certain sense this is not a new strategy. Cooperation with local firms and/or the installment of subsidiary companies in target markets has been one of the main features of the marketing policy of American firms in Europe for a long time. In addition future IT markets will experience intense involvement of Japan and the overall internationalization and globalization of firms or partnerships. The necessary scale of production of certain IT products cannot be achieved without cooperation in R & D and marketing which comprises firms in all three technologically advanced areas. The future of IT markets in Europe, Japan and the US will thus be characterized by new forms of competition and cooperation (see e.g. Grewlich 1988; Zysmann in this volume). Joint projects in so-called precompetitive research will become more common; competition will be influenced by tacit agreements on market shares.

Cooperation will not be limited to companies seeking access to the home market of their partner, but it will be especially important in R & D activities. Public research programs will have to finance studies which will not exclusively be carried out by national institutions. One possible framework for such supranational research is given by the large scale research projects of the EC. It is most likely that international cooperation in research will be based on agreements between groups of countries which in turn will gain relative advantages over countries that are excluded. From this, quite complex structures of competition might arise.

5. Competition between countries will focus on the location of regional centres for intercontinental communication links and of dynamic international providers of IT products and services

For the next decade the most dynamic markets for IT goods will be located in Western Europe, USA and Japan. South America, India and the South Pacific Area will follow as important providers of specific IT goods and services. Global IT networks are organized in form of main connections linking continents and smaller networks serving regional and local areas. The most favourable conditions for IT activities are found in places where the main communication lines start and end or are easily accessible. Especially in Europe, individual countries compete for becoming the hub of intercontinental communication links. Great Britain, in particular London, as the most important international telecommunication center seems to be ahead of France and Germany. This results from favourable communication conditions in Great Britain as well as from the fact that English is broadly accepted as a common language for international communication. National governments have only got indirect influence on international shifts of activities. Countries compete in terms of the most favourable conditions for the location of business, and they are concerned about balance of payments and long term positions in the global economy. The mechanisms of comparative advantage will be modified by technology policies which try to support local firms. Competition in industrialized economies includes as an important variable effective cooperation between governments and large firms in the field of technological strategies.

6. Technological leadership in future IT markets will be heavily contested between the US, Western Europe and Japan. The definition of norms and standards for information processing and transmission strongly influences this game

Due to the establishment of a Single European Market, the balance of payment problems in the US, and persisting export surpluses in Japan, competition will become more accentuated between the three geographical areas. The race for technological leadership for telecommunication electronics and software seems to be open for Japan and USA with Europe remaining slightly behind. A comparison of R & D expenditures seems as well to confirm the strong position of Japanese firms also in the long run (cf. Patel/Pavitt 1989).

Technological leadership will also depend on the results of negotiations on IT standards. Television norms (PAL, D-2 mac, HDTV) are a good example of the importance of standardization for the internationalization of IT based services. The advantages of firms/countries which succeed in imposing their standards on others could be observed in the past in the information technology sector. In the TV market competition seems to result in one or two dominant and other less significant norms. Thus there will be winners and losers. As far as data transmission is concerned, norm and protocol negotiations seem to aim at a more cooperative result. On the other hand, for many IT products norms and standards can be instrumentalized for protectionist purposes.

7. The geographical distribution of demand for IT goods depends to a large extent on the economic performance of the different countries and regions

Looking at the demand side, the prospects of future IT markets are determined by two questions: where are the most promising markets (or: who will buy IT products)? and how will IT products and services be used to produce a technological take off and spill over effects which induce growth and thus further demand for IT goods? Industrialized countries with dynamic paths of technological development will certainly continue to provide important markets for IT products. Possible saturation effects will be compensated by innovative product policies. The future prospects for IT markets are quite complex in third world and in socialist countries.

The potential for the absorption of IT products depends on the general economic performance of a country, the structure of its economy and its level of technological advancement. Structural determinants are the impact of information based activities in gross national products and the degree of integration in the world market. Since IT plays a central role in the dynamic development of the services sector in many countries, the relative size of this sector is an important indicator for demand estimates. Fast growing services sectors in GB and the USA have paralleled an expansion of IT markets, whereas Germany with a still high proportion of manufacturing also lagged behind in the use of IT. Thus diffusion rates and market volumes will not only differ between industrialized and third world countries but also within economically advanced areas, according to the varying dynamics of information based goods and services. It is necessary, however, not to consider only the relative contribution of services to the national product. The heterogeneity of this sector might bring about misleading results. In some less developed countries personal services make up for a large share of the national income. These services rarely use sophisticated IT goods. The availability of IT will be of no or negligible importance for this part of the services sector. On the other hand in some industrialized countries, the services sector may be relatively small statistically, because many production- or industry-oriented services are provided by the manufacturing sector in service departments which are fully integrated in manufacturing firms. Usually this type of services uses information intensively. It seems reasonable therefore to adopt sectoral analysis as an indicator for market potentials for IT goods only for a rough orientation. Better results can be obtained by analyzing input structures of manufacturing, services and agricultural sectors. High information inputs stand for promising IT markets. This is even more important because the same goods and services can be produced with very different amounts of information and communication. For example, the production of shoes will be much more information-intensive in Japan than in Chile, and a haircut in Germany is often accompanied by computer-supported consultation whereas in Morocco it is just a personal service requiring the information accumulated in the hairdresser's skill.

8. **One critical factor for the development of demand for IT goods is the debt crisis and the resulting scarcity of financial means. However, these factors will not severely hinder the expansion of IT markets**

A serious problem for further development of IT markets might arise from the international debt crisis. The chronic lack of capital will influence the purchasing power in many regions. But it can be observed that there is a strong preference for IT goods in the consumption patterns of third world countries. Thus a possible restraint in the availability of foreign currencies is more likely to influence imports of other goods. It will be of minor importance for the growth of global IT markets.

9. An analysis of relative factor endowments suggests that demand for IT goods will be concentrated in countries with comparative advantages in the supply of capital and skilled labour

The diffusion of IT is facilitated by a certain constellation of factor endowments. Use of IT seems to follow the same rules internationally as nationally. As Antonelli (Antonelli 1989) showed for the regional distribution of the adoption of selected communication services in Italy, the introduction of IT is paralleled by a reduction in the use of low skilled manpower, an increase in the use of skilled personnel and an increase in the use of fixed capital. Most less developed countries are characterized by an abundance of low skill manpower and scarcity of qualified people and capital. Assuming that the current distribution of factor endowments in the world will not change dramatically over the next fifteen years, it seems to be clear that the conditions for the adoption of IT products are not very favourable in less developed countries. Thus the world market for many IT products will be concentrated in industrialized capitalist countries which have relative advantages in the availability of capital and skilled labour, and in those developing (and/or socialist) countries which are able to provide cheap skilled manpower for the establishment of data processing and software industries.

10. The network character of IT links the demand for IT goods to the overall technological level reached in a country

The level of technological advancement is an important limiting factor for the growth of IT markets. This is even more so for IT than for any other good. Information and communication systems are to a large extent organised in networks and they require solid infrastructures. If only one firm in a certain country uses highly sophisticated data transmission equipment and its partners and customers do not, the IT investment is simply superfluous. Consequently, the more users there are for networks, the more probable it is that further demand for access will arise. This is particularly true for communication, but also for information technology, where common standards, qualified personal and service centers are needed. This network problem becomes apparent in countries where the overall economic performance does not allow for an approximately even distribution of technological potentials over the regions. It may also occur in technologically advanced countries, when the demand for certain telecommunication services is blocked because there are not enough participants to communicate with.

Obviously it is much easier to solve the problem if it is due to information marketing or product design deficits than if it is due to deficits in the general economic and technological achievement.

It has been argued that "appropriate technologies" tailored to the needs of countries in various stages of development will improve the poor absorption capacities for IT goods in economically backward countries. Indeed IT comprises all sorts of equipment from simple analog telephones or pocket calculators to high speed mega-computers and digital switching systems. In assessing the prospects of future IT markets in terms of demand potentials and their geographical distribution it is certainly necessary to look at the different sub-markets separately. Apart from the fact that - wherever they were introduced - "appropriate technologies" have had only quite limited fields of adoption[2], a strategy of product diversification according to the absorption potentials of various countries can mitigate the problem, it does not automatically mean that the technological gap will decrease.

11. The demand for IT goods is not only dependent on prices for certain products but also on their cost of adoption

The analysis of IT adoption and of demand for IT goods has to consider diffusion rates and market volumes. But it also has to investigate how IT goods are used and what the conditions for efficient use are. In the article mentioned above, Antonelli distinguishes "cost of adoption" from "cost of purchasing", stressing the importance of externalities[3] for firms which have to learn how to use IT. Cost of adoption includes the creation of an adequate environment for the use of IT. Starting with the necessary network infrastructure and sufficiently high penetration rates, factors are listed which are not decided upon by the investor himself but usually provided by state monopolies or the market. Cost of adoption in the entrepreneur's sphere of responsability comprise planning of internal IT networks and systems in order to reach high levels of integration and compatibility. Infrastructural externalities might for a long time remain a major obstacle for the development of IT markets in less developed countries.

---

[2] It would lead too far to discuss to reasons for these disappointing results any further here. In this context structural heterogencity and strong imbalances between metropolitan and rural areas should be mentioned, because they are directly linked with decisions about technology and communication requirements.

[3] One of the externalities Antonelli refers to is the network problem discussed above.

The concept of "cost of adoption" could be extended: A successful, productive use of IT does not only require the purchase of adequate hard- and software. The critical phase begins when the new equipment has to be inserted in existing processes and procedures. In many cases business structures have to be reorganized in order to fully exploit the advantages of IT products. Isolated use of IT "machines" in one area of an office or a firm can turn out to be counterproductive for the company as a whole if the new technology is not part of a whole system of technical and organizational innovations (Pogorel et al. 1989). To realize these changes a considerable degree of administrative and managerial skill is needed. It is exactly this sort of skill which is comparatively scarce in underdeveloped countries. Therefore most probably the complicated process of inserting IT productively in existing organizational patterns will be managed more successfully in industrialized than in non-industrialized countries. Since successful introduction of IT innovations stimulates further demand in the same market, the more dynamic markets for IT products will continue to be centered in economically advanced countries.

12. Integration in the world market for goods and services stimulates demand for IT goods

Integration in world markets for goods and services facilities the participation of a countries' economy in technological progress going on in other countries. Demonstration effects influence consumption patterns and management philosophies. Imported IT goods stimulate demand for complementary products or create additional fields of adoption. Exports have to meet international standards of quality and technological performance. Many non-IT goods contain quite sophisticated IT components (e.g. lorries with bordcomputers or toys with electronical functions). Countries which export these goods will have to buy IT components abroad or to develop an IT sector of their own.

Another form of integration in the world market which pushes on internal demand for IT goods is the presence of foreign firms from technologically advanced countries. The effects of integration in the world market on the growth of IT markets can be demonstrated in the cases of China and the GDR. Both countries are interested in a more pronounced participation in international markets. In order to compete with other countries, they have to make intensive use of IT in their products and production processes. Combined strategies of developing domestic IT production and importing know how and IT products are adopted. Similarly the Soviet Union can be expected to offer a promising market for IT goods, once it starts to open its economy towards international markets.

In summary, it can be said that the expansion of markets for IT goods will bring about new forms of competition and require new forms of cooperation. It will raise some critical questions concerning the international distribution of economic power, cultural identity and sovereignty as well as national security. The vision of a united worldwide information society remains unrealistic unless all countries are integrated in global information systems. The network character of IT and strong needs for standards and agreements for transnational IT systems accelerate the internationalization of IT goods and services, but makes life harder for those countries which are excluded from the main links of the global network.

References

Antonelli, Cristiano:
 Profitability and Externalities in the Regional Diffusion of Information Technology, in: Keio Communication Review, No. 12 (forthcoming).

Féaux de la Croix, Guy:
 The European-Japan-Initiative, in: European Affairs 2/89, p. 96-103.

Grewlich, Klaus W.:
 Positive-Sum Game USA - Japan - Europe, in: Außenpolitik III/88, S. 216-233.

Langdale, John:
 International Communications and trade in services: policy perspectives, in: Telecommunications Policy, Vol. 13, No. 3, September 1989, S. 203-222.

Patell, Pari/Pavitt, Keith:
 European Technological Performance, in: European Affairs 2/89, p. 56-63.

Pogorel, Gérard/Allouche, José:
 Technological Strategies in Large Corporations, mimeographed, Nancy/Paris June 1989.

COMMENTS ON
FUTURE WORLD MARKET FOR INFORMATION TECHNOLOGY PRODUCTS

Seisuke Komatsuzaki
Tokyo University of Information Sciences, Tokyo

In response to very comprehensive and excellent overview of the market for Information Technology Product presented by Professor Melody, I would like to comment on it focusing on the following three points which seem the most relevant to forecasting the world market of the Product.

1. What is Information Technology Product?
2. Trends of Information Technology Product
3. Prospects of Information Technology Product

What is Information Technology Product?

As is widely understood, "Information Technology" means the happy marriage of two independent factors such as "Information Processing" and "Telecommunications". The Convergence of computer and telecommunications has brought us wide variety of "intelligent" services and systems, and consequently has restructured each industrial activity in Western countries for few decades.

Rapid and continuous progress of information technology accelerated, in turn, the development of new kind of electronic means to rationalize aspects of information activities in office and at home such as production, processing, transmission, storage and retrieval of information. They may be called "Information Technology Product".

One of the noticeable characteristics of Information Technology Product is its "intangibility". It has been pointed out that the number of "software" also has increased tremendously. Now it is becoming very difficult to control the distribution of the Product by applying existing rules for tangible goods.

Trends of Information Technology Product

One of the most significant characteristics of Information Technology Product is the drastic change in production cost, as shown in the case of Japanese word processor. When it was first introduced into the market, it costed over five million yen. Now it is sold under 100,000 yen at discount shops in Akihabara, one of the most active markets for Information Technology Product.

Internationalization of market for Information Technology Product can be the second major characteristic of it. The Economies of Scale in the production of micro-electronics has been so significant that competition to develop products in advance of other competitors has been becoming more and more intensive.

Applications of Information Technology Product have diversified and expanded year after year since it has become cheaper and better. Information activities have been electronized by using "intelligent" means, such as the Japanese word processors. Not only has the productivity of information activities been remarkably improved, but decision making process has also been enhanced and quicker in responding to global competitors.

Prospects of Information Technology Product

Under the rapidly globalizing and mutually interdependent international circumstances, we are now confronting various kinds of problems on Information Technology Product such as "intellectual property right " and "technology transfer". As shown in the process of negotiations at the current GATT round, Information Technology Product has become one of the major items to be discussed.

Balance of "competition" and "cooperation" among industrialized countries, the NIEs and developing countries should be considered, even if it is not easily achieved.

On the other side, new type of literacy for better communication among the above mentioned countries at various levels of economic development is becoming an urgent goal. Utilization of Information Technology Product to overcome barriers separating nations, generations, classes, cultures and interest groups should be developed and accepted by all nations and other institutions.

INFORMATION AND RELATED TECHNOLOGIES AND THEIR IMPACT ON EAST-WEST RELATIONS

Peter Havlik
The Vienna Institute for Comparative Economic Studies, Vienna

1. Introduction

There is a vast amount of literature dealing with the gap in technology between East and West.[1] Information and communication technologies (electronics, computers and software, satellites, modern mass media technologies, etc.) form one of the most advanced, fastest growing and increasingly important parts of modern technology in general. Despite this being recognized also in the East there are some signs that the common perception regarding the fact that the countries of Eastern Europe and the USSR (the East) have already "missed the train" in modern technology is particularly valid for the area of information technologies. Later on I deal with measures which these countries undertake, both individually and collectively, in order to change this undesirable state of affairs.

Ambivalent as the spread of every new technology is, an attempt will be made to outline the challenge which information technologies may bring to the still rather ideologically rigid societies of the East. The various restrictions on the transfer of technology from the West to the East, limiting inter alia the transfer of information technology, are not unequivocal. Given the potential impact of the spread of information technologies on the Soviet bloc societies, it is by no means certain that more spread of such technologies would not benefit the security considerations (which lie behind Western technology transfer restrictions) more than the ambiguous, and not always very effective control efforts of, e.g., COCOM. Whereas more restrictions could perhaps help to broaden the Eastern technology gap, increased free trade would probably lead to more Eastern dependence on the West while maintaining simultaneously a certain lag in most advanced areas anyway.

Western reaction to Gorbachev's reform policies depends to a great degree on the evaluation of the potential role of new technology in this process. Increased liberalizati-

---

[1] For an overview of the literature see, for instance, H. Wienert, J. Slater, East-West Technology Transfer. The Trade and Economic Aspects. OECD, Paris, 1986.

on, enhanced by the spread of information technologies, could bring an easing of East-West tensions and more democracy for the peoples in the East. But modernization alone, aiming at the reconstruction of Soviet power under a changed environment, may also lead to an increased military threat to the West and to more efficient controls by the State, and would therefore rather require a tightening of export controls. Any decision is complicated by the nature of likely socio-economic effects of modern technology, its dual use character and, as far as the information technology in particular is concerned, by its global character. At the moment it is too early to judge the outcomes of current Soviet (and East European) reforms. It seems, however, that exactly because of the inevitable spread of information (including information technologies), the profound changes towards more liberalization must eventually come. Western stimulation of these processes appears therefore desirable.

2. The Gap in Information Technologies Between East and West

There is no need to describe in detail the Eastern technological gap in general since a number of recent studies have done so. The gap finds its expression in the low productivity in the East as compared with the West, in low and decreasing shares of the East in world manufactured exports, in continuous Eastern efforts to close this gap and, finally, in numerous (particularly recent) claims in this respect in Eastern mass media. The recent OECD study summarizes the results of a detailed evaluation of Soviet technological innovations in key industrial sectors - iron and steel, machine tools, high voltage electric power transmission, chemicals, industrial process control, computers, military equipment and automobiles - as follows: "There is no evidence of a substantial diminution of the technological gap between the USSR and the West in the last 15-20 years".[2] The economic structure - organization, prices, incentives - negatively affects the process of domestic innovation. Imports of Western technology largely paralleled poor performance in using domestic technologies. Interviews with suppliers of technology suggest that the assimilation period and lead-times remained long and planned production levels were often not achieved.

---

[2] See East-West Technology Transfer, op. cit., p. 121. Another study, concerned mainly with military technology, shows that out of 20 selected basic technologies the Soviet Union reached parity in 6 (aerodynamics/fluid dynamics, conventional warheads, directed energy, nuclear warheads, optics, power sources) and gained in 4 other (high weight, strength and temperature materials, propulsion, radar sensor, submarine detection) - see Joint Chiefs of Staff, US Military Posture, Fiscal Year 1987, p. 16.

As far as productivity differentials are concerned, various estimates show a lag between 30 and 50% below the levels attained in the West. Even the official Soviet statistics admits that labour productivity in the Soviet industry amounted to slightly more than half, in agriculture to less than a fifth of the US level in 1987.[3] But lagging Eastern technological performance is clearly visible also in shrinking market shares in total imports and in imports of manufactures of leading Western countries: the CMEA market share in the West dropped from 3.19% (1980) to 2.38% (1987) in total imports. The already very low share of machinery and transport equipment (SITC 7) of 0.88% in 1980 almost halved by 1987 (0.48%). Compared with the 1970s, the East lost, during the decade, its position not only in trade with machinery and transport equipment; a similar trend is now becoming visible in miscellaneous manufactured goods (SITC 8) as well. Here the Eastern market share peaked in 1975 (2.8%), but dropped continuously since then: to 2.39% in 1980 and 1.60% in 1987. This drop has been caused by the low competitiveness with respect to the developing - mainly newly industrialized - countries.

a) Telecommunications

Turning to information technology in particular, the situation regarding the gap behind the West is perhaps even worse than in other fields of technology. Telecommunications services in the CMEA countries are provided exclusively by the State post companies. Belonging to the so-called non-productive sphere, such services have traditionally been neglected as far as the allotment of centrally distributed investment resources is concerned.

Low density and poor quality is characteristic of the CMEA telecom networks. In the middle of the 1980s there were on average slightly more than 100 telephones per 1000 inhabitants in the CMEA area (USSR: 98, Poland: 109, CSSR: 226, GDR: 212, Hungary: 140), much less than in the West (USA: 760, Japan: 535, FRG: 599, Sweden: 890).[4] Density of telephone networks in Eastern rural areas is about five times lower than in the cities. Automatic dialling is a remote dream in most regions in the East

---

[3] See Narodnoye khozyaystvo SSSR 1987, Moscow, Finansy i statistika, 1988, p. 623.

[4] See The Telecommunication Industry. Growth and Structural Change. ECE, United Nations, New York, 1987, p. 86.

(exceptions are Czechoslovakia, the GDR, and partly Hungary).[5] In the USSR an (incomplete) automatic dialling system with abroad has been disconnected under Andropov in 1982 and since then not yet been fully restored. 30% of international calls are currently handled mannually, there were only 7 international calls per capita (USA: 100, FRG: 66) in the Soviet Union. In Moscow and other big Soviet cities there are even no public telephone registers. In 1988, there were 35 mn telephones in the Soviet Union (of which 21 mn in households). 4.5 mn new telephones were installed during 1987-1988, but the waiting line for telephones (15 mn applications in 1988) grew longer.[6]

In data transmission the problems are aggravated not only by unavailability of terminals but also by the poor quality of communication networks. Hungary, which is a relatively advanced country by Eastern standards, lies in the middle of the European field as far as communication services are concerned: she possessed slightly more than 11000 telex terminals in 1986. First teletex sets started to operate (via FRG) in 1986, but still no more than one or two hundred terminals will operate by 1990. The package-switched networks, an even more advanced communications technology, which already operates in 15 countries in Western Europe (and naturally also in America and Japan), should be introduced in Hungary with the help of Western firms. Hungarian Post Office recently started a program for telecom modernization: first digital switching centre (for 27 th lines) opened in February 1989, it will be expanded to 90 th lines by 1990 with the help of Austrian technology and credits.[7] In Czechoslovakia, during the 1981-1985 period, 433000 new telephone lines have been installed and the number of telephones per 1000 inhabitants increased to 246 by 1987. However, almost 200,000 applicants queued for the telephone line because of construction delays in the communications network.

In the course of Gorbachev's reform campaign, one of the ministries criticized for poor performance was also the USSR Ministry for Communications. Not only is the number of home telephones extremely low, even in many public places there are no telephone boxes at all. Moreover, because of outdated equipment, there are long connect times and successful calls are often being disrupted since the lines are overloaded. The number

---

[5] The GDR, as the most advanced CMEA country, introduced the automatic dialling system at the beginning of the 1960s. However, due to lack of funds, the share of automated telephone communication lines still does not exceed 60% - see Materialien ..., op. cit., p. 377.

[6] The density of the telephone network is very low outside Moscow: whereas 87% of Muscovite households have a telephone, in other big cities only 10-15% and the situation in the countryside is even worse - see Pravda, Feb. 6, 1989, p. 2.

[7] See Der Standard, Feb. 28, 1989, p. 12.

of telephones should increase in the perspective by 60 mn, but the capacity of switching networks forms a serious bottleneck. Domestic production of such networks is insufficient: an electronic switchboard plant which had to be completed in 1985 will not operate before 1993. Similar problems face also the production of coaxial cables.[8]

Satellite communication is being developed under the auspices and with the technical assistance of the USSR. The Soviet Union uses her own satellite communication system ORBITA. For the joint-CMEA satellite communication a regional organization, INTER-SPUTNIK, has been established in 1971, serving also non-European CMEA members and associates (Cuba, Mongolia, etc.).[9] Though impressive in volume, the Soviet satellite program faces similar quality bottlenecks as in other areas of high technology.[10] At the same time, the East is largely independent in space technologies. Today, the Soviet Union even attempts to capitalize on Western markets with some of its achievements in the area of space satellites.[11] First breakthrough in this area occurred in February 1988 when the US company Payload Systems Inc. signed a two-year contract with the Soviets for performing pharmaceutical experiments on the space station MIR starting from 1989.[12] In March 1988, the Soviets launched for the first time a satellite (for India) at a "higly competitive" price.[13]

---

[8] See Pravda, Feb. 6, 1989, p. 2.

[9] In addition, all CMEA countries are members of the International Organization for Satellite Communication (INTELSAT).

[10] As of December 1982, the Soviet Union has launched 2069 satellites into space, compared with only 997 satellites for the United States. By mid-1983 only 5% of Soviet satellites were still in orbit, compared with 18% of the American ones - see Lavoie, L., "The limits of Soviet technology". In: Technology Review, Nov.-Dec. 1985, p. 72.

[11] See, for instance, the Soviet offer to sell space photographs that are superior to any commercially available in the West - International Herald Tribune, Sept. 28, 1987, p. 1.

[12] See International Herald Tribune, Feb. 22, 1988, p. 5.

[13] See Izvestiya, March 18, 1988, p. 6.

b) Computers

The Eastern computer industry had a difficult start not only because of Western Cold War embargoes, but also because of ideological prejudices in the Stalinist period (at the time cybernetics, similarly like genetics and sociology, was classed a "bourgeois pseudo-science"). By 1964, the USSR started to produce computers of the second generation; at the beginning of 1970s about 30 different kinds of computer systems were in production in the CMEA.[14] Even contemporary Soviet mainframes are still confined to the IBM 360/370 architecture and marginal modifications thereof; minicomputers are variations on themes originally scored by Digital Equipment Corporation or Hewlett Packard; personal computer designs also stay close to the "international standards" of the IBM PC or Apple II and semiconductors borrow heavily from Intel, Texas Instruments, and Motorola.[15] Since 1973, the CMEA countries (except Romania) have entered on the production of third generation computers - largely independently of each other. As a result of such autarky a rather chaotic situation with largely incompatible equipment emanated. In addition to machines from domestic and CMEA sources, computers imported from the West have been in use as well[16] and small East European countries bought a number of licences from various Western companies.[17]

In May 1986 a new CMEA cooperation agreement for the period 1986-1990 in the area of a unified basis for electronic products has been signed. The plan calls for the joint development and production of more than 200 specialized technologies for the production of LSI and VLSI integrated circuits which are used in 16- and 32-bit computer chips. The tasks are divided between individual CMEA countries: Bulgaria concentrates on automatic management and control systems of technological processes, Hungary on control and measurement complexes, GDR and the Soviet Union work on silicon semiconductor plates, Czechoslovakia and Romania on apparatus maintaining the

---

[14] 10 in the Soviet Union, 5 in Czechoslovakia, GDR and Poland, 3 in Hungary, 2 in Bulgaria and 1 in Romania - see Lebkowski, M., Monkiewicz, J., "L'informatique dans les pays du CAEM". In: Révue d'études comparatives Est-Ouest, Vol. 17, No. 4, 1986, p. 6.

[15] See Judy, R.W., "The Soviet Information Revolution: Some Prospects and Comparisons". In: Gorbachev's Economic Plans. Joint Economic Committee Study Papers, Vol. 2., Nov. 27, 1987, p. 163.

[16] Thus, for instance, Czechoslovakia reported for 1970 58 different types of computers out of a total stock of 236 (152 of Eastern and 84 of Western proveniency) - see Statistical Yearbook CSSR 1972, Prague, Alfa, 1972, p. 154.

[17] The Western embargo has been gradually eased during the sixties. The following licenses have, for instance, been acquired: Romania for the production of integrated circuits (Thompson CSF), Hungary for automatic control equipment (Bosch), Bulgaria for magnetic tapes and discs (Wang), Czechoslovakia for VLSI circuits (Intel), Poland for high speed printers (ICL), etc. - see Lebkowski and Monkiewicz, op. cit., p. 8.

necessary clean production environment. The volume of mutual deliveries of integrated circuits should triple during 1986-1990.[18]

Despite such efforts the intra-CMEA sources will apparently not suffice to cover total domestic demand. Czechoslovakia, for instance, will be facing a considerable gap between available supplies and demand by integrated circuits at least till 1992 as the produced quantities cannot meet rapidly increasing demand. Czechoslovak users need roughly 760 types of integrated circuits. About 370 types are produced domestically, another 60 are being obtained from the GDR and Poland under the framework of agreements on specialization and production cooperation. In addition, a further 330 types are imported on a commercial basis (mostly from the USSR, but also from Bulgaria and Romania). Apart from the fact that East European suppliers are not over-enthusiastic about increasing such supplies (mainly because of problems with intra-CMEA prices), the quality of currently produced circuits leaves much to be desired, too.[19]

The Eastern lag in computer technology behind the West may lie anywhere between 4-10 years. Western estimates put the number of mainframes (including minicomputers) in the Soviet Union at one tenth of the USA (currently about 100,000 installations). Lower stocks are combined with poorer quality and other performance characteristics. Soviet computer users complain that domestic instruments are several times larger and more expensive than comparable Western analogues.[20] The gap is even greater in personal computers: about 25 mn units in the USA, whereas there are only a couple of hundred thousands - mostly quite simple - home computers in the Soviet Union. It seems that this is also a result of Eastern preference for mainframes which, contrary to personal computers, can be more easily controlled.[21]

---

[18] See Socialistická ekonomická integrace, No. 12, 1986, p. 19.

[19] The Czechoslovak Minister of Electrotechnical Industry, Mr. M. Kubát, estimated the likely gap between supply and demand at nearly one-third of the expected demand during 1987-1990 (the assumed supply level includes both domestic production and contracted supplies from other CMEA countries) - see Hospodárské noviny, Nov. 28, 1986, pp. 1 and 7.

[20] See EKO, No. 2, 1986, p. 37. For a detailed overview of Soviet computer industry from the beginning to present see Logé, Y., "Les ordinateurs soviétiques. Histoire obligée de trois décennies". In: Revue d'études comparatives Est-Ouest, Vol. 18, No. 4, 1987, pp. 53-76.

[21] Similarly will - according to one of the participants at 1986 NATO colloquium on Soviet R&D - the linkage of information networks and databases hardly be achieved because of socio-political bottlenecks. See APA-Ostwesthandel, No. 75, Oct. 13., 1987, pp. 6 and 7.

The dissemination of PCs is further hindered by prohibitively high prices. A Czechoslovak clone of IBM-XT (produced by Tesla Bratislava since late 1987) costs about Kcs 160,000, more advanced IBM-AT (produced by Agrocombinate Slusovice) costs as much as Kcs 260,000 plus additional equivalent of Kcs 100,000 in hard currency. At such prices the machines are obviously out of reach for private users since an IBM-XT clone costs an equivalent of more than four average annual salaries.[22] Similarly, the Soviet outdated PC model ISKRA-226 costs Rbl 18,000, i.e. more than seven average annual salaries.[23] The Soviet plan calling for the production of 1.1 mn of PCs during the 1986-1990 period is in danger and leading Soviet officials seriously consider the possibility of joint production with the help of Western firms.[24]

The socialist countries also experience grave problems with the development of more sophisticated 32 bit instruments which are not yet developed for commercial production, either in the Soviet Union or in any other CMEA country.[25] Furthermore, domestic software for Soviet PCs is not yet available either, although there are about 300000 programmers in the USSR.[26] The main bottlenecks are, however, in the poor quality and limited availability of the hardware.

Not withstanding scattered efforts the information revolution that already has taken off in the West cannot be easily triggered in the East. The underdevelopment of Eastern telecommunications networks prohibits, at least in the medium term, the intimate linkage of computers which currently brings about revolutionary changes in the way all manner of social and economic activity is conducted in the West. Other impediments lie in deeper systemic reasons as well as in the complex prerequisites for the favourable climate for innovation which are not fully understood and mastered even in the West. The Soviets point out bitterly that the backwardness of their information technologies

---

[22] See RFE Situation Report on Czechoslovakia, Jan. 20, 1989, p. 21.

[23] See Izvestiya, April, 3, 1988, p. 2.

[24] According to Academician Naumov, an official from newly created State Committee for Computer Technology and Informatics - see Pravda, Aug. 20, 1987, p. 2. The imports, e.g. of 100,000 of IBM XT clones produced in Peru over the rest of 1980s, will play an important role as well - see East-West, No. 402, January 1987, p. 4. The imports of PC turnkey plants still are banned by the COCOM.

[25] The technology is much more difficult to copy - see EKO, No. 4/1987, pp. 89-119. On the other hand, the recognition of respectable Soviet research results leads some Western businessmen to proposals for forming joint ventures with the Soviets, combining results of Soviet fundamental research with Western management and production know-how.

[26] See Ekonomicheskaya gazeta, No. 19, 1988, p. 18.

does not matter very much as long as there are no usable databases in the Soviet Union anyway.[27]

c) Consumer electronics

As may be seen by the example of personal computers some modern high technology consumer goods may easily revolutionalize existing systems of information distribution and control. Numerous examples are known of ideologists from the Soviet Union, Bulgaria, Czechoslovakia or GDR complaining about negative impacts of Western music, literature and related cultural phenomena, especially on the youth. Literature (both fiction, Western newspapers and periodicals) is the most searched for item on borders of East European countries. Western radio broadcast (Radio Free Europe, Radio Liberty, but occasionally also Voice of America, BBC Foreign Service and Deutsche Welle) used to be jammed at great costs by most communist governments until very recently.[28] The use of copying and other printing machines which could serve to disseminate independent information is tightly controlled by the State. In the Soviet Union as well as in the majority of East European countries the unauthorized use of photocopying and offset machines is prohibited. In Romania even typewriters must be registered with the police.

Television broadcast may be relatively easily controlled - even in the age of satellite TV - as long as receiving antennas are relatively expensive, difficult to build and too big to be easily hidden.[29] Despite attempted administrative controls and technical problems, a significant proportion of the population in Western parts of Eastern Europe and the Soviet Union (mainly in the Baltic republics) regularly watch Western television broadcast.[30] In the GDR, where the West German TV may be received almost on the whole territory and where, moreover, there is no language barrier, West German TV

---

[27] See Izvestiya, Aug. 15, 1988, p. 2.

[28] The jamming costs were estimated at US-$ 750 mn annually - see The Economist, June 6, 1987. The jamming has stopped only in December 1988 - see International Herald Tribune, Dec. 1, 1988, p. 1.

[29] In the Soviet Union the sale of parabolic antennas to individuals is prohibited and the use of high-frequency radio equipment or antennas requires special permission - see Collection of USSR Laws, Official Gazette, Vol. 8, pp. 396-400.

[30] An Estonian Communist Party leader recently acknowledged that "about a quarter" of his republic's population watched Finnish television - see Radio Helsinki, June 14, 1987. Concern has been expressed that Iran had begun transmitting religious programmes in Turkmen for the inhabitants of Turkmenistan - see Turkmenskaya iskra, Sept. 3, 1987.

is regularly watched by the majority of the populace. Still, the barriers limiting the free flow of international broadcasting are serious. Eastern bloc countries use different technical norms and broadcasting frequencies (e.g. the French SECAM system for video and different frequencies for TV sound broadcast) so that ordinary TV sets from domestic production cannot be used straightforwardly for the reception of Western programmes (mostly PAL system). Direct satellite broadcasting is being strongly opposed by the East mainly within a campaign for a New Information Order in the framework of the United Nations. Nevertheless, the policies of individual governments show an increasing diversity.

Video poses a somewhat greater problem, from the point of view of attempted Eastern central controls. Again, though some Eastern ideologists warned of the forthcoming technology and its potential "subversive effects" as early as in the middle of the 1970s, the spread and possibilities of the video caught the planners obviously unprepared. There are currently about 300,000 video recorders in the USSR - most of them imported from abroad. The Soviet Union started to produce video recorders on a large scale only in August 1984; the plan is to produce 200,000 pieces of this model (Elektronika VM 12) until the year 2000. The production of another model, turned out in cooperation with Finland in Voronezh, will reach 100,000 pieces annually by 1990.[31] Again, not only is the number and quality of domestically produced recorders very low, but the video cassettes are hard to obtain and very expensive, too.[32] As a result of insufficient attractiveness of home-made videos an extensive black market in Western video cassettes has developed. Recent changes in attitude to private services (see below) led to the opening of first private video saloons which, however, have been banned soon again.[33]

In other socialist countries the situation is similar. Czechoslovakia and Hungary produce video recorders in cooperation with Western firms. The Hungarian company Videoton assembles video recorders from Japanese parts (Akai since 1984 and Panasonic since 1985); Videoton's output in 1986 has reached 3000 units. Recently, Czechoslovakia (Tesla) signed a contract with the Dutch company Philips for a licence production of video recorders in Bratislava.

---

[31] See Izvestiya, May 18, 1987, p. 1. Current Soviet production of videos is 35.5 thousands (1987), resp. 73 thousands (1988) annually - see Izvestiya, March 21, 1987, p. 4 and Pravda, Jan. 22, 1989, p. 3.

[32] One video recorder costs Rbl 1200-1800 (6-9 average monthly salaries) and one blank videocassette Rbl 50 - see Izvestiya, March 21, 1987, p. 4.

[33] Since January 1st, 1989 - see Izvestiya, Dec. 31, 1988, p. 2.

3. Eastern Policies Aiming at Reducing the Technology Gap

So far we have seen that Eastern countries have been following a mixed strategy in their efforts at reducing the gap in high technology. Traditional policy has been the attempted development of own production, sometimes with the help of Western licences, combined with the use of (both legally and illegally) imported technology and know-how. However, these efforts were not particularly successful because of various systemic, institutional and other reasons. The very nature of scientific and technological development seems incompatible with existing institutional arrangements of rigid Party control, State monopoly in production and trade and with central planning. Distinguishing economically unsound innovations from profitable ones - a major problem for industrial managers everywhere - is further complicated in Eastern economic systems since here the relevant success indicators are either biased or completely missing; in some cases - like the still overwhelming priority of plan fulfillment - they even act contrary to the successful implementation of innovations.

a) Joint efforts

Similar problems - often even multiplied by difficulties resulting from diverging interests of national bureaucratic bodies - have been encountered in joint bilateral and multilateral cooperation within the CMEA. The recently adopted "Comprehensive Programme of Scientific and Technological Progress up to the Year 2000" currently faces the same problems as similar efforts in the past. The Programme, adopted on Dec. 18, 1985 at the 41st Session of the CMEA, aims at catching up in science and technology with industrially developed countries by the year 2000. Five priority directions in science and technology are to be marshalled by coordinated efforts of CMEA countries: electronization of the national economy, comprehensive automation, accelerated development of nuclear power, new synthetic materials and technologies and the development of biotechnology.

A major weakness of the Programme is that it follows the traditional implementation procedures. Main emphasis is put again on the coordination of planning and other activities in the field of planning. The actual procedure is to work out agreements for specific projects included in the Programme, such agreements then being taken into account in the coordination process of the five-year and annual plans of each country.

The individual CMEA countries are obliged to provide the necessary material and financial resources for the cooperation measures agreed upon; they also pledge to ensure favourable conditions for developing direct contacts between participating institutions and enterprises. The cooperation measures are to be financed from national funds and credits taken at the CMEA banks. An overall absorption of modern technology, leading to distinctly increased efficiency in the national economy of the CMEA countries, is not to be expected as long as the existing planning systems are not radically overhauled.

The 43rd CMEA Session in 1987, however, could not agree on anything but verbal commitments to create conditions for new cooperation forms. Apart from this, the CMEA Secretariat is to be streamlined and the CMEA organs shall concentrate only on problems requiring inter-governmental agreements (economic and scientific-technological policy coordination, programmes of strategic importance, integration mechanism, etc.). In one of the most problematic areas, namely in the convertibility of common currency (transferable Rouble), even a setback apparently occurred: an (unspecified) group of CMEA countries will "experimentally use national currencies" for accounting purposes related to direct production cooperation and to the bilateral joint ventures, as well as in the realization of tasks envisaged in the Comprehensive Programme. The practical problems related to a gradual transferable Rouble convertibility will be "studied".[34]

b) Individual reform efforts

Gorbachev's reform attempts, which are not limited to the economic sphere, but which also proclaim a "democratization" of society as one of the basic prerequisites for economic reform, may potentially lead to significant changes not only in the Soviet Union but elsewhere in Eastern Europe as well. Within the economy, the Soviet Union has recently adopted a programme aiming at decentralization and modernization. At the end of June 1987, an important Session of the Central Committee of the CPSU adopted "Basic Principles for a Radical Reconstruction of Economic Management".[35] These principles envisage numerous changes in planning, pricing, organization of material and technical supply, and finance, as well as in the structure of management organs. In essence, the changes should be implemented by the end of the 1980s, in order to

---

[34] See Pravda, Oct. 27, 1987, p. 4.

[35] See Izvestiya, June 27, 1987, pp. 2-3.

prepare the next five-year plan (1991-1995), already reflecting changed systemic conditions. The aim is to proceed from currently prevailing administrative management methods to the economic management at all levels as well as to the "democratization of management".

Simultaneously, a reform in foreign trade is being undertaken, too. Starting from January 1st, 1987, 21 ministries and about 70 large enterprises have obtained the right to perform foreign trade operations, from April 1989 all state enterprises and cooperatives are entitled to trade with abroad. Separate decrees have been issued on the regulations relating to the establishment of joint ventures with foreign (also Western) partners on Soviet territory.[36] One of the aims of these new initiatives is to "acquire advanced technology, know-how and management experience" from abroad. More than 160 joint venture projects with Western firms (though not exactly of a "high-tech" character) have already been signed by the end of 1988.[37]

Encouraged by the Soviet Union, various reform attempts were either started or intensified in most smaller East European countries as well.[38] Hungary and Poland adopted the most radical reform path, Bulgaria and Czechoslovakia undertake only hesitant steps, whereas the GDR and Romania practically reject the necessity of any market-oriented reforms.

c) Brief assessment of reform limits and likely socio-economic outcomes

Generally, short-term economic outcomes of the latest reform waves are uncertain. An important aspect of the current Soviet reform (which already leads to various spill-overs in Eastern Europe as well) is the accent on the socio-political dimension of the reform, namely on democratization. Indeed, the "perestroika" (a synonym for the Soviet reform) is virtually always connected with "glasnost'" (mostly translated as "openness" in the West) in the official Soviet political vocabulary. As a matter of fact, so far "perestroika" has indeed advanced more in cultural areas while its impacts within the economic sphere

---

[36] Latest revision of joint ventures regulation was issued in December 1988 - see Ekonomicheskaya gazeta, No. 51, 1988, pp. 17-18.

[37] See Pravda, Jan. 22, 1989, p. 5.

[38] For an overview of Eastern economic reforms see "Economic reforms in the European centrally planned economies", ECE/W-IIW Symposium, United Nations, New York, 1989.

are practically nil. Soviet mass media report now more openly and with less delay on most earlier taboo subjects (like, for instance, natural catastrophes, misuse of psychiatry, drug addiction, etc.), though in some instances flagrant cases of selective reporting for domestic (usually more restrictive), and foreign audiences still occur. Soviet television became the primary communication medium of the Gorbachev era: actually, he is the first Soviet leader to use television to popularize his political goals.

At the same time, various efforts to limit the impact of free information flows increased as well. Important new steps have been undertaken in order either to curtail foreign "hostile propaganda" or to hinder uncontrolled contacts with foreigners. Apart from propagandistic measures, disciplinary measures of a legal character that render unlawful any undesired contacts with foreigners or exchange of information with abroad were tightened as well. New regulations provide that any kind of information critical of the regime (in addition to state, military and economic secrets) that is passed on to foreigners can be deemed as punishable. On the other hand, numerous publications from so called "special funds" of libraries have recently been freed from restrictions; limited number of Western newspapers and journals is currently on sale in selected Soviet cities as well.[39]

Nevertheless, the uncontrolled exchange of information has always been classified as a crime against the state. The tightening up of the legal situation appears to be a reaction both to post-Helsinki relaxation of human contacts and to the challenge posed by new information technologies. Beside considerable travel restrictions, the bundle of measures aiming at screening off the country and its citizens from "harmful" outside influences shows that the East is on the defensive since Helsinki (1975) at the latest.[40] It is no longer a matter of carrying Marxist-Leninist ideas into the world, but rather of defending those ideas against new challenges.

There is no doubt that technology plays a decisive role in these new evaluations. Challenged by the worldwide spread of information technologies - which affect world economic and social development, threaten the roots of the communist system not only because they find their way, despite attempted controls, into the countries of the East,

---

[39] See Izvestiya, Nov. 3, 1988, p. 3.

[40] At the same time, several East European countries (notably Hungary, Poland and, to some degree, also Czechoslovakia, GDR and the Soviet Union) eased their travel restrictions recently.

but because they threaten the Soviet superpower position - the Soviet system faces hard choices indeed: either to continue on safe old paths and face the prospect of economic decline with all social and political consequences, or to dare the unknown way of fundamental changes which, though potentially leading to economic improvements, may cause undesirable systemic changes as well. While only the latter seems to be a viable option for a realistically thinking Eastern politician (Gorbachev seems to be the one), the question is whether the system as such is suited for this type of change without simultaneously causing major social unrest.[41]

At the same time, the dangers resulting from the new information technologies employed by repressive governments with the purpose of more effective and extensive controls must not be dismissed. With a combination of skilful propaganda and selective access to information (technology) the "liberalization impact" resulting from the spread of modern information technologies could be neutralized to a considerable degree. The eventual shift will be a subtle one, stretched out over years. But even the dissidents quickly grasped the new possibilities. A new generation of self published journals, some of them produced with personal computers, have already appeared in the East. The authorities, however, are not prepared to retreat from their positions regarding information monopoly. The creation of independent publishing and printing cooperatives was banned in the Soviet Union as "contradictory to decisions of the party and the government on this matter" so that the spread of independent information will for the time being remain the domain of dissidents.[42] Professionals, working in established structures, will press for easing restrictions, too. While this may not be of much help to the organized dissent, increased contacts with the West within (and outside) officially sanctioned channels will doubtlessly have positive effects as well.[43]

Finally, the impacts of information technologies on societies in the East should not be overestimated either. As mentioned above, the missing linkage of computers via an extensive and reliable telecom infrastructure considerably diminishes the effects resulting from the mass spread of personal computers. When - in addition - PCs are supplied without printers and the discettes are either unavailable or prohibitively expensive, then

---

[41] For a discussion of Gorbachev's options see Goldman, M., Gorbachev's Challenge. Economic Reform in the Age of High Technology. Norton & Co., New York, 1987, pp. 227-262.

[42] The instructions banning the independent publishing were issued already in 1987 by the Council of Ministers, but have not been published in the official press until the end of 1988 - see Izvestiya, Dec. 31, 1988, p. 2.

[43] See Dizard, W., "Mikhail Gorbachev's Computer Challenge". In: The Washington Quarterly, Spring 1986, pp. 157-163.

the State has relatively simple and effective control over the whole process. But such controls would damage the free innovation climate with the consequence of seriously impeding the whole process of attempted technological modernization and would be counterproductive to the success of reforms.

4. Implications for the West and East-West Relations

The information revolution threatens the foundations of systems which have, so far, been based on repressive measures of control. The Eastern dilemma may be summarized as follows:

"On the one hand, the Western lead in the new communication technologies makes possible a greater circulation of information from the West to and among Soviet-bloc populations, despite regime efforts to keep it out. At the same time, these technologies are becoming increasingly indispensable to the industrial and military strength, and to the growth and smooth functioning of all developed countries, including the Soviet Union, if it aspires to retain its advanced status. Thus the information revolution is exerting both a push and a pull toward greater openness in communist-controlled countries. Whatever the ultimate fate of communism as a system of rule, there is an absorbing challenge for the West to maintain policies and programmes which will encourage a more open flow of information within these societies and thus contributing to modifying the very nature of these regimes."[44]

The West has only limited possibilities to exert an influence on the development of societies in the East. The more important is the use of these possibilities in an optimal way. Information technologies form one of the few powerful tools which the West has at its disposal. No less important is the continuation of the East-West dialogue which maintains and improves necessary socio-political prerequisites. A promotion of the process started in Helsinki in 1975 is one of the crucial points since it deals with both dissemination of material technology and information in proper. The West should insist on a minutious observance of then agreed principles which, inter alia, include also a free movement of ideas and people. In the field of technology, the principles of export restrictions should be reviewed, too. Positive changes in international climate which

---

[44] Roberts, W.R., Engle, H.E., "The Global Information Revolution and the Communist World". In: The Washington Quarterly, Vol. 9, No. 2, Spring 1986, p. 142.

follow recent US-Soviet disarmament approaches from a good starting point for this purpose. Without the continuity in East-West dialogue the Western influence on how the information revolution in the East will be mastered would be much more limited.

The problems of technology transfer, its pros and cons, are much debated at present and will certainly have to be reviewed, too. Whereas Western positions with respect to information exchanges mostly favour the more free transfer, related issues of technology are by far not resolved yet. Even in the East are the opinions controversial. In an important change of position, prominent voices in the Soviet Union spoke out recently against "illusions from Western technology" and called for increased reliance on domestic technological developments.[45]

High technology plays an increasing role in international trade.[46] As far as technology transfer to the East is concerned, the greatest supplier has been the FRG with more than 33% market share in OECD high technology exports to the CMEA countries in 1986.[47] Japan became the second most important hi-tech supplier recently (11.0%), followed by France (10.6%) and Italy (8.3%). In absolute terms, OECD countries shipped high technology worth more than US-$ 3.1 bn to the East in 1986 (1.5% of their total high technology exports and only 8.7% of their total exports to the East). Out of selected information technology products, the OECD countries, in 1986, exported to the CMEA: automatic data processing equipment (for US-$ 173 mn), telecommunication equipment (for US-$ 193 mn), electronic measuring and controlling equipment (for US-$ 457 mn) and switchgear (for US-$ 309 mn). During the 1980-1986 period - for various reasons - the importance of CMEA as a market for OECD high technology products slackened.

Apart from the transfer of embodied technology, reflected in international trade statistics, there are also various grey and black channels in which advanced technology flows from the West to the East. Recently, selected spectacular cases of technology smuggle evoked much interest in international news media. Problems are posed

---

[45] See speeches by Prime Minister N. Ryzhkov and by the former President of USSR Academy of Sciences, Academician Alexandrov, at the XXVII Party Congress of the CPSU in 1986.

[46] See Barisitz, S., Stellenwert der Hochtechnologie im österreichischen Ostexport und im internationalen Vergleich. WIIW Forschungsbericht No. 154, Vienna, February 1989.

[47] Note that the market share of FRG is significantly underestimated since it does not include inner-German trade (i.e. trade with GDR).

particularly by dual-use products and technologies regulated by COCOM, but also by possibilities to extract classified information from Western computer databases.

Western export controls of high technology products were eased in September 1988. COCOM regulations on specific less advanced telecommunication equipment, personal computers and coaxial cables were lifted.[48] This has opened new possibilities for Western exports, e.g. for the above mentioned modernization of Hungarian Post, for various joint ventures in the Soviet Union, etc. The potential for Western exports of high technology products to the East is high: only by bringing the share of high technology in total OECD exports to the East (8.7% in 1986) to its average share in total OECD exports (14.4%) would theoretically lead to additional hi-tech exports to the East amounting to more than US-$ 2 bn, and even to considerably more exports if existing development lags should be eventually eliminated. Whether such export expansion would occur will depend not only on further improvements in East-West climate, but on Eastern financial possibilities as well. Eastern reform attempts open new and more vistas for Western action. A more liberal global approach, to various issues in both East and West, seems therefore desirable for the sake of improved understanding between the nations living in different, but increasingly interdependent, socio-economic systems. Such an approach could stimulate economic progress on both sides as well as positive political and social changes in the East.

References

Barisitz, S., "Stellenwert der Hochtechnologie im österreichischen Ostexport und im internationalen Vergleich". The Vienna Institute for Comparative Economic Studies (WIIW), Forschungsbericht No. 154, February 1989.

Bergson, A., "Comparative Productivity: The USSR, Eastern Europe and the West". In: The American Economic Review, Vol. 77, No. 3, June 1987.

Brandstetter, W., "Export Control Reform and Western Security". WIIW Forschungsberichte No. 135, November 1987.

Dizard, W., "Mikhail Gorbachev's Computer Challenge". In: The Washington Quarterly, Spring 1986.

Economic Survey of Europe in 1986-1987. ECE, New York, 1987.

---

[48] See Die Presse, Aug. 24, 1988, p. 1.

Ehrlich, E., "Comparison of Development Levels: Inequalities in the Physical Structures of National Economies". In: Bairoch, P., Lévy-Leboyer, M.,(eds), "Disparities in Economic Development Since the Industrial Revolution". The Macmillan Press Ltd, London, 1981.

Goldman, M., "Gorbachev's Challenge. Economic Reform in the Age of High Technology". Norton & Co., New York, 1987.

Hanson, P., "Trade and Technology in Soviet-Western Relations". Columbia University Press, New York, 1981.

Hardt, J.P., "Perspective Normalization of East-West Commerce: A View from Washington". Congressional Research Service, Manuscript, Dec. 1987.

Hardt, J.P., Boone, J.F., "U.S. Export Control Policy and Competitiveness". Congressional Research Service, April 30, 1987.

Havlik, P., "Comparison of Real Products Between East and West, 1970-1983". WIIW Forschungsberichte No. 115, April 1986.

Judy, R.W., "The Soviet Information Revolution: Some Prospects and Comparisons". In: Gorbachev's Economic Plans. Joint Economic Committee Study Papers, Vol. 2, Nov. 27, 1987.

Lebkowski, M., Monkiewicz, J., "L'informatique dans les pays du CAEM". In: Revue d'études comparatives Est-Ouest, Vol. 17, No. 4, 1986.

Lendvai, P., "Der Medienkrieg". Ullstein, 1980.

Logé, Y., "Les ordinateurs soviétiques. Histoire obligée de trois décennies". In: Revue d'études comparatives Est-Ouest, Vol. 18, No. 4, 1987.

"Man, Science, Technology. A Marxist Analysis of the Scientific-Technological Revolution". Academia, Prague, Moscow-Prague, 1973.

"Materialien zum Bericht zur Lage der Nation im geteilten Deutschland 1987". Bundesministerium für innerdeutsche Beziehungen, Bonn, May 1987.

Roberts, W.R., Engle, H.E., "The Global Information Revolution and the Communist World". In: The Washington Quarterly, Vol. 9, No. 2, Spring 1986.

Schmid, K., "Einschränkungen des grenzüberschreitenden Informationsaustausches in der UdSSR". In: Berichte des Bundesinstituts für ostwissenschaftliche und internationale Studien, Cologne, Nos. 2 and 26, 1985.

"The Telecommunication Industry. Growth and Structural Change". ECE, United Nations, New York, 1987.

"The Technobandits". In: Time Magazine, Nov. 23, 1987.

Wienert, H., Slater, J., "East-West Technology Transfer. The Trade and Economic Aspects". OECD, Paris, 1986.

THE UNBALANCED TRIAD

Francois Bar and John Zysman
BRIE, University of California, Berkeley

1. Introduction

We have been asked to discuss the effect of the United States on European Japanese relationships in telecommunications and trade. In fact, the real issues are different. They are the balance and evolution of two bilateral relationships; that between the United States and Europe on the one hand and between the United States and Japan on the other. The triad, very simply, is unbalanced.

The American influence in telecommunications on each of its partners has come through three different channels. First it has come through deregulation. The United States became early on a source of experimentation in telecommunications use, experimentation in alternative ways to develop and configure the networks. Second, that deregulation which opened the American market to alternative suppliers also opened it to foreign suppliers. Together these channels created pressure on regulatory policy, monopolies, and producer cartels in Europe and Japan. Now, through more general trade legislation, a third channel of influence is opened. The recent American trade bill suggests that the United States Congress has become uneasy with the evolving balance in trade, principally with Japan but also with Europe. In this bill, telecommunications becomes a metaphor for the American situation and our relations with our major allies. That bill introduces and presses notions of reciprocity, changing the language of trade debate in what is now being called a post-Gatt world. It encourages in a supposedly global economy the emergence of political arrangements for regional markets.

The first task though is to set the context, clarify the parameters of our discussion. Indeed it is a central purpose of a conference such as this. We must consider in turn the patterns of trade and the outlines of American, European, and Japanese policy. Some of the elements of the context seem well-known and agreed, but what seems evident to us may be questionable for you. As we turn to the specific arguments here, we want to emphasize that we speak as analysts of the American scene, not as advocates of her policies.

2. The Trade Context

Before we turn to the telecommunications issues, we must set the basic trade context and consider the trade patterns among our trio. Europe and Japan have quite limited trade or investment relations. Professor Schütte's paper has shown the limited number of technology agreements in the information technology area between Europe and Japan.[1] In telecommunications both the Japanese and European markets have been essentially closed to each other; however, Japanese firms may now seek presence in the European market.

The U.S.-European trade relationship is quite deep and has historically been quite balanced both in quantity and form. Above all there has been relatively open access on both sides for direct foreign investment. While there have been irritating elements and trumpets that periodically announce trade wars, the relationship has been on sound footing. Indeed, until recently the United States maintained a steady surplus with Europe. That has not been the case with Japan.

The American Japanese relationship is troubled. It is now characterized by an overwhelming import by America of manufactured goods from Japan and a surge of Japanese direct foreign investment into the United States. Critically, to an American eye the Japanese market is impermeable, whatever the reason. The relative closure of the Japanese market rests on a mix of policy, business practice and arrangement, and client demands. At one point that closure was clearly intentional and a product of policy; now it is partly the result of past policy but is equally a function of continuing practice and purpose.[2] This creates an economically strategic asymmetry that is politically unstable and which is likely to bring about a series of crises in different forms.[3]

Asymmetric markets, closure in the markets of major competitors in high technology industries, pose strategic problems. Policy can shape both outcomes in specific sectors

---

[1] See Professor Helmut Schütte's paper for this conference.

[2] Zysman's position on these matters is argued out more fully in Laura Tyson and John Zysman in "Developmental Strategy and Production Innovation" in Politics and Productivity: How Japan's Development Strategy Works Ed. Chalmers Johnson, Laura D'Andrea Tyson, and John Zysman.

[3] Ibid.

and in the nations technology trajectory. The huge American trade imbalances, we should emphasize, are not a product of policy abroad. If anything our partners policies have loosened during the years that our trade problems have become aggravated. At the root was a huge budget deficit and a rapid rise in the value of the dollar that priced many American goods out of established markets. However, those price increases simply revealed the inability of American firms to use established production practices to respond to rapidly changing markets. As the dollar came down, the deficit - quite unexpectedly for many - remained. The U.S. trade deficit will be resolved by import substitution. The only question is how that process will work. That is, the dollar depreciation has not brought about the surge of exports and shrinking of imports needed to create an equilibrium. Now that our factories are operating at high capacity levels, further currency depreciations will not bring much trade adjustment, but will perhaps bring considerable inflation. In any case, import substitution will be forced by the adaptation of American firms in the long term or by political pressures that compel domestic investment to service this market.

We must consider the telecommunications story against this backdrop. Entangled with the debate about telecommunications is a discovery of the changing place of services, both in trade and in the economy. To a large extent, this requires a reconsideration of our old intellectual models. The GATT (General Agreement on Tariffs and Trade) system was constructed around problems of trade in goods, not services. Services were internal matters, not problems of international trade. Therefore telecommunications policy, because it addressed primarily telecom services, was first and foremost a domestic question. International discussions merely dealt with interfaces as telecommunications, like other services, were inter-connected at the border. Similarly, trade issues merely were the consequences - intended or not - of the interfaces between domestic policies.

For years, this system had been remarkably stable. In all developed countries national monopolies - whether their name was ATT, PTT or NTT - owned and controlled the networks. National policy was the affair of technocratic elites. With a handful of domestic suppliers, they agreed on what to design, what to offer, and at what price. They focused on the construction and the operation of their national network, paying relatively little attention to the international consequences of their decisions. Moreover, services were then simply considered passive adjuncts to manufacturing. To the firms using them,

---

[4] This argument is developed in a number of places. See for example Giovanni Dosi, Laura D'Andrea Tyson, and John Zysman "Trade, Technologies, and Development" in Op. Cit. Politics and Productivity.

telecoms simply were utilities, like electricity or water, rather than an infrastructure upon which to build strategic advantage.

This static picture has now dramatically changed. First, the national monopolies have been challenged; some must now deal directly with competitors, others must accommodate competition on the margins of their domain. Many telecom services have become internationalized and as a result have pushed their place to the center stage of trade negotiations. As national equipment markets became increasingly open to international competition, national borders no longer contained telecom policy issues, which spilled over into international arenas. In short, domestic telecom policies are being recast within a more open environment, and their international consequences have become harder to ignore.

Second, the economic role of telecommunications, like other services, is being re-interpreted. We are beginning to understand that while the world is not moving to a Post Industrial economy in which services are the organizing feature, we are watching a reconfiguration of production. One critical element of that reconfiguration is that services, intimately linked to the production and development of goods, become increasingly critical constituents of the production system.[5] Perhaps more than any other, telecommunication services are vital inputs to the emerging economies which rely increasingly on the processing and transmission of information. How they are delivered to the users and how the national communications infrastructure is organized have become fundamental determinants of corporate and national competitiveness. It is in this context that we must assess the changes in national telecommunications policies: the American deregulation, the Japanese and European re-regulations.[6]

3. Telecommunications and American Policy

American deregulation and the AT&T divestiture were driven by two interrelated efforts. The first dominant and successful effort was, at the level of industrial

---

[5] See Stephen Cohen and John Zysman Manufacturing Matters, Basic Books, 1987.

[6] For an elaboration on the telecommunications policy changes, see Michael Borrus, Francois Bar, et al. Telecommunications Development in Comparative Prospective: The New Telecommunications in Europe, Japan, and the US, BRIE Working Paper # 14, May 1985. See also Francois Bar and Michael Borrus, From Public Access to Private Connections: Network Policy and National Advantage, BRIE Working Paper # 29, September 1987 and Michael Borrus et al., The Impacts of Divestiture and Deregulation: Infrastructural Changes, Manufacturing Transition, and Competition in the United States Telecommunications Industry, BRIE Working Paper # 12, September 1984.

development and firm strategies, waged by major users and producers of telecommunications equipment progressively to remove control over the structure, evolution and uses of telecommunications from regulatory and judicial constraints.[7] The second drive, at the policy level, was the gradual abdication of government responsibility over the equitable development of the nation's telecommunications infrastructure and the delegation of that role to market competition (i.e. to the control of major users and producers). The desire for rapid and efficient exploitation of technological change, in particular the development of new transmission technologies and the convergence of computing and communications, provided both the opportunity for AT&T, its competitors and major customers to push government policy toward deregulation and divestiture, and the necessary justification for the government to turn toward the market as its easy way out of the difficulties of maintaining control over the national telecommunications infrastructure in a time of rapid technological change.[8]

The most dramatic consequence of American deregulation was to permit unprecedented experimentation with the new telecom technologies among users and producers. Users have discovered the power of networks to reconfigure their operations, more critically to allow new strategic approaches to markets and production.[9] If producers seeking new markets forced the initial judicial decisions; users who can implement new networks were their most ardent supporters.

Equally important, the US deregulation unilaterally opened the American market to foreign competition, while foreign markets remained largely closed to US firms. The asymmetry in market access was created as an unintended result of purely domestic American policy. This policy, grounded in the belief that market competition could best guide the evolution of the US telecommunications infrastructure, saw no reason to limit such competition to US participants. If anything, it assumed that domestic competition would stimulate innovation among US firms, making them more competitive abroad. It further assumed that American economic preeminence on the international scene would

---

[7] The interventions of major corporate and public users, that provoked change and determined its form, in the regulatory and judicial decisions leading to deregulation and divestiture, are amply documented in Dan Shiller, Telematics and Government, Ablex Publishing, NJ, 1982, part one, p. 1-96.

[8] This analysis is fully elaborated in Michael Borrus, Francois Bar et al. The Impacts of Divestiture and Deregulation: Infrastructural Changes, Manufacturing Transition, and Competition in the United States Telecommunications Idustry, BRIE Working Paper # 12, 1984.

[9] Francois Bar and Michael Borrus, From Public Access to Private Connections: Network Policy and National Advantage, BRIE Working Paper #18, September 1987.

naturally force foreign emulation of American policies. Deregulation would be "contagious" and foreign countries would relax their hold on domestic telecom markets, under the combined pressures of their domestic users envious of the new possibilities offered to their US counterparts, and of increasingly competitive US producers. Overall however, the focus of US deregulation was to transform the domestic status quo, and its trade consequences largely went unexamined. On his own and without attention to the international consequences, Judge Green made one of the most critical trade decisions affecting high technology.

Such "unilateral disarmament" is difficult to explain. Its consequences however, quickly became obvious. From a $1 billion trade surplus in 1980, the US telecom trade balance deteriorated to a $700 million deficit by 1984.[10] Having initially focused on promoting competition, diversity and experimentation within the US, American telecommunications policy is now turning its attention to trade. Having given away their most powerful bargaining chip, access to the American market, American policy makers are now insisting on reciprocity and equal access to foreign markets. Certainly the telecommunications elements of the trade bill grow from frustration with a self generated problem. But its approach by no means assures American success either in trade or the widespread use of the new technology. The policy, and the US dissatisfaction at its unintended consequences, did however put pressure on both Japan and Europe to reconsider and reevaluate their policies.

4. Reregulation and Deregulation in Japan and Europe

Understandably, Japan and European countries have not found the American exhortations to emulate its deregulation policies very convincing. Indeed they had painlessly gained access to the American market and saw little need to repay the favor. More fundamentally, their developmental policies of the past had served them quite well, and they disagreed on the very premise of the US policy: they believed the state, rather than the market, could best guide the evolution of their national telecommunications infrastructure.[11] However, domestic telecom policies in Europe and

---

[10] Source: American Electronics Association.

[11] Of course this oversimplifies and there are variations among these countries' positions on this issue. Great Britain for one, would be more easily convinced than its European neighbors to inject a dose of deregulation in its domestic policy.

Japan are not static and their evolution will undoubtedly have new consequences on telecommunications trade.

In Japan, telecommunications policy has been part of a broader developmental policy to facilitate and accelerate development and diffusion of electronics. That policy combined three elements: 1) difficult access to domestic markets, reserved for local producers; 2) controlled but real competition among Japanese firms on the Japanese market; and 3) limited but real and crucial subsidies. This arrangement served to develop the Japanese electronics industry and produced competitors with powerful advantages in global markets. By contrast with the US situation, the asymmetry of access to the Japanese market was strictly intended. It has proved a crucial element of development in the past and there is every reason to believe that it will continue to be in the future.

The reregulation of the Japanese telecommunications system and the reconfiguration of NTT networks will certainly prove to be an important part of development of the Japanese electronics industry.[12] It remains to be seen whether foreign producers participate in those developments and whether Japanese policy remains an element of international dispute. We suspect however that foreign entrants will only be permitted as the result of conscious political bargains, and that the areas open to foreign competition will be carefully selected not to interfere with Japanese developmental policies. The continued asymmetry in market access simply is no longer politically tolerable. While the change may not result in an opening of the Japanese market, it will certainly result in responses from Europe and the United States that will press toward a set of regional markets.

In Europe of course domestic policy changes are inscribed within the movement toward 1992. Certainly the Commission has encouraged technological collaborations and an environment in which quite dramatic alliances have been formed.[13] However, in the telecommunications arena equally significant changes are being driven at the national level. Those national changes involve refashioning the role and operations of the primary service providers, the PTTs. In each national setting there has been some introduction

---

[12] Taka Yamada and Michael Borrus are working on analyses of this issue.

[13] See for a good analysis of this Wayne Sandholtz's dissertation, Crisis and Collaboration in European Telematics, University of California, Berkeley, 1989.

of limited competition in service and equipment. The policy focus remains on maintaining network coherence under overall PTT control (even when, like in the UK, the PTT has been transformed from a public monopoly into a private quasi-monopoly).

The United Kingdom led the way and Mercury was allowed to compete with British Telecom in the provision of basic telecom services. It also deregulated the market for Value Added Networks (VANs). France, Germany and Italy are progressively following suit and are relaxing constraints on the provision of advanced information services over their national networks. Throughout Europe, new options have emerged for the purchase of terminal equipment, and new services such as cellular telephony now become available.

The consolidation of equipment vendors, certainly encouraged by European policy, has the consequence of altering the logic of national procurement debates. The question of who is a national supplier suddenly becomes much fuzzier and the technological learning from several markets can accumulate more easily in a few European vendors. Further, it may be difficult politically to sustain double standards and treat foreign-but-European producers differently from US or Japanese companies.

There is clearly change and movement in European telecommunications, but the form and direction of that change is still unclear. Two dimensions are interesting here. First, each national system has consisted of a monopoly purveyor of services and a cluster of "family" firms supplying equipment through that PTT. Will the European market consist of a competitive market for services and equipment or a highly cartelized and regulated market? The European market, cartelized or competitive, we might add is certainly finding a place for outside suppliers including Northern Telecom, ATT, and depending on what we call an outsider, Ericsson. The real choices of course are not reflected in the choice monopoly/cartel on the one hand and competition on the other. Rather the choices are about what form of regulation and which areas of competition.

Second, what is the balance between user and producer needs? In telecommunications the experimentation in the United States has unquestionably contributed to the demand for new services and equipment. By serving the user needs, the producers have - in some dimensions - been served as well. Which concerns - those of producers or users - will have priority? Or perhaps we should put this question differently. There are different groups of users. Priority in the United States has been given to the freedom of large users to innovate in applications and networks, with the attendant risk that service to other groups, most notably small and medium size businesses, would be damaged. How will the balance between the needs of firms which have the financial and technological resources to fashion and operate their own networks be set against other groups. That balance in Europe may only be settled by the construction of very elaborate and general broad-band ISDN networks, but the demand for and the uses of such an infrastructure are far from clear. Of course, there is always the Minitel case to point too in support of a form of Say's law for telecommunications. An innovative infrastructure creates its own use.

Once again, the primordial telecom policy issues are domestic ones - or, rather, in the case of Europe, regional ones. Trade issues emerge at the interface of these regional policies. But as each national policy focus is redefined, so will be the resulting trade issues.

The American policy of deregulation and market opening has at least contributed to the European and Japanese experimentation. Now that both are moving, there is a substantial chance that the United States government and firms will be uncomfortable with their position in the European market and will provoke tensions in a variety of domains. American policy, as we have suggested, has been foolish in these domains, giving up unilaterally what it would require to obtain its objectives by negotiation. American companies, equally, have not always displayed an understanding of the communities, not just the markets though that as well, in which they are trying to begin or expand business. Europe is complicated, but readily accessible to foreign business. Japan is relatively impermeable. In any case asymmetric outcomes, whatever the rhetoric of free trade, are not - we emphasize - going to be politically stable.

5. The Crucial Fact Left Out

Yet there will be a disjuncture in American influence on Japan and Europe in telecommunications. The discussion so far, one might argue, rests on outmoded premises or leaves out crucial elements. It is rooted in a notion of American centrality and power, a vantage which - when presented by an American - often is grating.

The presumption of American economic and technological dominance is no longer appropriate and consequently the logic of American influence will change. It cannot be assumed that America will be central to the next generation of developments in telecommunications. This has several dimensions. First, America's position in the global economy has been altered by both the trade deficits of the 1980s and the competitive weaknesses of firms that underlay those deficits. The risk is that problems will be cumulative. Markets lost because of production weakness contribute to a weakening of the continued development of technology and product. America is not being transformed from unchallengeable giant into feeble pygmy. Nonetheless, while once our power in trade, money, and technology was overwhelming and could serve as a resource for foreign and security policy, now our position is much weaker. The change in America's position, our relative decline, is not simply a matter of other countries rebuilding in the post war years or catching up to our leading position. Rather, in the last decade the capacity of American industry to respond to shifts in global markets has deteriorated.

The message of the 1980's for the American government may be that the capacity to manufacture is a national asset, its erosion a national problem. For companies the lesson was equally simple, you can't control what you can't produce. Indeed, after World War II there was merit to the argument. The United States made things others could not; and products others could make we often made better and cheaper. The advantage rested on real innovations in the late 19th and early 20th century. A system of mass production and divisionalized management underlay our position. Other countries tried to catch up. They sought to imitate what we did; they saved and invested to do so. In a real sense they never did imitate the United States, rather they created their own sets of innovations, and from their own set of innovations built a basis for advantage in global markets. There were two sets of innovations abroad, one in policy and one in production. The second set of innovations lie in production. In countries as diverse as Japan, Italy, and Germany we can see that in varied forms a new approach to production has emerged. Its advantages are not to be listed by element, though it does provide lower costs, higher quality, and tighter delivery times. It is not an issue of incremental or even radical improvement in an old system, but a new approach - a new paradigm as one IBM engineering manager called it. He labeled it velocity manufacturing, but it is not a story of speeding up the line. Rather, it is a story in which the central codeword is flexibility. Importantly, these production innovations do not stand alone. It is not simply that cost is reduced, though it is, or that quality is improved, though it is an inherent product of the innovations. Rather, rapid introduction of new products - dynamic flexibility - and rapid variation of established products - is also facilitated. That package of advantages becomes a powerful competitive weapon allowing a whole variety of new marketing strategies to translate production advance into market position.

The question of course is why did these second set of innovations occur in Europe and Japan and not in the United States. The first answer is simple and obvious. A dominant and effective system existed in the United States. Until that system was challenged, there would be little need, understanding of the need or incentive to alter existing practice. However, that still leaves open the question of why the challenge emerged as it did. The answer is that the logic of firm choice in Japan and parts of Europe generated that response.[14] Take the Japanese case. After the war Japan's market was protected and growing rapidly. Its firms were technology followers borrowing technology abroad. For companies, that meant that firms faced the need to borrow and implement rapidly technology from abroad. Each market increment that came through growth allowed the possibility of borrowing and implementing another round of technology. In essence in quite traditional industries, Japanese firms faced conditions Americans associate with high technology industries. Learning curve economies dominated, making the pursuit of market share a necessity to sustain short term profits. In that environment and with capital short, a system emerged of semi-market ties between assemblers and component producers that organized production in new ways. The organizational innovations, including the use of statistical process control, moved firms into the fourth of Jaikumar's stages and laid the foundation for the implementation of NC machine tools. That technology was shaped by the new choices, rather than driving them, can be seen in differences in American and Japanese machine tools. What seems common to the Japanese, German and Italian cases - for we clearly cannot trace out each instance here - are broad definitions of job responsibility and highly skilled and educated workforces.

The problem for America lies not in the pressure from abroad, which is advancing production and product development to our advantage as well; rather the difficulty is in our response. Our response has been driven by mythologies that have been very difficult to shake off, mythologies that have affected both government and firms. In the policy arena the notion of sunrise and sunset industries distorted our understanding both of

---

[14] For the Japanese case see Tyson and Zysman in Politics and Productivity. For the Italian case see Charles Sabel, Work and Politics, Cambridge University Press. For the German case see Gary Herrigel's dissertation and his article in Pater Katzenstein Industry and Politics In West Germany Cornell University Press 1989.

trade and the economy. We were slow to grasp that the bulk of the sunrise industries produce intermediary goods used in the products and production of other industries. Consequently, the so called sunset industries were the clients of the so called sunrise industries. The problem was how to use the new transformative technologies to alter traditional industries. Similarly, the notion of a post-industrial society kept us from understanding that we were witnessing a transformation in industrial production, a shift in the role of services in manufacturing, not a move up and out of industry. However, Steve Cohen and we have argued both of these matters elsewhere.[15]

Similarly there were a set of corporate myths that are worth mentioning if not developing here. The first was the notion that one could win with technology, leaving the dirty business of production to others. Certainly, this led firms to cede parts of the market where production mattered most to foreign companies that then built distribution channels from which to attack the technology intensive segments of the business. Equally, it deceived firms about the nature of product innovation. Product and process knowledge are not that separable, and except for a few disjunctures, new products are built from knowledge accumulated in early generations. Cede production and you limit innovation. A second myth was the notion that competitors advantage lay with cheap labor. That hid from view the powerful evolutionary steps in manufacturing going on abroad. It led to moves offshore that established networks of production that made Asian production cost effective quite apart from direct labor costs. A third myth was the notion that capital costs alone kept American firms from an effective use of technology, when - as the General Motors case reveals clearly - the central obstacle was an understanding of what to do.

In any case, the current American industrial decline will encourage Europe and Japan to assert the validity of their own approaches and to establish their own policies as models. In the telecommunications sphere in particular, they are unlikely to accept the United States approach as a blu-print of their future. This is especially true as these countries believe that their telecom policies are essential to shaping and controlling the development of the information infrastructure which underlies the current reorganization of their industries and economies.

---

[15] See Manufacturing Matters, Op. Cit. and Stephen Cohen and John Zysman sections of "Business Economics and the Oval Office: Advice to the President and Other CEOs," Harvard Business Review, Vol. 66, No. 6 (Nov.-Dec. 1988).

6. New Issues for American Policy

Very simply, the fact left out is the broader shift in global trade patterns. The changed global relationship affects American choices in a wide range of arenas that bear on telecommunications and influence the future of the triad. Consider the question of High Definition Television. Here the American position and that of Europe and Japan is suddenly reversed. The United States for years has told its allies that their economic development could be assured by American subsidiaries in critical sectors or by technology licenses from America. They did not have to exclude American firms and develop their own companies and technology. Now America finds itself without a strong entrant in the consumer electronics sector. The one American entrant assembles in Mexico using substantial doses of Japanese components. The American market is dominated by European and Japanese firms.

Suddenly some American officials call for the same policies we deplored elsewhere, promotion and protection. But they must ask difficult questions. The first question of course is what is America's public interest. Assuming they can answer that question, and we believe America has an interest in the development and diffusion within the United States of the components and production skills that will be developed in the HDTV industry. Then the issue rises of who is an American producer. Is ownership the only issue. Perhaps we can close the American market, but do we close it to those who assemble abroad - Zenith; - those whose components are developed abroad - Sony. Should we develop or rather redevelop our industries in alliance with foreign firms? If so what - from a public vantage - do we expect from them? The risk of course is that simple value added or domestic content rules will result in plants design abroad, operated semi-automatically by production systems developed abroad, and assembling foreign developed and produced components.

We certainly believe the future of HDTV in the United States lies in American alliances with foreign producers. But the particulars of policy are not central to our concerns here. The policy problem for the United States is suddenly similar to the choices of its allies in earlier periods. We act with the same narrow vision and often unthinking reactions.

7. A Changing Structure of Telecommunications Policy

The simple point is that the basic pattern with which we began our discussion no longer holds. America can no longer singlehandedly drive developments in international trade, at the center of two dyads. Following a decade of discussion of the global economy in which America was at the center, now we confront the emergence of competing regional economic blocs. A global economy and regional economic blocs will not be alternatives in fact. Rather there will be a mix of global firms and regional markets in a form yet to be settled.

We face a multipolar global economy; the era of the American empire is over. Instead of the pinion or hegemon, the United States may become the wildcard. The recent trade bill and earlier trade debates suggest that both the coalition for and the ideology of free trade are being challenged. Any serious move to closure in the American market, even if practically our market remained substantially open, would almost certainly provoke a formal construction of regional trade blocks.

Telecommunications would almost certainly follow the general same pattern. US deregulatory policy will not be automatically copied abroad. At the same time, the various domestic telecom policies have become more inter-dependent and national decisions can no longer be taken in isolation. Very schematically, the 1980s begun with separated national telecommunications systems interconnected by interfaces. Telecommunications policy was a matter of monopoly professionals and engineers building the national network to their conception of appropriate technology. We will not go back to that era. Telecommunications has become a matter of broad public concern and will not be the exclusive domain of government professionals. Equipment markets are being pried open and monopolies loosened so that global firms will participated in each regional market. Yet technology rarely dictates social organization. Global technology networks can be reshaped by politics into regional balanced regional ones.

W. Klenner, University of Bochum (Ed.)

Trends of Economic Development in East Asia

Essays in Honour of Willy Kraus

With contributions by numerous experts
1989. X, 554 pp. 28 figs. Hardcover DM 198,–
ISBN 3-540-50048-0

The economic success achieved in the last decade in East Asia has brought about a fundamental reorientation in the Western view of the region. In order to contribute to a better understanding of present events and future developments in the area, leading East Asia economists and men of experience in Asian business from Asia, America, and East and West Europe have written papers on their reseach or business fields for this volume. The individual articles deal with problems common to the East Asian region and the Pacific area as well as with specific economic problems of Japan, China and South Korea.

The volume is divided into four parts:

East Asia and the Pacific Basin includes articles on supranational issues, for example on the international economic relations of Japan, China, Taiwan and Korea.

Japan includes articles on Japanese industrial and business structure, technological policy, exports and other issues.

China includes articles on structural change, economic reforms, fiscal policy, agriculture and other issues.

Korea includes articles on economic and industrial policy, restructuring, protectionism and other issues.

The occasion of the publication of this volume is the 70th birthday of Willy Kraus, who for many years has been actively concerned with the questions of development in the East Asian region.

Springer-Verlag Berlin Heidelberg New York London Paris Tokyo Hong Kong

H. Hax, W. Kraus, T. Matsuda, T. Nakamura (Eds.)

Pacific Cooperation from the Japanese and the German Viewpoint

1990. Approx. 190 pp. 16 figs. 46 tabs. Hardcover DM 59,-
ISBN 3-540-51694-8

The Pacific Rim includes highly industrialized countries like the USA and Japan and a number of developing countries ranging from South Korea to Indonesia. This economic region has over the last decade shown the highest dynamic growth of any region in the world. The consequences for the world economy are far reaching, and affect not only Japan as a part of the region but also the countries of the European Community.

The papers in this volume are the result of a Japanese-German seminar. They deal with some of the most important aspects of the new situation, such as the reaction of commodity markets and corresponding trade flows, the impact of regional cooperation upon free international trade, the role and development of financial markets, and management problems arising in connection with direct investments. Each of these points is examined by a Japanese and a German expert. Their partly contrasting views result in a comprehensive survey of the whole set of problems.

G. Pfeiffer, DETECON, Bonn; **B. Wieland,** University of Cologne

Telecommunications in Germany
An Economic Perspective

1990. VIII, 199 pp. 23 figs. 8 tabs. Softcover DM 68,-
ISBN 3-540-52360-X

This book describes the German telecommunications market and its regulatory environment and contains four case studies showing how forms in Germany employ telecommunications in their corporate strategies.

The book describes in detail the recent regulatory reform in Germany and compares the new environment with the old. It also presents a systematic analysis of the corporate uses of telecommunications usage in Germany. The book is based on work done for an internatioanl research project organized by the OECD and the University of California, Berkeley.

Springer-Verlag Berlin Heidelberg New York London Paris Tokyo Hong Kong